"KIKE!"

Books by Michael Selzer

THE ARYANIZATION OF THE JEWISH STATE: A Polemic

THE WINESKIN AND THE WIZARD: The Problem of Jewish
Power in the Context of East European Jewish History

ZIONISM RECONSIDERED: The Rejection of Jewish Normalcy

POLITICS AND JEWISH PURPOSE

ETHNIC PREJUDICE IN AMERICA SERIES

General Editor—Michael Selzer

A Documentary History of
Anti-Semitism in America

Edited and with an Introduction
by Michael Selzer

Foreword by Herbert Gold

A Straight Arrow Book

"KIKE!"

A MERIDIAN BOOK
WORLD PUBLISHING
TIMES MIRROR
NEW YORK

Staff members of the American Jewish Committee, of the Jewish Division of the New York Public Library, and of the Library of the Graduate Center of the City University of New York provided advice and assistance which were invaluable in the preparation of this volume. Their services are gratefully acknowledged, as are those of Adam Isler and of Lonnie Selzer, both of whom helped in the dreary task of transcribing materials.

A Meridian Book

Published by The World Publishing Company

Published simultaneously in Canada

by Nelson, Foster & Scott Ltd.

First printing—1972

ISBN 0-529-04495-1

Library of Congress catalog card number: 74-183095

Printed in the United States of America

WORLD PUBLISHING
TIMES MIRROR

Contents

Foreword

Confessions of a former dark stranger with soft hands and curving fingers now grown frank, boyish, and goyish in the service of the republic

The dense world is a walkie-talkie. Every Jew has his little anthology of anti-Semitic lore from the receiving end. Every non-Jew has a little repertory from the sending end. (Sheeny! All the money! Stinks! Bah! Roger and over . . . God will avenge me. *Shema Yisroel Adonay Elohenu,* feh, roger and over.) And the situation is electronically complicated in those marvelous meat computers, our brains, by the fact that every Jew is also a non-Jew, and most non-Jews sometimes, in the heart of hearts, and not just when they're in love, know that theirs is the situation of the Jew, abandoned and wandering on earth, with no hope of salvation except through the good luck they make themselves. How odd of God to choose . . . Everybody!

Nonetheless, despite our historical joining and sharing in this problem, there is an important difference between the rock-thrower and the rock-throwee. The rock-thrower thumps, and gets it off with his hatred. The rock-throwee is thumped, and turns his hatred wildly in all directions, and sometimes figures that the safest procedure, in a difficult world full of rocks, is to hate himself. Alas, the self-hating Jew.

My feet still ache when I hear about Jewish overvisibility, because I remember the meek, bent back of the shoeman, fitting me with my Buster Browns in Lakewood, Ohio, and lecturing my mother about how two Jews, Brandeis and Cordoza, were too many. "I've lost business," he said. "People talk. They don't like."

"Then get off the Supreme Court!" I yelled at him, and wouldn't wear the shoes, just cutting holes in my sneakers until my pushy ten-year-old Jewish toes lapped the ground.

Clearly the centuries of diaspora and persecution were a test of emotional survival, and not everyone survived. Perhaps those who survived were tempered in the crucible. Surely the weird stubbornness of Israel—some call it gallantry, some are merely bewildered—is one of the things the Jewish people have come to after so much otherwordly idealism, dreamy attending on the Messiah, making do in feudal, capitalistic, or socialistic Christian orders. They are saying: Okay, salvation if at all, here below. Okay, we'll save ourselves, since no one else will, and the Messiah is one of those brilliant specialists who neither makes appointments nor keeps them.

When my father came to visit during my student days in France, and at Orly airport they asked him to fill out a form, including his nationality, he wrote, "Jewish."

"No, they mean American," I said.

He looked at me pityingly. "When anyone asks that question, what they want to know is this: Are you a Jew?"

His experience was different from mine. It was a life lived

in function of the disability of nationality, mitigated by its pride and integrity. During the Great Depression, varieties of paranoids, lovers of uniforms, questers after easy explanations, and suffering isolates gathered together to march at night and complain during the day. Depending on sartorial or other minor conditions, they called themselves the Black Legion, the German-American Bund, or the Silver Shirts, and they took a position about the Jews similar to that of the Ku Klux Klan about the Negroes. They explained all evil; down the hatch with 'em. My life as a boy in that time was one of rebellion and combat against the disability. When we were refused service in a roadside tourist camp near Sandusky, Ohio, my father drove on morosely; I wanted to set fires. "How do they know, Dad, how do they know?"

"They know," he said. He gave Them magic powers, though of course it was a simpler matter, with a middle-aged Russian Jew signing the register "Gold" and speaking with his hard *t*'s and a confusion of *v*'s and *w*'s. And how did he get the name of Gold? He had heard that there was gold in the streets of New York. I am a man who came close to being named Streets. It would have changed my whole life.

Well, getting a bed in the motel is not a problem any more. Perhaps the world has evolved, or American vitamins and tennis make all white American travelers look more or less alike, or world wars and the Israeli Air Force have bombed out the paunchy, narrow-eyed naturalization officials who once decided if you could or could not buy a cabin for the night near Lake Erie. I can put my tongue between my teeth in the casual, sophisticated, sporty way essential to correct pronouncing the *th*. No hard final *g*'s.

Nevertheless, that history is still alive. There is a boiling of both righteous anger and dread, in varying balances, in most Jews, though some may not admit it, and in many the righteous anger has been converted into moral fervor for causes as far afield as Africa, the Cherokee Nation, and the Palestine refugees. Anxiety and dread are base metals which can be converted into moral coin. The tormented Maoist Jews of Al Fatah are brothers to the bearded patriarchs of Mea Shearim, those ultras of piety, who marched toward the Jordanians in 1948, wanting to open the gates to the Arab Legion because the rule was: No return to Jerusalem till the Messiah comes. The babes born on communes with names like H. Rap Shapiro and Stokely Epstein mean to say Justice for Everybody, no matter how fashionable and unlikely.

Finally in the 1970s, of course, Jews are no longer the prime targets. A miracle of history, Jewish survival through persecution, seems to be in the process of being replaced by a still greater miracle—Jewish survival through lack of persecution. At last, leaving the Soviet Union and the Arab tyrannies out of it for the moment, Jews are having their chance to live like others. The American melting pot produces a stew rather than any homogeneous mush, but those promiscuous lumps are surely a lot healthier for everybody. Jews, Chinese, Irish, the Japanese are cooking nicely; it's the Indians, the Chicanos, and especially the blacks who are making the trouble of human beings demanding the full right to be human.

In the past, the Jewish role was chiefly to be outrageous, to stimulate outrage. Money, sex, power, occult rites. Communion with the devil. And loud talking in summer resorts.

Now the burden of outrage has been lifted from the shoulders of the Jew. Others fulfill the needs of blue-collar dread; the greasy Jewish seducer is replaced by the hairsome hippie and the electric black man. The German-American Bund, the Black Legion, and William Dudley Pelley's Silver Shirts, those social clubs which elicited the happy cries of Christ-killer from my schoolmates, seem to have sunk into the ashes of history. Other times, other enemies. In my day I have lived through the evolution of the squirmy little sexpots of Lakewood. They used to have the mission to make Jewish men miserable; then they had the mission to make them happy; and now they mostly don't care one way or the other. Jews are accepted in most clubs and in the parking lots of A&W Root Beer stands all across this nation. The fine young gentleman of the Mosaic persuasion, whom Pattie or Sharon brought home to drive her parents nuts, has now been replaced by the fine young gentleman of the, er, colored persuasion. Jews just aren't exotic enough to be well hated any more. Those marginal differentiations which produced a special preeminence of Jews (peace to Thorstein Veblen) have been shaved into the middle class. The form of slavery created to suit the American Jew has been suburban white-collardom. Allergies, ulcers, and sick headaches—repression of desire in the interests of ranch-style, picture-window visibility—have replaced the blood and smoke of pogroms. The pack on the peddler's back is now filled with freeze-dried steaks and trail maps. He is hiking in the mountains with everyone else. Credo in ecology! Nobody here but us kids, the herd of independent minds.

Not to be smug about it, of course. The Jew is still a stranger. But he is no longer the Dark Stranger, the Wandering Traducer, the Prime Enemy. It would take heavy changes to give him back his former stature. In the meantime, the commie red bastard hippie spade junkie kid will have to serve the uses of American unease.

Hatred of the stranger seems to be, alas, natural to human society. The bitterest steady prejudice I've ever met was in Haiti, the black republic, where black hated mulatto, mulatto hated white, and black, straight hair resented kinky hair, broad nose resented narrow nose, and there were dozens of words to name the differences of blood between pure African and pure Caucasian. I used to be taken by mulatto friends to the Bourdon Country Club, which admitted neither blacks nor whites as full members; only the lovely browns were allowed to pay dues. And I knew a beautiful girl, niece of a former president, who claimed that there were no blacks in her family.

"You're descended from an infinite series of mulattoes?"

"*Oui.*"

And in Africa I've seen the despising of Arab and black, Ibo and Hausa, Yoruba and everyone else—and a brutal war of extermination waged in Biafra against the Ibos and their friends.

In California, free, lovely California, and in San Francisco, where nobody came first, there is still that certain feeling between the Chinese and the gentry perched a little higher on Russian Hill. If I see a man warming up his motor for ten minutes while I wait in honking traffic for his parking place, I think, Gee, the Chinese peasant mentality doesn't really understand about warming up motors and people being kept waiting. . . . Which is a hare's breath from : "DAMN CHINK MOVE YOUR DAMN ASS OUTA THERE!" The Native Son feels a bit cleaner and fresher than the dusty new arrival from Oklahoma or New York, and the United Airlines pioneer who got here a whole year ago feels like a native son when he sees the clumsy tourist trying to climb with his billowing Hawaiian shirt and his jabbering bubble-haired wife onto one of "our" cable cars.

But normal xenophobia is not the full explanation for the special persistence of complex paranoias against the Jew. I once read of a courageous medieval pope who defended the Jews against the charge of cooking Christian maidens for holiday fare by issuing a formal reminder: "Their religion forbids the eating of animals with claws." Crabs and pigs, my mother told me, were not kosher; nor were the Patties and Sharons next door. My mother and the culinary pope understood each other. Nothing but chicken fat in our matzo balls. Your runaway daughter couldn't be found in our pantry.

Things seem to have changed even in sex. It used to be the fate of the pretty little round-headed country club girls to be mean to Jews, because they have those cloven hoofs and horns and devilish tails curled into their gabardine pants. Consequently it was also their fate to be especially nice to the Jewish kids on the block, for the same reason—horny hoofs, the cunning tail of the devil. Just because sex with the devil was magic and forbidden, it naturally became magic and supremely desirable. Many a giggle herein implied.

Now, with a new generation, there is a benevolent indifference to the devil's emissary in every small town. Sexual liberation has meant an end to Jewish slavery in the rice paddies of Eros. Why play hospital with Marvin Schneider down the street when you can sneak past the Trailways Station, cross the tracks, and visit young Floyd Washington, someone who *really* has the devil in him, according to your parents. . . .

Curiously enough, through all the sad and comic history of anti-Semitic abuse, one facet of Jewish life generally got a good word or at least a mournful sexual okay. It can be called the Beautiful Rachel Syndrome. The daughter of the usurer is ashamed of her greasy dad; think of Jessica, of course, but she, Jessica or Beautiful Dark-Eyed Rachel, fills the melodramas of three centuries. But who now is the last remaining villain of Jewish lore? It's no longer the Yiddish mama, who has definitely been shot down by a generation of squirming Jewish writer-sons. It's the JAP, the Jewish American Princess, the beautiful Rachel finally getting hers, too. She is depicted as greedy, prudish, calculating, middle class, devoted to adoration of her mirror. The one whom Dickens and Shakespeare spared has come to her day of reckoning.

Sartre's ingenious idea that the anti-Semite hates Jesus, the burden of Christianity which Jews have put on him, helps to explain some of the special bitterness of the recent two thousand years. Clearly the Christian world has never lived up to the holy ideals of meekness, generosity, loving thy neighbor, peacefulness. There is some bad conscience about it, bad faith, to misuse the Sartrean language. Besides the positive injunctions to love and make peace, Christianity has also asked Christians to repress desires, and there it was more successful. Pleasures were suppressed, sinning was explored and ramified as a way of life, confession continually emphasized how Jesus hated all those things you liked to do in the dark. And what happens to repressed desires? They break out in violence, and violence especially against the dreamy other who seems to be the cause of the anxiety. The Jews gave the anti-Semite this knotty, knobby Christian hair shirt to wear, and they themselves don't wear it! What an injustice. How presumptuous. The chosen people is exempt from so many sins. They are free to do all the nasty things we want to do, make money, wallow in luxury, do funny things to women. Oh, it hurts. Ow, ouch. Let's throw a rock.

The air is not so filled with rocks as once it was. I was a busy kid in Lakewood, Ohio, living the life of a symbol but dodg-ing palpable stones. Now there is only an occasional flurry of the action there used to be, but of course history is a movie which never ends. There are intermissions and reel changes; the movie goes on.

My non-Jewish wife was never taken to be a Jew until she married me. Now it's creeping up on her. A friend asked her if it's true that Jewish babies have a black spot in the middle of their backs. *Yes* is the answer, and if you take a magnifying glass to it, you can read the tiny, dimpled words: *This offer not valid in Moscow or Cairo or other states where prohib-ited.*

Another time she heard a lovable Carolina student come up to me and say, "Mistah Gole, Ah useta be a anti-See-mite," —let me now depart from dialect comedy—"until about six months ago. I just got turned on to Jew-beauty." And he smiled beatifically and waited for me to tell him all about Jew-beauty, that frequent discovery of the last literary gener-ation.

This book is filled with the marvelous murderous comedy of anti-Semitism, as in the image of the French duke showing his half-Jewish son a gold coin and calling out notice to see how the kid's eyes start from their sockets. Or the distinctions between high-minded Nordic courage and sticky Hebrew persistence. Or the note about how Jewish accomplishment in the arts of literature and music is merely "expressiveness," while Christian creativity is manifested in more serious en-deavors, such as soldiering. Or the Wisconsin sociologist calmly predicting that Jewish adaptability will eventually lead the Jew to enjoy camping out, cooking over open fires, and tramping in forests, just like Nordic nature-lovers. The Jew's "soft hands and curved fingers," a surprisingly recur-rent theme, are sometimes running with Galician slime, sometimes suspiciously clean of honest toil. Hardly a single aspect of his being or persistence on earth fails to come under attack by some glinty paranoid. Looking for simple explana-tions for the troubles of life on earth, many have found joyous revulsion in contemplating the Dark Stranger, the Wandering Jew, total villain and devil's best emissary. The Beautiful Rachel theme, the sloe-eyed Jewess ashamed of her evil daddy, provides the single relief. (T. S. Eliot doesn't even like Rachel, however.)

The American anti-Semite usually claims to be a Christian, and he is meek and mild. "We have been accused of being Jew-baiters. . . . This is not true. We despise only villainy, and our aim is to direct the attention of Americans to the danger that lurks in the Jews." There is something sweet and innocent in this declaration. When he speaks of the danger lurking *in* the Jews, he perhaps means to objectify the menace of the devil which is merely given housing by the Jew's unfortunate body. Perhaps he is not a Jew-baiter at all, but merely needs to destroy the Jew-host in order to kill the devil-tenant. Morality everywhere. Morality even in chagrin, spite, and the will to murder.

If the devil didn't exist, surely the godly would invent him.

—HERBERT GOLD

"KIKE!"

Several years ago a large exhibition commemorating two thousand years of Jewish life on the Rhine was held in Cologne, Germany. In reviewing the catalog of this exhibition for the *Jewish Observer and Middle East Review*, I was struck by what seemed to me then to be the rather "Germanic" thoughts on the problem of tolerance expressed in its introduction. "Tolerance," it declared, "is not a question of sympathy or of hindsight and, above all, not of indifference. Tolerance is a question of self-discipline and of spiritual and moral maturity."

To introduce the categories of "self-discipline" and "maturity," and to deny the value of common human sympathy in this respect, appeared to me to be tantamount to chiding bigots for lacking some of the very qualities to which the Third Reich had exhorted its supporters—it was something like saying that intolerance is not "manly." What is more, the emphasis on such factors seemed to divert attention from the wider social contexts of which I had been trained to regard anti-Semitism as a product. As such, it had at least the potential of denigrating the value of "social engineering" as the strategy for improving the human condition to which I was, as a liberal, committed.

A consideration of the history of anti-Semitism in the United States, however, and of attempts to account for it, now leads me to question whether these moral criteria are not, after all, the categories in which bigotry is most aptly examined.

Saying this is not to deny the role that social forces and historical developments have played in shaping the nature and determining the intensity of anti-Semitic feeling at any given moment in time. From the middle of the nineteenth century, and in particular during the period from about 1880 to 1920, the immigration of large numbers of Jews to the United States from Eastern and Central Europe engendered the kind of tensions which normally accompany the mass migration of any group to another country[1]; the declining power of the White-Anglo-Saxon-Protestant elite group from the end of the nineteenth century, as Baltzell has shown, gave rise to fears and frustrations which vented themselves in acute, aristocratic distaste for the Jews[2]; the urbanization and industialization of America brought about a vicious populist reaction against "big city" capitalism that pitted the virtues of Jacksonian pastoralism against the vices of an allegedly Jewish modernity during the first quarter of the twentieth century, in particular[3]; the tensions of American life during the Depression, and the fear of involvement in the gathering conflict in Europe, both vented themselves in the widespread anti-Semitism of the 1930s: the Jews were to blame.[4]

Since the end of the Second World War, on the other hand, there has been marked decline in anti-Semitism as a social force in American life. The cessation of mass immigration and the acculturation of the children and grandchildren of the immigrant generations are factors in this development, as indeed are wider changes in the social structure of American life. Conceivably, horror at events in Nazi Germany and admiration for the exemplarily American virtues of industriousness and martial competence displayed by Jews in Israel may also have contributed to this result. More immediately, the rising pressure for social, economic, and cultural equality by blacks and other groups in America has led to new alignments of social and political tensions and to the diminution of Jewish "visibility."

From a historical or sociological point of view it is possible, therefore, to link anti-Semitism to wider developments in American life. From such a point of view, moreover, it is beyond dispute that anti-Semitism, formerly a widespread and, to an extent, even a respectable attitude, has become a relatively negligible factor. Opinion polls conducted over the course of the past thirty-five years establish the decline of anti-Semitism beyond question.[5] What is more, discrimination against Jews—i.e., the behavioral manifestations of anti-Semitic prejudice—has fallen off dramatically. During the first half of this century the exclusion of Jews from hotels, vacation resorts, clubs, housing developments, universities and university fraternities, and from a wide range of employment opportunities, was a pervasive and seemingly immutable fact of American life.[6]

This pattern, it should be said, still persists; there are still hundreds of clubs from which Jews are barred (a fact which, because of the convention of conducting business transactions in a social setting, has serious economic implications, and has often been used to justify the non-hiring of Jews in senior managerial positions), and thousands of upper-echelon jobs in industry and commerce which no Jews have ever filled; nor can one overlook the fact that there are less than five university presidents who are Jews in the country today.[7] Nevertheless, these forms of discrimination are far less notable than before, not only because of the enactment of antidis-criminatory legislation from which the Jews have benefited, even if they were not intended as the prime beneficiaries, but also because the attitudinal factors which lead to dis-crimination are far less in evidence than before. It would, quite simply, be unthinkable for a president of Harvard pub-licly to announce, as Lowell did in a commencement address in 1920, the imposition of a Jewish "quota."[8]

From the perspective of the social historian, then, Ameri-can anti-Semitism is a relevant focus of study only during the period stretching from the middle of the nineteenth to the middle of the twentieth century, when its prominence as a fact of American life was indisputable. Nevertheless, there are certain obvious limitations to this approach. Anti-Semitic attitudes were to be found in America in the middle of the seventeenth century, and Jews were denied even elemen-tary rights in the colonial period.[9] In modern times, more-over, survey after survey has shown that a large number of Gentile Americans are anti-Semitic, even though their anti-Semitism does not always manifest itself in their actual behavior. A survey of white church-members conducted in 1963, for example, revealed that 33 percent of Protestants and 29 percent of Catholics agreed that "Jews are more likely than Christians to cheat in business,"[10] and that 36 percent and 35 percent, respectively, agreed that "Because Jews are not bound by Christian ethics, they do things to get ahead that Christians generally will not do."[11] Forty-three percent of Protestants and Catholics alike agreed that "Jews tend to wear flashy clothes and jewelry."[12]

The same study concluded that 33 percent of affiliated Protestants and 29 percent of affiliated Catholics ranked "high" or "medium high" in anti-Semitic beliefs, and that only 20 percent and 26 percent, respectively, appeared to be free of anti-Semitic attitudes altogether.[13] A related study conducted in 1964 showed that among whites with only a grammar school education, 30 percent in the North and 36 percent in the South were "high" or "very high" in anti-Semitism; among those with at least some high school educa-

tion, 20 percent of Northerners and 24 percent of Southern-
ers fell into the "high" or "very high" categories; and the
same holds true of 8 percent of those with at least some
college education.[14] The findings of survey research are not
always accurate, of course, particularly when they are aimed
at measuring attitudes which are held in public disrepute
and which respondents are unlikely to acknowledge freely
(this no doubt holds true to an even greater extent for those
with at least some higher education). In such an event, however, one must assume that the actual incidence of, in this
case, anti-Semitism, is somewhat higher than indicated by
the data. But whatever the incidence of anti-Semitism down
to the last percentage point may be, all surveys agree that
anti-Semitism *as an attitude* continues to be widespread in
this country—even though, for social historians, it is no
longer considered a significant focus of study.

Does anti-Semitism that fails to manifest itself in anti-
Semitic behavior *matter?* The answer is surely yes, it does
matter, and from at least two equally important points of
view. We have seen that social historians have traced, and by
implication tended to explain away, the emergence of manifest anti-Semitism as the product of certain social forces and
political events. It is beyond challenge that these factors have
indeed played a role in the story of anti-Semitism in the
United States and that even in the present time anti-Semitism is linked to regional and sociological factors (i.e., an
uneducated Southerner is likely to be more anti-Semitic than
an educated Northerner). Anti-Semitism, however, enjoys (if
that is the word) a life independent of such factors. At times
it can emerge, unpredictably and with remarkable vigor,
from the murky recesses in which it is concealed.

In a sudden outbreak inspired by vandalism in Germany,
swastikas and other anti-Jewish obscenities were painted on
synagogues and Jewish cemeteries across the United States;
Jewish homes and stores were similarly vandalized and Jews
were insulted and even assaulted. A total of 643 such inci-
dents were recorded within a span of three months and then
ceased, as suddenly as they had begun.[15] The episode was

relatively harmless. No Jews were killed and nothing of irreplaceable value was destroyed. But the fact that the perpetrators of these deeds were young Americans rather than nostalgic, aging fascists, and that the indescribable brutalities of the Nazi era served as an example to inspire rather than to horrify them, is surely an object lesson in *what can happen* in the United States. There is no reason to believe that from the vast reservoir of bigotry, and specifically of anti-Semitism, that exists in this country, a new wave of Jew-baiting, perhaps even of persecution and murder, may not arise.

Tens of millions of Americans dislike Jews, fear or mistrust them. By one of the absurdities of the human personality, many anti-Semites can indeed claim that their "best friends are Jews," or at least that they enjoy cordial relations with Jews. However, many surely also manifest their Jew-hatred, causing pain, fear, and shock. Thousands, and no doubt millions, of lives in America today are warped by this hate, or by exposure to it. This mistrust and bitterness *is* a fact of life in America today; there are, apparently, people who are taught to believe that Jews have horns[16] and are guilty of indescribable perversities. One cannot be indifferent to such enormities, or insensitive to the anguish which they cause. *Anti-Semitism matters,* even when it does not appear as an explicit and uncensured fact of public life. It matters if you are a Jew and encounter it. It also matters if you are a Gentile and demean your humanity through it.

The fallacy underlying much social history and the social sciences in general is in the last resort a moral one. One aspect of this has already been discussed: what is significant to the social historian or to the social scientist is not necessarily significant to individuals living in society. But this tacit denigration of the individual inherent in the sociological method has even wider moral repercussions in terms of the notion of human responsibility which it implies. Where bigotry, in this case anti-Semitism, is seen primarily as a function of certain social or historical forces, it is easy for the individual to absolve himself of blame for his own bigotry, which he can attribute to factors beyond his own control. That those forces do indeed play a major role in shaping his attitudes is beyond dispute. But saying this is not to accept the view of the individual as a passive object devoid of will and incapable of surmounting the evils which surround him.

Anti-Semitism is not, as Simmel insisted, a "social disease"[17] but a moral aberration; it is a denial of the humanity of other human beings and the responsibility for it lies with those who are guilty of it. Maimonides, one of the greatest Jewish thinkers of all time, attributed it quite simply to the desire to "thwart God's will,"[18] and the extraordinary persistence of anti-Semitism across time surely entitles us to regard it as one of the more prevalent and hence significant manifestations of man's pervasively (but not ineradicably) evil nature. As a moral aberration, anti-Semitism defies the categories of sociological analysis: it exists, in greater or lesser measure, among all classes of persons and at every period of history. A Henry Adams or an F. Scott Fitzgerald will express it with more eloquence than some of the crude pamphleteers whose inspirations are also presented in this book; and all of these will be more articulate than an epithet-hurling John Doe; not all will manifest their Jew-hatred as obviously as the officers of a club who deny Jews admission, let alone as cruelly as those who lynched Leo Frank. But however it is manifested, and even where it is not explicitly manifested at all, anti-Semitism is something which arises out of the hearts and minds of individual human beings, and must in the final analysis be understood as such.[19]

The notion that "To fight racism effectively means to fight to abolish the social structures which engender it" not only contains this tacit denigration of the individual's responsibility to himself but, in view of the tenacious survival of anti-Semitism in virtually any kind of social structure, holds out scant promise of any final resolution of this problem. The only palliative which can ultimately effect the emancipation of mankind from the devastations of bigotry is that of the individual's moral will exercised, first and foremost, against his own will to evil: to cite the title of Tolstoy's greatest polemic, "The Kingdom of God Is Within You."

But if the Kingdom of God is within us, then so too is the Kingdom of Satan. By calling attention to the attitudinal dimension of bigotry, and by documenting it as vividly as possible, the readings contained in this volume, and in the other volumes of this series, will enable the reader to identify some of the dynamics that have informed the tragic history of ethnic prejudice in the United States. But this is not the sole purpose of this volume, or of the series of which it is a part. Rather, our intention has also been to identify attitudes which are to be found in most people but which many of us, in turn, hide even from ourselves. By bringing these to the fore and presenting them in all their stark and sometimes brutal reality, we invite the reader to ask whether he can find in them any reflection of himself.

—MICHAEL SELZER

1. Anti-Semitism in Early America

Prejudice toward the Jews, and even overt discrimination against them, have from the outset been a part of the Jewish experience in America. Despite this fact, however, the Jews have managed to take root in this country and have succeeded in making theirs the most important community in Jewry. In this contrapuntal theme of rejection and resurgence is sounded the lietmotif of American Jewish history.

There is therefore some symbolic significance—and irony, too—in the fact that the first recorded instance of anti-Semitism in North America relates to the attempt made in 1654 by Peter Stuyvesant, the governor of New York, or of New Amsterdam, as it was then called, to banish Jews from that city.[1] That attempt failed; and in due course New York was to become the home of a vast Jewish population and the center of an extraordinarily creative and vital Jewish culture.

Peter Stuyvesant Requests Permission to Expel Jews from New Amsterdam, September 22, 1654.

The Jews who have arrived would nearly all like to remain here, but learning that they (with their customary usury and deceitful trading with the Christians) were very repugnant to the inferior magistrates, as also to the people having the most affection for you; the Deaconry also fearing that owing to their present indigence they might become a charge in the coming winter, we have, for the benefit of this weak and newly developing place and the land in general, deemed it useful to require them in a friendly way to depart; praying also most seriously in this connection, for ourselves as also for the general community of your worships, that the deceitful race—such hateful enemies and blasphemers of the name of Christ—be not allowed to further infect and trouble this new colony to the detraction of your worships and the dissatisfaction of your worships' most affectionate subjects.

Samuel Oppenheim, "The Early History of the Jews in New York, 1654–1664," *Publications of the American Jewish Historical Society*, XVIII (1909).

The Directors of the West India Company, Amsterdam, Rescind Stuyvesant's Order, April 26, 1655.

. . . We would like to have agreed to your wishes and request, that the new territories should not be further invaded by people of the Jewish race, for we foresee from such immigration the same difficulties which you fear, but after having further weighed and considered this matter we observe that it would be unreasonable and unfair, especially because of the considerable loss sustained by the Jews in the taking of Brazil and also because of the large amount of capital which they have invested in shares of this company. After many consultations we have decided and resolved upon a certain petition made by the said Portuguese Jews, that they shall have permission to sail to and trade in New Netherland and to live and remain there, provided that the poor among them shall not become a burden to the Company or the community, but be supported by their own nation. You will govern yourself accordingly. . . .

> Oppenheim, "Early History of the Jews."

The West India Company Defines the Status of Jews in New Amsterdam, March 13, 1656.

. . . The permission given to the Jews to go to New Netherland and enjoy there the same privileges as they have here has been granted only as far as civil and political rights are concerned, without giving the said Jews a claim to the privileges of exercising their religion in a synagogue or at a gathering; as long, therefore, as you receive no request for granting them this liberty of religious exercise, your considerations and anxiety about this matter are premature and when later something shall be said about it, you can do no better than to refer them to us and await the necessary order. . . .

> Oppenheim, "Early History of the Jews."

The West India Company Rebukes Stuyvesant and Defines Further Restrictions of Jewish Rights, June 13, 1656.

. . . We have seen and hear with displeasure that against our order of the 15th of February 1655, issued at the request of the Jewish or Portuguese nation, you have forbidden them to

trade to Fort Orange and the South River, also the purchase
of real estate, which is granted to them without difficulty
here in this country, and we wish it had not been done and
that you had obeyed your orders, which you must always
execute punctually and with more respect; the Jews, or Portuguese people, however shall not be employed in any public
service (to which they are neither admitted in this city), nor
allowed to have open retail stores, but they may quietly and
peacefully carry on their business as before said and exercise
in all quietness their religion within their houses, for which
end they must without doubt endeavor to build their houses
close together in a convenient place on one or the other side
of New Amsterdam—at their own choice—as they have done
here. . . .

Oppenheim, "Early History of the Jews."

Resolution of Peter Stuyvesant and the New Amsterdam Council to Exclude the Jews from Military Service, August 28, 1655.

The Captains and officers of the trainbands of this city
having asked the Director General and Council whether the
Jewish people who reside in this city should also train and
mount guard with the citizens' bands, this was taken into
consideration and deliberated upon; first the disinclination
and unwillingness of these trainbands to be fellow-soldiers
with the aforesaid nation and to be on guard with them in the
same guard house, and on the other side, that the said nation
was not admitted or counted among the citizens, as regards
trainbands or common citizens' guards, neither in the illustrious City of Amsterdam nor (to our knowledge) in any city in
Netherland; but in order that the said nation may honestly
be taxed for their freedom in that respect, it is directed by
the Director General and Council, to prevent further discon-
tent, that the aforesaid nation shall, according to the usages
of the renowned City of Amsterdam, remain exempt from

general training and guard duty, on condition that each male person over 16 and under 60 years contribute for the aforesaid freedom toward the relif of the general municipal taxes 65 stivers every month, and the military council of the citizens is hereby authorized and charged to carry this into effect until our further orders, and to collect, pursuant to the above, the aforesaid contribution once in every month, and in case of refusal, to collect it by legal process. . . .

> Oppenheim, "Early History of the Jews."

At a somewhat later date, and with rather more success than had met Peter Stuyvesant's efforts, certain of the British colonies also denied settlement and other rights to Jews. The following is a document ordering the expulsion of Jews from Georgia in 1734.[2]

The Expulsion of Jews from Georgia, January 5, 1734.

Ordered. That the Secretary do wait on Messrs. Alvaro Lopez Suassa, Francis Salvador, Jr. and Anthony Da Costa with the following Message in writing:

The Trustees for establishing the Colony of Georgia in America having receiv'd a letter from Messrs. Alvaro Lopez Suassa, Francis Salvador, Jr. and Anthony Da Costa, in answer to a message sent for their Commissions, which letter does not appear satisfactory to the said Trustees, they think themselves oblig'd not only to insist on the redelivery of their Commissions, but as they conceive of the settling of Jews in Georgia will be prejudicial to the Colony, and as some have been sent without the knowledge of the Trustees, the Trustees do likewise require that the said Messrs. Alvaro Lopez Suassa, Francis Salvador, Jr. and Anthony Da Costa, or whoever else may have been concerned in sending them over, do use their endeavors that the said Jews may be removed from the Colony of Georgia, as the best and only satisfaction they can give to the Trustees for such an indignity offer'd to Gentlemen acting under His Majesty's Charter.

Charles C. Jones, Jr., *History of Savannah, Ga.* (Syracuse, 1890), p. 52.

"By the middle of the eighteenth century," Higham reports, "a regime of freedom flourished so profusely that intermarriage was frequent and socially acceptable. Well-to-do Jews joined the same clubs and private libraries as their Christian peers, attended the same dancing assemblies, and sent their children to the same schools. Jews contributed to Anglican and Catholic undertakings and, on at least one occasion, solicited the aid of Christians for a synagogue."[3] There is much evidence to corroborate this statement. On the other hand—and this is something which we shall observe throughout the course of American history—the acceptance of Jews by some people was matched by the rejection of Jews at the hands of others. Even in the New England states, where a form of philo-Semitism was a part of the Puritan tradition, hatred of the Jews was, as Ezra Stiles observed, widespread.[4] In 1762, for example, as we see from the following source, Jews were actually denied naturalization in Rhode Island.

Jews Are Denied Naturalization in Rhode Island (1762).

The petition of Messrs Aaron Lopez and Isaac Elizer, persons professing the Jewish religion, praying that they may be naturalized on an act of Parliament made in the 13th year of His Majesty's reign George the Second, having been duly considered, and also the act of Parliament therein referred to, this court are unanimously of the opinion that the said act of Parliament was widely designed for increasing the number of inhabitants in the plantations; but this colony being already so full of people that many of His Majesty's good subjects born within the same have removed and settled in Nova-Scotia and other places; (the petition) cannot come within the intention of the said act.

Further, by the charter granted to this colony, it appears

that the full and quiet enjoyment of the Christian religion and a desire of propagating the same were the principal views with which the colony was settled; and by a law made and passed in the year 1663, no person who does not profess the Christian religion can be admitted free of this colony. This court therefore unanimously dismiss the said petition as absolutely inconsistent with the first principle upon which the colony was founded and with a law now of the same in full force.

> Quoted in Franklin B. Dexter, *Extracts from the Itineraries and Other Miscellanies of Ezra Stiles, D.D., LL.D., 1755–1794* (New Haven, 1916), p. 52.

The following poem, which evokes an image of the Jew which was to be widely propagated a century later, also suggests that anti-Semitic prejudice was by no means unknown in the latter half of the eighteenth century.

The Jew as an Economic Parasite (1790).

> Tax on tax young Belcour cries,
> More imposts, and a new excise.
> A public debt's a public blessing
> Which 'tis of course a crime to lessen.
> Each day a fresh report he broaches,
> That Spies and Jews may ride in coaches.
> Soldiers and Farmers don't despair,
> Untax'd as yet are Earth and Air.

> Quoted in Morris U. Schappes, *A Documentary History of the Jews in the United States* (New York, 1950), p. 73.

2. The Onset of Mass Immigration

Prior to the 1840s the Jewish community in America had been stable, bourgeois, and small, numbering perhaps fifteen thousand souls at the most. From that decade on, however, a very different type of Jew began to migrate to the United States, first by the thousands and eventually by the hundreds of thousands. The victims of persecution and deprivation in Central and Eastern Europe and, at least during the first few years after their arrival in the United States, still bound to the customs and traditions of Jewish Orthodoxy, these "huddled masses" of Jews were a source of acute discomfort to their American Jewish brethren and of no less acute distaste to many Gentiles.[1]

Whether as "wagon barons" peddling trinkets and utensils across the country, or as sweatshop laborers eking out a miserable livelihood in the slums of large cities, notably New York, the Jewish immigrants quickly became a byword as dirty, diseased, primitive, ugly, lazy, avaricious, irredeemably dishonest people, a threat to society and a menace to civilization. Anti-Semitism in America did not arise, as we have already suggested, with the onset of mass Jewish immigration, but the influx of large numbers of "dirty-looking" Jews unquestionably now led to the emergence of a new and virulent form of Jew-hatred.

An Anti-Semitic Incident (1835).

I continued my peddling until January 1835, when one evening, in deep snow and quite frozen, I came to Easton, a pretty little town in Delaware, and entered an inn. A number of guests sat around the glowering stoves; and as they saw me enter, a pale and snow-covered merchant, a feeling of compassion must have come over them, for nearly everyone bought something of me; and thus even in the evening, I did some good business, after I had run about the whole day in terrible winter weather, earning scarcely enough for a drink. While preoccupied with my business, I was watched by an oldish-looking, occasionally smiling but apparently unconcerned man behind the stove. He allowed me to finish the business in peace but then he got up, tapped me on the shoulder, and bade me follow him. Out of doors, his first question was whether I had a trade-license for peddling. I still felt so strange in America, and he spoke in so low a voice, that I did not understand him and, therefore, looked at him in astonishment. My long, ten-days-old beard struck him, and he asked me further whether I was a Jew. He did not want to believe me when I denied it. Fortunately, I had with me the passport of my homeland, which I presented to him. Now he grew somewhat better disposed, looking at me sympathetically, and said, "Since I see that you are an honest Protestant Christian I shall let you go, although I am losing twenty-five dollars through it. I have no kind feelings for the Jews, and were you one of them, I would not treat you so gently. If I wanted to arrest you, you would have to pay fifty dollars' fine or, until you were able to raise it, you would have to go to jail, and half the fine would be mine. Still, I shall forego that; but you better give up your trade and look for another one. Sooner or later you will be caught and then you'll be out of luck.

After having said this he shook my hand and went away. . . .

When I stepped again into the room, the friendly innkeeper was able to observe my embarrassment and guess what had taken place. He praised the humane constable, laughed at his Jew-hatred, but he, too, advised me to quit my trade.

> G. F. Streckfuss, *Der Auswanderer nach Amerika* (Zeitz, 1836), quoted in Rudolf Glanz, "Source Materials on the History of Jewish Immigration to the United States, 1800–1880," *YIVO Annual of Jewish Social Science,* VI (1951).

A Pogrom in New York (1850).

Who would believe that the wild appetite for Jew-baiting crosses even to North America? And who brings it here? Irish emigrants, or rather dregs. . . . The *Weserzeitung* reports the following: A shocking event occurred last Sunday. It was the eve of the great Day of Atonement of the Jews and they were all in the synagogue. The house in which the synagogue is situated is occupied by both Jewish and Irish families. During the gathering of the congregation someone brought a street woman in to the rear of the building: a short time later, a rumor spread that the Jews had murdered a Gentile girl for their holiday. About 10:30 a crowd of some 500 men burst into the house, broke down the doors, and literally pulled from their beds sleeping women, one of whom was in childbed next to a sick husband. A most shocking riot was perpetrated; everyone who resisted was knocked down, a little box of jewelry to the amount of 63 dollars was stolen from a peddler. The remarkable thing about this affair is that three Irish policemen were the leaders of this raging mob, and the tumult thereby acquired a sort of official character, whereas, after all, the authorities had remained totally ignorant of this riot.

Allgemeine Zeitung des Judentums (1850), p. 593, quoted in Glanz, "Source Materials on the History of Jewish Immigration," *YIVO Annual of Jewish Social Science,* VI (1951).

A Bizarre Disturbance (1849).

There are some 12,000 or 14,000 persons of the Jewish persuasion in this city, and finding it difficult to obtain burial grounds within the city limits, they have purchased land on Long Island and in other places. A German (Jewish) congregation purchased a burying ground near East New York, and one day last week, having occasion to bury an aged member, the German population of that place, with stones, guns, and clubs, dispersed the members, ordered them off, wounded several persons severely, and compelled them to deposit the body in the Cypress Hills Cemetery. Complaint was made of the outrage to the authorities of Brooklyn, and we presume the parties will be arrested and made to answer for their conduct. These German emigrants imagine that a free country means the privilege of doing what they please, and violating law and order whenever it suits their purpose. A lesson or two will let them understand in what their rights consist.

Sunday Times and Noah's Weekly Messenger, August 12, 1849, quoted in Morris U. Schappes, *A Documentary History of the Jews in the United States* (New York, 1950).

Discrimination in Employment, and an
Editorial Comment (1849).

A Bohemian writes to ask us what we meant by saying in our article yesterday on the secret of success, that in this country *all are equally encouraged and protected;* for he says he is a Hebrew by race, though a naturalized citizen, and that certain persons, tradesmen, in advertising in a journal of this city for a number of shade painters, put in as an exception, "No Jews wanted here." Bohemian, being a Jew, and a shade painter, thinks the doctrine of equal encouragement and protection don't work here. We did not expect any such interpretation. We meant simply that the *government and institutions* of this country hold out the same inducements and chances to every citizen—in thus much and thus far they are equally protected and encouraged. If individuals, or members of different races and clans will disagree and battle with each other, the quarrel is theirs, and the more pitiable and shameful is it to him who draws the weapon first and uses it furthest. We apprehend the spirit of our institutions and government is often more liberal and generous than that of many individuals who enjoy its blessings and who ought to imitate its example.

> New York Sun, March 17, 1849, quoted
> in Schappes, *Documentary History of
> the Jews.*

The identification of Jews as petty criminals seems already to have become widespread by the middle of the nineteenth century, as the following extracts reveal. In 1867 a cause célèbre came into being with the adoption of discriminatory practices against Jewish shopkeepers by certain insurance companies.[2]

The New York City Police Gazette Indicts the
Jews (1862).

The developments of almost every day serve to show the extent to which the German Jews are acting as receivers of stolen goods . . . a very general suspicion prevails against this people, and it is not surprising. Many of them are professional lifters, burglars, and swindlers. Those in business find it difficult to effect an insurance upon their stock because of the frequency with which fires occur in their stores and the suspicious circumstances attending them.

New York City Police Gazette, as quoted in *The Israelite* (vol. 5, 1850), cited by Glanz, "Source Materials on the History of Jewish Immigration," *YIVO Annual of Jewish Social Science,* VI (1951).

A Jewish Swindler (1860s).

Thus they journey from one saloon to another until the greenhorn is already in need of his friends' support to set him on his feet; and they too are grateful enough not to leave him lying. They know well why. In the Bowery they pass by a jewelry store. Moses is standing at the door, and is examining some precious stones. "Sir," says the chap, "here we can do some business. I myself am a good hand at jewelry, these damned Jews buy the stuff cheaply and are delighted if they can get rid of it again at a small profit." "So?" "Then we better go inside," replies the greenhorn, whose tongue is getting to be somewhat heavy. "What is the price of this pin?" "Thirty dollars, sir!" "You're crazy, I'll be damned if I give you more than half that much." "Not a cent less, gentlemen, a diamond of the first water." Here the chap returns to the greenhorn and whispers into his ear, "Don't excite the Jew, offer him twenty-five dollars, he will let you have it, and the thing is worth fifty dollars between brothers!"

"All right then, five dollars more!" The Jew smiles. "Five dollars still more, or don't annoy me." At a sign from the chap, the Jew hesitantly gives in and the sale is closed. Thereupon the greenhorn opens his pocketbook, in which there is unfortunately nothing but Illinois banknotes. The Jew won't accept them and the buyer is just about ready to start another dispute when the man in the blue coat pushes in between them, saying: "Hand me that fifty-dollar bill. I'll give you good bills for it and still ask only 2 percent. Here are the twenty-five dollars for the pin, and twenty-four dollars for you, with the 2 percent discount make it fifty dollars." The greenhorn gets the pin and with a "damn those Jews" lets himself be dragged out of the store.

(The next day)

Further, it turns out that the banknotes he had received are all counterfeit, that the pin is worth hardly fifty cents. In indignation, he runs to see the Jew, but the latter coolly denies ever having seen him, and threatens to call the police if he does not clear out immediately.

> Georg Teckla, *Drei Jahre in New York* (Zwickau, 1862), quoted by Glanz, "Source Materials on the History of Jewish Immigration," *YIVO Annual of Jewish Social Science,* VI (1951).

The Jew was condemned for being an alien, and for very blatantly violating the norms of American society. The process of acculturation to American values, however, was rapid and it then became possible to denounce the Jews, not for being different but for trying to assimilate to American life. While acts of overt discrimination against Jews were to become far more frequent from the 1880s on, the following extracts reveal that the impulse to exclude Jews from the mainstream of social life was already manifesting itself by the middle of the century.

The Jew at the Theater (1848).

For a paltry few cents he can make himself at home here. . . . This is the place where he finds recognition, where no one can make him feel he is a Jew. And how the jewelry glitters in the magnificent illumination! Rebecca and Sarah can lean over the balustrade of the first balcony, showing themselves to all. They are on the first balcony! And all for fifty cents apiece! . . . You will, dear reader, recognize them at a glance by the way they carry their elbows. But should your eyes not recognize them—well, then, your nose will let you know in the midst of which species you find yourself!

Theodor Griesinger, *Lebende Bilder* (Stuttgart, 1848), quoted in Glanz, "Source Material on the History of Jewish Immigration," *YIVO Annual of Jewish Social Science,* VI (1951).

The Jew Blackballed (1866).

. . . There are certain people who consider themselves intelligent upon whom, however, the philosophy of centuries and its fruits—spiritual emancipation, humanism, and religious tolerance—have left no mark whatsoever. Among the many educated and enlightened members of the Arion society these are those whose fundamental principle is: "We want no Jews . . ." It so happened that a Jew had been proposed for membership in the society. His candidacy was enthusiastically sponsored by many members. Your correspondent, too, who is a friend of the candidate and can only speak of him in praiseworthy fashion, was advised that it would be regrettable to place him in the embarrassing circumstance of failing to receive the requisite number of votes because he is a Jew. Your correspondent stood his ground and declared that he would leave the society where the candidate refused admission because of his faith. Other progressive members sought to enlighten the benighted members of the society, but in vain. . . . My candidate was defeated because he is a Jew. This occurred in the land of freedom of conscience in the year of our Lord 1866. Naturally, I could no longer remain in this society.

New Yorker Handelszeitung (1866), no. 879, quoted in Glanz, "Source Materials on the History of Jewish Immigration," *YIVO Annual of Jewish Social Science,* VI (1951).

In 1862, during the Civil War, a furor was caused by discriminatory measures ordered against Jews, and particularly against Jewish traders, by General Ulysses S. Grant. Grant's instructions were eventually countermanded after an appeal to the president in Washington.[3]

Grant's Anti-Jewish Directives (1862).

> LaGrange, Tenn.,
> November 9, 1862

Major-General Hurlbut,
Jackson, Tenn.:
Refuse all permits to come south of Jackson for the present. The Israelites especially should be kept out.

> LaGrange, Tenn.,
> November 10, 1862

General Webster,
Jackson, Tenn.:
Give orders to all the conductors on the road that no Jews are to be permitted to travel on the railroad southward from any point. They may go north and be encouraged in it, but they are such an intolerable nuisance that the department must be purged of them.

> Holly Springs, Miss.
> December 8, 1862

General Order
On account of the scarcity of provisions all cotton speculators, Jews, and other vagrants having no honest means of support, except trading upon the misery of the country, and in general all persons from the North not connected with the army whatever, and having no permission from the Commanding General to remain in town, will leave in twenty-four (24) hours or will be put to duty in the entrenchments. By order of Col. Jno. V. Du Bois, U. S. Army.

> Hdqrs. Thirteenth A.C.,
> Department of the Tenn.,
> Oxford, Miss.,
> December 17, 1862

Hon. C. P. Wolcott,
Assistant Secretary of War,
Washington, D.C.:

I have long believed that in spite of all vigilance than can be infused into post commanders, the specie regulations of the Treasury Department have been violated, and that mostly by Jews and other unprincipled traders. So well satisfied have I been of this that I instructed the commanding officer at Columbus to refuse all permits to Jews to come South, and I have frequently had them expelled from the department, but they come in with their carpet-sacks in spite of all that can be done to prevent it. The Jews seem to be a privileged class that can travel everywhere. They will land at any woodyard on the river and make their way through the country. If not permitted to buy cotton themselves they will act as agents for someone else, who will be at a military post with a Treasury permit to receive cotton and pay for it in Treasury notes which the Jews will buy up at an agreed rate, paying gold. . . .

> Hdqrs. Thirteenth A.C.,
> Dept. of the Tenn.,
> Holly Springs,
> December 17, 1862

General Orders,
  No. 11.

The Jews as a class violating every regulation of trade established by the Treasury Department, and also department orders, are hereby expelled from the department within twenty-four hours from the receipt of this order.

Post commanders will see that all of this class of people be furnished passes and required to leave, and anyone returning after such notification will be arrested and held in confinement until an opportunity occurs of sending them out as prisoners, unless furnished with permit from headquarters.

No passes will be given these people to visit headquarters for the purpose of making personal applications for trade permits.

By order of Maj.-Gen. U. S. Grant.

> Jno A. Rawlins,
> Assistant Adjutant-General.

> Joseph Lebowick, "General Ulysees S. Grant and the Jews," *Publications of the American Jewish Historical Society,* XVII (1909).

Anti-Semitism in the Ranks (1864).

Norfolk Jail 12th April.

To B. F. Butler
Maj.-Genl. Comdg.

General

I hope you will excuse the liberty I thus take in addressing a letter to you. My name is Max Glass. I served honorabl in the Italien and Austrian arme. After Asperemonte where Garibaldy was woundet I resigned. Last year I succidet in coming to America, and to offer my service for the country. I arrived 12th August in N. Y. My intention was to remain a few days in the city, and then to present myself before the Govenor, show him my papers, and to offer him my service. Unfortunate after being three days in the City I made an acquaintance with a man dressed in a dept. uniform, and as he spoke German I questioned him, wath I would have to do in such a case. He advised me not to go to the Govenor, because everyone who desires a comition has to help to re-cruit a company, and that would need a great deal of money, and as I dont speak English my way would be useless, but if I wanted to join the service I must give him my papers which he would show his Colonel, and assured me after being inser-vice a short time that I would recievd a comition and the benefit of a bounty, he said he belongd to the 12th N. Y. Cavl: and that I should go with him to Norwich wher his Regt. was recruiting. As I had no money and faith in the word of an officer I followed him to that place wher we arrived the next morning. After taking my papers he left me and returned with a citizen and told me to go with the citizen, and that all was right. I was carried to an office wher I was told to sign my name, after doing this I was carried befor a doctor and sworn in. I was astonished to be brought in a room where I was guarded; I questioned but no one understood me. Later I found a man in the clothing office who spok the French language and to my surprise I found that I had been de-cieved. I was brought as a substitute, and the man who brought me was no Capt. but a N. Y. Swindler. Without frind being in America 5 days, I had no aide. I was sent to New Haven and ther I complained me to colonel commanding, but he said as I now not the man who brought me he could do nothing, but detail'd me for Prof. guard duty, which duty I have done faithfull. As I later desired to be sent for the enemy, I was sent to the 8th Con.V. Arrived at the regt: I was abused for reason that I never understand. It may have been because I did not make them my companions in drinking, or as I am a Jew. If I went in the street or any wher I was called Jew.Christh killer & such names. I also had stones, dirt thrown at me. I complained me to the comp. office & the Colonel, begged to be transferred, that no man that had feeling could stand such treatment; but no one would investi-gate. I wnt to General Heckman but could get no hearing. Five weeks ago we had a skirmish drill. A prt of the Regiment only was going through drill, and we were reposing, as usual many of them becan to abuse me by throing mud at me & calling me some of the most infamous names. The officie. in charge Lt. Radburn acted not as with his duty by stoping the abusement, and as my feeling was very much mortified I started to the camp in order to report it to the commander of the regt., but as I made about twenty pases the named offic. cried after me halt Dutchman, and as that was no way to order a soldier I kept on, and the offic. sent after me a corp.

with the tow men who had abused me, they caught me by the collar & dragged me back., befor the whole company of man so they could make fun of me. After finishing drill I reported the whole affair to the comd. of the regt. Capt. Hoyt, demanded a court-marshal for the offence and myself, I waited some time but no court-marshal was given to me and I was still abused. After seeking in every way for Justice & not recieving it I resolved to go to Norfolk and stay eight days and reported myself as a deserter in order to get a courtmarshal. Arrived at Norfolk I learned that man were wanted in the navy & I entlisted for a Gun Boat, thinking I was doing no wrong. I was arested ther by an offic. of my regmt; and brought to this prison.

General! I hope you will take this into your kind consideration, and I beg you heartily concerning this that I was decieved, il treated, no justice given to me and therefor needed to leave the regiment, that you shall not find me guilty to suffer now in prison.

I cant be called a deserter from the service of the U.S. I cant be called a bounty jumper, I never recieved a bounty. As I would be more useful in the field than in prison I emplore you to transfer me from my Regt. to another taking again 3 years service without any bounty. Closing this I have no more to say, that all that I said I cane prove by witnesses officer and privates. In hope of your pity for unfortunate man whose intention are the best.

I remain your humble servent

Max Glass

Quoted in Schappes, *Documentary History of the Jews, pp. 48–50.*

Possibly nothing highlights images of the Jew prevalent in the period from the 1840s on more vividly than many of the dime novels of the time which featured Jewish characters. As artistic creations they rank on a level with the soap operas and *Peyton Places* of television today; sociologically, however, they are probably no less revealing of their times than the effusions from the electronic wasteland are of our own. That the Jew emerges from the pages of the dime novel as an incomparably sinister and avaricious personage is at once apparent. Other motifs also recur with considerable regularity. As Shakespeare, in *The Merchant of Venice*, created Jessica as a counterpoint to Shylock, so too do we find in many of the dime novels that the ugly and evil Jew is played off against the beautiful and compassionate Jewess. This would tend to suggest that the Jewess figures, somehow, in the whole complex conundrum of repressed sexuality on the part of the Gentile, in much the same way, perhaps, as the Negress has. Also of great curiosity is the recurrent theme, in many of these novels, that the Jew is never what he at first sight appears to be. The appearance he presents to the outside world is merely a mask designed to hide a very different reality; the Jew's true nature therefore emerges as something mysterious and impenetrable. He is an enigma: one can never be sure who and what he is, but must always assume that he is not what he appears to be. This assumption enables the Gentile to invest the Jew with the wildest attributes of his—the Gentile's—fantasy world.[4]

Who Is Herman Stoll? (1871).

Was the taunt of his foes truth or not, Herman Stoll indignantly denied that Jewish blood flowed in his veins, although after one look into his face—one quick glance at the high cheekbones, curved nose, piercing black eyes, and short, crispy curling hair—anyone gifted with the skill of "reading faces" would surely have concluded that Herman Stoll was lying when he declared that no blood of that scattered nation, who cannot claim a country of their own, ran in his veins. . . . If [he] was not a wealthy man, he acted like one, and spent money as though it were as easily got as water. . . .

> Albert W. Aiken, *The White Witch; or the League of Three* (New York, 1871), p. 11.

"The Jew Solomon" (1861).

"Dost thou know where the Jew Solomon dwells?"
"I do, my master."

"And canst thou show me where one Lord Tarncliff re-
sides?"

"I can, my master."

"Then I shall need no guide but thee, good Malak! I will go
first to deliver my letter to the Jew, and after that I will visit
the lord whom I named."

"Malak awaits his master's orders," replied the black.

The young man first looked to his letters, and seeing that
he still had them, at once sallied out, and soon, under the
guidance of his servant, stood before a miserable-looking
dwelling, in a narrow and most ungainly street.

"Surely, no man of wealth can live here," he muttered

"It is the Jews' quarters, and they are men of wealth," said
Malak. "The Jew Solomon, whom my former master has dealings with, dwells here."

"A *Jew* may live in such a den, but a *Christian* would not,"
said Morgan contemptuously. "Knock, good Malak, and ask
if the Hebrew is at home, if thou art not indeed mistaken in
the spot."

The Negro struck the oaken door heavily with the hilt of
a broad-bladed dagger which he wore in his belt.

After some delay, a small wicket upon one side of the door
was opened, and a pair of keen black eyes could be seen to
glitter from within.

"What seek ye?" asked a sharp, querulous voice.

"Does the Jew Solomon dwell here?" replied Morgan, impatient that the door was not opened instead of the wicket.

"Yes. Who wants to see him?" replied the person from
within.

"I do," replied Morgan, still more impatiently.

"What is thy business with him?"

"That he will know when I see him."

"He will know it, Sir Stranger, before his door is opened to
thee. These are not over-peaceful times, and the Jews have
few friends, save those of their own sect."

"Out upon thee for an unmannerly churl!" cried the young
man angrily. "Had I not promised Ethelbert the Hermit to

deliver a letter to the Jew Solomon, I should not wait to cool my heels before his kennel."

"Why didst thou not say before that thou wert a messenger from him?" replied the person from within. "Tarry but a moment, and I will admit thee."

There was a sound as of loosening chains and removing bars, and then the door was opened; and an old man, whose hair and long beard were white as snow, but whose jet-black eyes glittered like the orbs of a serpent, stood upon the threshold. His tall, slender form was dressed in a habit of coarse brown cloth, which descended nearly to his feet; and his appearance, as well as that of the apartment before the young man, indicated extreme poverty—a poverty which did not appear to require to be guarded so securely as it was by bolts and bars.

"Be seated, sir, and let me peruse the letter which thou bearest. I am the Jew Solomon!" said the old man, pointing to a wooden bench while he secured the door, after Morgan and his servant had entered.

The young man took the letter from within his surcoat, and handed it to the Jew, but remained standing; for in truth, he neither liked the man, nor his reception, nor the appearance of the dwelling, which was squalid and filthy in an extreme.

The Hebrew hastily broke the seal, and a look of pleasure and surprise exhibited itself on his wan face, as he perused the letter.

"Pardon me, young master!" he said, turning to Morgan, with a look of humility and respect. "Pardon me that I did not know who thou wert. My esteemed correspondent bids me treat thee as if thou wert his own son. I pray thee to follow me to a more pleasant apartment."

And rising, he unbolted another strong door, which opened inward, and revealed a far better furnished apartment. But without pausing, he passed through this room into another, which was furnished in a style of magnificent splendor and oriental luxury, which fairly dazzled the eyes of the young man.

"I pray thee to be seated, and excuse my presence for a

moment; I will be absent only for an instant," said the Jew, pointing to an ottoman of crimson velvet.

Silent from surprise, Morgan took the seat while the Jew went into another room. He was absent only a few moments, when he returned, garbed in a much richer style than before, and accompanied by a young female of that rare and striking beauty so peculiar to women of the Jewish race.

"This is my daughter Miriam, Master Morgan!" said the Hebrew. "She will command refreshments for thee; and, perchance, while away an hour or two with a song for thee, or some music from the harp. I must absent myself for a brief while, to fulfill a command sent by my good friend Ethelbert. Thy servant knows the way to the kitchen, and will, doubtless, take care of himself until my return."

Young Morgan bowed low to the Jewish maiden; and ere he glanced a second time at her lovely face, he looked at the mysterious ring upon his finger as if it were, indeed, an amulet to protect him from the magic power of beauty.

E. Z. C. Judson, *Morgan: Or, The Knight of the Black Flag* (New York, 1861), pp. 14–16.

Moloch, the Jewish Extortioner (1845).

He kept on his way, enveloped to the mouth in his cloak, and with his cap, which was an ordinary French traveling-cap, pulled down over his eyes as if to escape recognition. On reaching the extremity of the lane up which he had come, he did not turn to the right into the wide and spacious avenue which led towards the better part of the town, but deviated to the left, taking a close, crooked street which seemed to wind through the very heart of the oldest and most obscure portion of the metropolis. As he advanced along this tortuous thoroughfare his step was quicker and his arm moved beneath his cloak as if he was grasping the hilt of a dagger. The place was by no means calculated to increase the confidence of one passing through it. The houses on either side were very high and seemed to be crowded with tenants like a beehive, though without the bee's industry; for all seemed to be steeped in poverty, idle and vicious. The lower stories were converted into miserable stalls and drinking taps, the doors of which were thronged with a motley set of both sexes, who seemed congregated around them for no other reason than to quarrel and cause confusion. Police officers were seen at intervals slowly promenading the sidewalks, but their familiar presence there scarce seemed to check the confusion of oaths, obscenity, and drunken laughter!

It was with difficulty the commander of the yacht kept his way without contact with these filthy crews, from whom, if he jostled anyone by chance, he received the fiercest execrations. He, however, continued his course with a firm, prompt tread, disregarding their menaces yet with an eye and hand ready to discern and guard against any ruffianly attack.

At length he reached the end of this vile thoroughfare and passed by, turning to the right into one that was little wider but scarcely of better appearance. Its aspect and features, however, were different. The sidewalks on both sides were lined with rows of shops dimly lighted. The windows and the inside of the doors were hung with every possible variety of cast-off clothing from a rich court-suit down to a poor scriveners threadbare black coat. Chapeaus and round hats, military caps and even swords and pistols were displayed upon the shelves. The interiors were filled with articles of wardrobe, and behind each counter could be seen old men with dark visages, arched eyebrows, large black eyes, high aquiline noses, generally mounted with a pair of iron-rimmed spectacles. They were Jews, and this street was the quarter where they did business not only in cast-off wardrobes, but also most of them were money-dealers; for wretched as some of their shops and the habitations above them for their families were, they were far richer than they seemed, and many of them had thousands of pounds loaned at usurious interest to the merchant and the noble.

Tudor Dauling, for such was the name of the personage whose progress we are now following, after entering this thoroughfare of the Jews slackened his pace and kept his eyes scrutinizingly fixed on the opposite side of the way; for although the lamps of the street were far apart, and gave but dim light to the dark pavement, yet the murky light from the farthing candles in the shop windows enabled him to distinguish one sign from another, though with some difficulty. He seemed to be endeavoring to ascertain the location of some one of the tenants of the shop in particular, as if not sufficiently familiar with the place to recognize its exterior. At length he stopped and searchingly regarded the one opposite to him, and succeeded in making out the half-obscured letters on the sign. It was "Enoch Moloch, Jeweler, and dealer in apparel."

It was but five steps across the street to the sunken doorway of this tenement, which was half shop, half habitation. The stories of the ancient row of houses to which it belonged rose one above the other to a great height above the low doorway of the ground story, which appeared to have been pressed into the ground full four feet by the superincumbent weight of the black mass of damp and moldy bricks above it.

Over the door and the square window of the side projected a sort of roof or "stoop" which turned off the rain from the "old clothes" which in the daytime hung from a hundred nails driven into the shutters and into the mortar between the corroding bricks. This projection was at a level lower than the heads of the passengers, so that a person entering a shop would have to stoop to avoid bringing his head into contact with it: and to get fairly within the shop he would have to descend two steps. As it was now night, Enoch Moloch the Jew had taken in, or rather his two apprentices, black-eyed Israelitish youths of his own blood, had done it at his command, all the motley array of scarlet, green and blue, gray-black and mixed garments that served to the passerby as an advertisement of the occupation of the keeper of the shop.

The neighbors of the Jew were all his brethren, dealers in the same commodities, and the captain of the yacht as he crossed the street towards the shop of Enoch saw them variously occupied in their stalls, some in smoking huge German pipes, others in bargaining with customers, others standing in their doors talking, and waiting for customers to come in and buy. In Enoch's shop he could discern no one but a Jewish lad in a red cap who sat upon a high stool smoking a short pipe, his black eyes shining like stars through the clouds of tobacco in which he was enveloping his brown face.

As Dauling stooped and descended into this stall the lad jumped from his elevated seat on which he was perched and, in a shrill voice, while he bustlingly displayed upon the short counter a handsome, half-worn court-dress which Enoch had no doubt bought at a bargain: "Sheep sir at doo poun'sax shaylin! worn birt-day last, by te kreatest Dook in te hoal kingtom! Puy it, sir! Jis' fit a nople shentleman like you as!"

"Where is the Jew?" demanded Captain Dauling with an impatient manner, still keeping his features closely concealed as if fearful of being recognized by any chance passer by the door, though the dimness of the two yellowish tallow candles that were stuck up in rusty iron sockets in the shop afforded sufficient security.

"Fader!" cried the lad in a shrill octave, directing his voice towards a narrow staircase, the door of which was half-hid by hanging garments: "Dere ish a shentlemans in te shoop as don't want to puy nothin' put to see you!"

In answer to his call a young girl made her appearance, with fine Jewish eyes and an air of the most finished coquetry. She was not more than eighteen but was tall and nobly formed. She wore a scarlet satin closely fitting her finely developed bust, and affording by its bright cherry hue, a striking relief to her jet-black hair and nut-brown complexion. A necklace of rubies sparkled upon her beautifully molded neck, and on her bare arms were bracelets the stones of which emitted the same rich crimson light. Her shoes, which were wonderfully small, were crimson and covered with spangles, and the heels being full two inches in height, gave her, perhaps, a false height.

"My uncle desires to know what your business is, sir?" she said with a searching investigation of her eyes, to discover the features that belonged to the stately figure before her. She spoke in a richly keyed flutelike tone that fell upon the ear with delightful cadences; while her manner was at once graceful and refined, while it partook, perhaps, something of independence and price of conscious beauty.

"I have been here before, Mademoiselle Rachel! You do not seem to recollect me," answered the commander of the yacht in a voice that was accompanied by a slight smile. As he spoke he raised the visor of his cap.

"I will tell my uncle who it is," she said smiling with recognition and assuming an air of profound respect.

"But do you *know,* fair Jewess?" he demanded quickly.

"I know that you have been here before and that you are one of his friends!" she answered with an emphasis on the last word.

"Yes, one of his *friends!*" he repeated in a tone of haughty contempt, as she re-ascended the stairway. "To do business with these money-dealers, one must be content for the time being to stand on a level with them. Money makes all upon an equality when we trade in it! Nay, it sometimes makes slaves masters. The poor noble may sue to the rich Israelite, aye, fawn upon him to handle his vile gold without which nobility were mockery! But I am not troubled with nobility, though scarce a nobleman in England has such blood flowing in his veins as——"

Here the return of the Jewess interrupted his soliloquy.

"My uncle desires me to conduct you to him," she said, descending to the shop and directing him with a gesture of her hand to mount the stairs, while she drew aside a Scottish plaid that half-obscured the passage.

The captain of the yacht passed her slightly bowing in deference to her sex and beauty, and aided by a glimmer of a light at the top of the stair, which was both narrow and angular, he succeeded in reaching the landing, though the planks bent beneath his heavy tread as he ascended.

On reaching this place she passed him, took up the lamp, which was a curious silver one, and leading the way along a sort of common hall, came to a heavily made door at which she tapped with her fingers.

"Come in," answered a deep voice in a strong Jewish accent.

The Jewess threw open the door and the captain passed in, the entrance being immediately closed behind him upon the outside by his conductress.

The room into which the commander of the yacht was ushered by the beautiful young Jewess was of a very different character from the other parts of the interior of the dwelling already described. It was large and spacious, and furnished with the luxury of a nobleman's private chamber. Gold mingled with crimson met the eye in the drapery of the windows and the richest colors covered the chairs and ottomans. The general style of the room and its furniture was oriental rather than English. At a table covered with an embroidered scarlet cloth sat a man about fifty years of age dressed in a loose black gown. A brazen antique lamp suspended above the table cast its beam downward upon his majestic head and features. His high, columnlike forehead shaded with short black locks, his strong, arched brows, and large, full, piercing black eyes, his high-bridged and slightly arched nose, and the red fullness and flexibility of his lips betrayed him to belong to the tribe of Israel. A jet-black beard mingled with gray descended from his chin to his breast. His size was large and his air noble and imposing. But there was an expression in his eyes of profound avarice, and about his mouth played deceit and cunning. Physically the Jew was a noble specimen of his finely formed race; but morally, he looked in every lineament the usurer. As the captain of the yacht entered, he was busily summing up a column of figures in a book before him. He did not look up from his occupation until he heard the door close again and the step of the visitor advancing towards him. He then raised his face from the accounts, keeping his forefinger upon the column he had been calculating and fixing his gaze upon him, said with a strong Jewish accent,

"You are velcom, my lort. Pe-pleesh to take a shair! So, you haf come vor more monish?" he added, with a scarcely perceptible glimmer of satisfaction in the expression of his eyes.

[After much haggling, Dauling finally agrees to accept the extortionate terms being demanded by Moloch.]

"Goot night, my lort," answered the Jew; and taking up a little silver bell that stood before him upon the table, he rang it and the beautiful Rachel came into the chamber.

"Niece, see this gentleman downstairs and through the shop," he said to her.

"I am honored by so fair a guide, charming Jewess," said Tudor Dauling, bowing with an air of gallantry to her; although this courteous manner sat ill with the haughty and sinister expression that was upon his features, as if he despised the race to which the young girl belonged, while he admired her physical beauty.

"My niece little understands the fair words of flattery, my lort," said the Jew coldly as if displeased.

"Nay, Enoch, I am no gallant for the sex. Little care I for any of them, else might I seek to mend my fortune," he added in a tone meant only to reach the Jew's ear, "*by taking a wife.* But seldom have I given them more than a passing glance, for rare must be the beauty that causes my eye to linger. Such beauty is that of thy niece! But good night. Tomorrow at eleven! Fair daughter of Abraham, I follow thee."

Thus speaking, the captain of the yacht, preceded by Rachel, who all the while had stood silent and down-looking, left the sumptuous private chamber of the rich moneylender, Enoch Moloch, and, passing down the dark staircase, emerged into the shop below. Then with a slight bow he took leave of the Jewess, and wrapping his cloak closely about his face went forth into the street and rapidly pursued his way in the direction of the Strand.

Rachel lingered a moment, with her forefinger placed upon her lip, as if reflecting upon the mingled indifference and admiration towards her of the dark-featured noble-looking stranger, when the sound of the silver bell recalled her to her uncle's presence.

"Well, Niece, what think you of my noble visitor," said

Moloch, speaking in the Hebrew tongue with a dignity of accent and enunciation that singularly contrasted with the badly pronounced English he had made use of in his conversation with Tudor Dauling.

"Is he noble?" asked the maiden and she seated herself upon an ottoman opposite him.

"What dost thou think of him?" repeated Moloch with a half smile; for during the brief interval that had elapsed since the departure of the commander of the yacht he had conceived a thought in his inventive brain, which the last words of the other had given both spark and fuel.

"I think him a man of large stature, about eight and thirty years of age, with a haughty air and a countenance exceedingly noble and handsome yet at the same time singularly forbidding."

"Could you love him, Rachel?"

The Jewish maiden started slightly, and then, opening her large black eyes, rested them upon the face of Moloch with an expression of surprise and alarm. "Love him! Oh no! I should fear him were he powerful and I in his power."

"Yet methinks he looked kindly upon thee!"

". . . Would you have me marry him indeed, Uncle?" she asked earnestly.

"Truly I would."

"He would scorn me. Besides I know him not. Nor could I wed a man I have no love for, much more a Christian," she said jeeringly; and rising up she walked the space before the table with a quick tread and a look much more excited. Moloch, in the meanwhile, sat perfectly composed yet with a firm aspect.

"Know you, Rachel, that this man is not only noble, but Royal?"

". . . I will hear you, Uncle," she replied, reseating herself upon the ottoman and folding her arms upon her bosom with a haughty air that exceedingly became her.

John H. Ingraham, The Clipper Yacht
(New York, 1845), pp. 8–17.

3. Anti-Semitism Emerges as a Major Social Force

From the late 1870s on, the mass migration of Jews to the United States gained momentum as social and political conditions in Eastern Europe, the great heartland of Jewish settlement, deteriorated. Anti-Semitism, too, gained momentum, and indeed now emerged for the first time as a major social force in American life.

Several factors, not all of which were directly bound to the rising tide of Jewish immigration, contributed to this development. Most Jews arrived in the United States penniless. The hostility which their poverty engendered, and the frequently appalling conditions in which they lived in the urban slums, was a major ingredient in the new anti-Semitism of the period.

What made this anti-Semitism truly new, however, was the growth of nativist hostility to unrestricted immigration into the United States, its conjunction with racist scientific thought, and the emergence of ideological anti-Semitism. The Jew, along with other groups, was considered to be racially inferior to America's earlier Anglo-Saxon stock, a presumption to which social Darwinism and eugenics alike were called in defense.

It is not, however, sufficient to condemn the Jew for threatening to dilute the racial purity of the American stock. Anti-Semitic ideology, originating largely in France, Germany, and Russia, taught many Americans that the Jews posed another type of threat to their society and civilization, too. For even where this ideology did not confirm the genetic inferiority of the Jew, as compared with the Aryan, it depicted him as an evil and purposeful parasite, bent on the destruction of white Christian values, the enslavement of society, and the control of its economy. The bitter economic crisis of the 1890s confirmed, for many, the urgency of the Jewish threat. All these factors together also contributed in a marked degree to the rising pressure for restrictions on immigration from Europe, restrictions that were finally enacted after the Great War.

It is during this period, too, that another facet of anti-Semitism also came to the fore. The Jews, as already mentioned, were denounced for the festering sores of American urban life, for the slums and squalor and crime which were such a marked feature of the large cities of the time. At the same instant, however, other Jews were no less viciously denounced for seeking to leave the slums to enter into the mainstream of middle-class American life. Discrimination against the Jews now became a widespread fact. Jews were barred from summer resorts and hotels, were discriminated against in employment, and were severely restricted in their access to universities and fraternities.[1] This discrimination was to remain a bitter fact of Jewish life in America until well into the 1950s.

The image of the lower-class Jew as a petty but inveterate criminal was widespread and tenacious, and never more authoritatively stated than in 1908, when Police Commissioner Bingham of New York City declared that "perhaps half" of that city's criminals were "Hebrews"—a charge he was subsequently to retract.[2]

The Jewish Criminal (1908).

The crimes committed by the Russian Hebrews are generally those against property. They are firebugs, burglars, pick-
pockets, and highway robbers—when they have the courage;
but although all crime is their province, pocket-picking is the
one to which they seem to take most naturally. Indeed, pick-
pockets of other nationalities are beginning to recognize the
superiority of the Russian Hebrew in that gentle art, and
there have been several instances lately where a Hebrew and
an Italian have formed a combination for theft in the streets,
the former being always selected for the "tool," as the profes-
sionals term the one who does the actual reaching into the
victim's pocket, while the other creates a diversion to dis-
tract attention, or starts a fight in case of the detection and
pursuit of the thief. . . . Among the most expert of all the
street thieves are the Hebrew boys under sixteen, who are
being brought up to lives of crime. Many of them are old
offenders at the age of ten. The juvenile Hebrew emulates
the adult in the matter of crime percentages, forty per cent
of the boys at the House of Refuge and twenty-seven per cent
of those arraigned in the Children's Court being of that race.
The percentage of Hebrew children in the truant schools is
also higher than that of any others.

> "Foreign Criminals in New York,"
> *North American Review,* CLXXXVIII
> (1908).

The Wolves of New York (1881).

In person he was about the medium height, apparently,
but he was so bent with age and toil that he appeared quite
undersized in stature, although almost as muscular in form as
a giant. His face was a peculiar one, the skin being as yellow
as parchment; the chin was covered with a heavy gray-black
beard, which was as kinky as the wool of an African; the hair
of his head resembled the beard, both in color and in character, although worn quite long; and from under his bushy

eyebrows looked eyes, ferret-like in their sharpness. . . .

His dress suited well his face; a very long coat, half "ulster" and half body-coat, rather the worse for wear, covered him from neck to heels. His long, muscular-looking hands were incased in dingy brown gloves which, somehow, gave one an idea of the talons of some fierce and rapacious bird of prey.

. . . Van Tromp, who rather prided himself on his judgement, took a good look at the man and in his own mind summed him up: No beggar, but a crafty, wily man of business who came upon serious matters intent, and who would not have come unless his business was important. . . . "Well, sir, you wished to see me?" the master of the house remarked.

"You ish Mister Van Tromp?" the man asked with a strong German-Jew accent.

"Yes, sir, that is my name."

"And mine is Solomons—Moses Solomons. I have an office in Wall Street; I am a broker and also do a leetle business in bill-discounting; anyting, you know, to make de honest penny," and the old fellow chuckled and rubbed his hands.

Van Tromp had never met one of this fraternity before, yet had often heard of them. As the jackals wait upon the lions, the vultures upon the battlefields, the camp-bummers on the march of the victorious army, so upon the outskirts of business a gang of disreputable wretches eager for prey and plunder. . . .

> Albert W. Aiken, *The Wolves of New York* (New York, 1881), p. 18.

The Jewish Informer (1884).

He was about to have dinner when a small man, unmistakably a Polish Jew, ambled into the reception room where he was and, approaching him, said, "Have I the honor of speaking to Mister Squeek?"

"Yes, who the devil are you?"

"My name is Aaron Moses Lackstein."

"Well, Aaron Moses Lackstein, how comes it that you know me?"

"I had a very good description of you, my dear," answered the Pole.

"Admitting that, how did you know where to find me?"

"Your friend told me," was the reply.

"You come from Anthony Pegg, then," said the Bow Street runner.

"Just so, my dear sir."

"Well, what message have you?"

"Whisper"—the Jew caught Dominick by the coat sleeve and placed his repulsive face very close to that of the detective—"I know where Tom Coddle has hidden the money. You understand . . . I spoke to your friend and told him that if he could give me a little something, I would help him. I am an honest man, Mr. Squeek. . . ."

"What do you mean by a little something?" asked the detective.

"A thousand dollars. . . ."

"That will be alright," replied Dominick.

With many bows and contortions of the features intended for smiles, Aaron Moses Lackstein backed out of the room.

> Gilbert Jerome, *Dominick Squeek, the Bow Street Runner, An English Detective in America* (New York, 1884), p. 24.

A Portrait of the New York Ghetto (1888).

New York, like Rome, has its Ghetto, or low Jewish quarter. And it is safe to most emphatically declare that in physical degradation, squalor, misery, and dirt, the New York Ghetto is unsurpassed by that of the Eternal City, or of any great metropolis on the face of the earth.

The New York Ghetto—and that is the name by which it is duly styled by the officials of the Board of Health, and of police headquarters—is situated in those narrow thoroughfares on the East Side, lying between Grand and Catherine and Ludlow and Division Streets. The houses in the Ghetto are all tall, narrow, noisome tenements, packed from basement to roof with swarming, unwashed humanity. The locality is practically given over exclusively to the descendants of Israel, the disgusting habits and extreme filth of the latter being such as to drive away from the immediate vicinage even the most miserable and lowest representatives of other races.

Enter one of these frightful tenements given over to the sons and daughters of Israel, and the nostrils are instantly assailed on the very threshold by the fearful stenches, which can best be compared to the odor arising from vegetables in a highly advanced state of decomposition. Pass a little further along the hallway, and the mal-odourous atmosphere becomes so thick with putrescent exhalations as to suggest the idea that you could cut it with a knife. The walls are disfigured with great streaks and blotches of foul moisture and dirt; and vermin—those faithful little companions of the Jews, even to the wealthiest—are to be detected at not infrequent intervals.

Turn into the apartments branching off from these ghastly hallways, and you will find them ill-ventilated, pestilential, and filthy in the extreme. So overcrowded are they as to suggest the worst portions of the Chinese colony in San Francisco. In many instances a father, mother, grown-up daughter and son, and several little olive-branches of Israel, big-bellied, big-nosed, and in more or less advanced stages of development and dirt, are to be found occupying the same sleeping apartment. Only a Jew could live in such an atmosphere of moral and physical debasement, and survive.

And yet poverty cannot be ascribed as the cause of the Jew of the Ghetto living in this way. He lives—yes, and thrives— in this wretchedness and filth, partly because filth is congenial to him, and partly from a desire to more rapidly save and accumulate the only thing in this world he cares for—dollars and cents. Many of these Jews of the Ghetto are far better off than Gentiles living in neat and well-appointed flats on the West Side. Some of them are, in fact, quite well-to-do. Later on, perhaps, they will branch out as merchants in leading thoroughfares, with social ambitions, and the regulation amount of Jewish ostentation, impudence, and arrogance. Their sons will figure at Delmonico's, and at the swell summer resorts, and clamor for admission at the fashionable clubs. But launch out as they may, array themselves in broadcloth and fine linen as they will, the stink of the Ghetto, and mayhap some of its vermin, will cling to them still.

No matter how wretched or how low he may be, the Jew rarely becomes a workman, a creator, speaking in a political-economy sense, of wealth. On the contrary, he almost invariably figures as a dealer, a jobber, a trader. Thus none of the Jews of the Ghetto are laborers or artisans, but are to a unit street salesmen, peddlers, and petty traders. One of the chief forms of avocation in the Ghetto is the peddling of fish, fruit, poultry, and meat.

And what fish, what fruit, what meat!! In his greed to acquire gain, the Jew does not hesitate at poisoning an entire community. The fish he sells is decayed, the fruit rotten, the mean putrid. Thousands of human beings are sickened and sent down to their graves every year in New York, by the fruit, the fish, the poultry, and the meat peddled by the Jew of the Ghetto.

And how does it happen that the food peddled by these miserable wretches is in this shocking condition? Happen! It is not a question of happening: it is a matter of design, for the Jew drags the four corners of the city to secure this putrid food. He haunts the markets of the city, buying up food which had become stale on the dealers' hands, and is either on the point of becoming decayed, or has already passed into a state of putrescence. He hangs around the docks at which vessels have arrived, and buys up remnants of stores which remain unconsumed after the voyage. The more rotten the food, the better it pleases the Jew, for it is so much the cheaper.

Having thus collected this filthy food, the Jew takes it to his dirty quarters in the Ghetto, where it is pawed over by the unwashed fingers of the other members of the household;

and after its cost has been duly quibbled over and discussed, it is fixed up in the best shape possible for sale. The Jew of the Ghetto has, of course, no storing-place; and, consequently, the food is kept in the overcrowded dwelling apartments, until such time as it can be hawked in the streets.

Imagine a couple of filthy rooms occupied by two, perhaps four, unwashed adults, and half a dozen dirt-bedaubed brats; the ceiling damp with slimy moisture; cockroaches and vermin crawling over the furniture; and great lines of decaying fruit, or fish, or meat, strung across from wall to wall—imagine such a scene and you have a picture of a Jew tenement in the Ghetto.

The day after making his purchases of the refuse of the markets, the Jew sallies forth with his hand-truck, or cart, to sell his unwholesome supply. He is usually accompanied by his wife, or by one of the elder olive-branches of Israel. He stations himself on some street corner in a poor but populous thoroughfare, and by his cheap prices tempts the unwary to buy. He sells his wares, laden down as they are with the germs of disease, alike to the unsophisticated housewife, and to the innocent child, without one touch of pity, without one sting of remorse. He is as a grinning skeleton, a figure of evil, standing by the wayside and scattering the fetid germs of disease and death among wayfarers, young and old, as they pass him by.

But sometimes retribution, sharp, sudden, and swift, sweeps down on him in the form of the avenging angels of the Board of Health. At repeated intervals, especially in the summer-time, the officials of the Health Department make wholesale and systematic raids upon the peddlers from the Ghetto, in the interests of the public safety. Then, upon such occasions, ensue scenes of indescribable confusion, and of dire weeping and gnashing of teeth in Israel. The fat and paunchy Jewesses will tear their hair, and call upon the God of Jacob and of Aaron to witness how sweet and pure is the food they sell, and how they are persecuted. They make the most wild and frantic efforts to save even the smallest portion of their disgusting wares; often sticking huge hunks of rotten fish or decaying meat under their petticoats, in the hope of saving them from seizure.

But the Board of Health officials are lynx-eyed and inexorable; and they ruthlessly seize the vile food, confiscate it, and, hurling it pell-mell into carts brought along with them for the purpose, carry it off for destruction. During the past year, seventy-four thousand pounds of unwholesome fish were seized upon in the Ghetto by the Board of Health; and upwards of one hundred and fifty thousand pounds of putrid meat, poultry, and fruit from the same quarter met with a similar fate.

But the Jew of the Ghetto is incorrigible. He repairs to his filthy tenement, weeps the bitter tears of avarice over his loss, and then returns to his trade of wholesale poisoner.

Very similar in his modes of living to the Jew of the Ghetto is the Jew of Baxter Street, New York—the famous "old-clo" Jew, who has been held up as a butt of ridicule by novelists and playwrights and newspaper writers from time immemorial. In Baxter Street, for a couple of blocks south of Pearl Street, the thoroughfare on both sides of the way is lined with an unbroken string of these "old-clo" shops. Old trousers, old coats, and old garments of every description hang from the walls of the houses, and flaunt in the breeze to a height of two stories.

Outside the doors of the dingy, ill-smelling shops, lounge men with black, beady eyes, swarthy skins, and the great hawklike noses of Israel, and fat Jewesses, heavy of jowl and paunch, who brazenly solicit the passerby to buy of their wares. Whenever a stranger enters the street, he is at once assailed by a running fire of solicitations that fairly overwhelms him.

"Don you vant to buy a fine bair of bants, meester? I sell you a nice vaistgoat for a keevarter. Kem and look at a suit of clothes I have me here for four tollars und a ha'f. It vill fit you like der baper on der vall!"

These and a thousand other similar exclamations greet the passerby; and in their avidity to close their long, clawlike fingers upon his money, these rival dealers in old clothes actually lay violent hands upon the wayfarer, and seek to drag him by main force into their shops. If he shows the least inclination to trade, he is in danger of being literally torn apart by the rival dealers. Enter one of the shops, and a fat Jewess will alike unhesitatingly and unblushingly measure the customer for a pair of trousers, or assist him in trying on a new vest or other garment.

The Jew in his eagerness to sell does not hesitate to heap ridicule even upon himself: "I vos an honest sheeny man. I geef you cent per cent value for your monish," is an expression frequently to be heard. An "honest sheeny." Just think of it!

But, if you know how to go about it, you can buy something besides old clothes in Baxter Street. Gold watches, enameled lockets, costly overcoats, sealskin sacks, and even diamonds may be bought in these same dirty little shops, if you are not too particular about inquiring into the history of these objects of value, and whence they came. For the old-clo dealer is, almost to a man, what is technically known in police circles as a "fence"; and in the cellars and hiding places of the old-clo dealer's shops, stolen goods are stored away in quantity.

"I haf a reech on-kel who vas in der bawn-proking beezness; I got dot from heem. I seel it to you cheap, and doant say a vord about it," says Fagin, in disposing of some ill-gotten article of value.

But the Jew of Baxter Street is probably the least dangerous and objectionable of his race. He is, it must be conceded, in his rightful sphere. Would that all the members of his race could be restricted to their natural element—the old-clo business!

Anon., *The American Jew* (New York, 1888), Chapter 2.

Jewish criminality, in the mind of the anti-Semite, could assume any and every form of depravity. The perverted sexual propensities considered characteristic of the Jews are illustrated, in somewhat astonishing detail, in the following extract.

The Jew Lecher (1888).

Next to his lust for money, the strongest passion in the Jew is his licentiousness. This, like every other vicious trait of which the Jew is possessed, takes a peculiarly prominent and objectionable form.

The average Jew is disgustingly bawdy in his talk, and interlards his conversation with filthy expressions and obscene words. On the verandas at summer resorts, in hotel corridors, in the lobbies of theaters, on steamboats, on railway cars, and in public places in general, the Jew indulges in this repulsive peculiarity, to the great annoyance and disgust of respectable Christian women and decency-loving Gentile men. This was one of the habits which made him so objectionable at summer resorts, and has led to his practical exclusion from almost every first-class summer hotel in the land.

The boldest and most offensive of that class of persons who lounge about the prominent thoroughfares of our principal cities and are known as "street mashers," are Israelites. Overdressed, with mincing gait and dandified mien, these Jew "mashers" are daily to be seen strutting up and down the leading streets, ogling, with amazing effrontery, every woman who passes them by. Young girls of tender age are especially marked by these Jew "mashers" as their particular prey. Some years ago, in San Francisco, the attention of the police was directed to a band of Jew "mashers" who made a point of following up the girls of a certain public school on their way from the classroom to their homes. These Jew scoundrels, whenever they were unable to make a girl's acquaintance, would follow her up in pairs, talking together in the most disgusting manner, so as to be overheard by the objects of their pursuit. Some of the children's male relatives, assisted by the police, finally succeeded in very effectually disposing of this band of wretches.

Almost any afternoon, in Kearny Street, San Francisco, knots of Jew "mashers" are to be seen hanging around the corners and ogling the women who pass. Some of these fellows have not merely lascivious propensities in view, but have their sharp and restless eyes open to any possibilities of blackmail that may present themselves. Some years ago, a young married woman who had been foolish enough to allow one of these foppishly dressed Jew scoundrels to make her acquaintance, was so mercilessly blackmailed, although her conduct had in no way passed into the bounds of criminality, that the unfortunate woman was driven into an attempt at suicide. The truth then leaked out; and she and her husband never lived happily together, and eventually drifted apart.

Upon one occasion, a young lady, while passing the corner of Park and Kearny Streets, was addressed by one of these Jew Lotharios of the street. Gazing upon the Jew dude with a pitying look, she drew a fifty-cent piece from her pocket and threw it at his feet, exclaiming, "You miserable thing! you don't look as if you were half fed. Go and buy yourself something to eat with that."

The Jew masher gazed for a moment at the coin as it lay on the sidewalk, and then the instinct of his race conquered him. He stooped, picked up the money, and pocketed it. A quick and efficacious way to get rid of the Jew masher is to throw him a little money. It will engross his attention, and secure a release from his importunities.

In Eddy Street, San Francisco, a Jew dentist established himself some time ago in business. One day, while a lady was under the influence of an anesthetic in the dental chair, this scoundrel, taking advantage of her helpless condition, committed certain improprieties. The lady regained consciousness more quickly than he had anticipated, and he was discovered. She went home, and told the whole story to her husband. The latter, arming himself with a stout rawhide, compelled his wife to accompany him to the dental parlors. Arrived there, he laid the lash justly over the Jew's head and shoulders—flogged him unmercifully. The Jew coward made no attempt at defense. He simply writhed and squirmed and screamed, like the whipped cur that he was. Finally, lest his humiliation should not already be sufficiently complete, he fell down on his knees before his assailant, groveling before him, kissing his feet and imploring him to desist the castigation. Then, still abjectly kneeling, he confessed his attempted crime in terms of sickening servility, and implored the wife's forgiveness. What a disgusting spectacle! But all Jew lechers should be treated likewise.

In another street of San Francisco, within a stone's throw of the famous "Poodle Dog" restaurant, a Jew kept a hairdressing establishment on a somewhat pretentious scale. In the window of the shop was an immense glass case, under which was a miniature garden most beautifully devised. In the midst of this garden was a quantity of white mice, which were wont to disport themselves in a most amusing fashion. The pretty miniature garden and the curious antics of the mice had the effect of drawing numbers of women and girls to the window, where they would stand contemplating the interesting spectacle. The spot upon which they stood was formed of boards in which large holes were pierced. Underneath this was the cellar. The Jew barber, as it subsequently transpired, was in the habit of passing a large portion of his time in the cellar, immediately under the woodwork, which, it was proved, had been specially perforated by his orders. This filthy "Peeping Tom" was finally betrayed by a Jew, one of his workmen. The barber had quarreled with the man, and discharged him; and the latter communicated the story to the police. The Jew was arrested. The story made quite a sensation, and more than one lady in San Francisco who had been interested in the pretty white mice in the Jew's window blushed long and deeply as she perused the particulars of his infamous misdemeanor.

In the same city, a big scandal was occasioned some years ago by the misconduct of a daughter of the wealthiest shirt-manufacturer on the Pacific Coast—an Israelite—with a Chinaman who was a servant in her father's household. What became of the offspring of this scandalous intrigue cannot be definitely ascertained, but the father offered a hundred thousand dollars to any young man of decent antecedents who would make the girl his wife. His offer was confined to Gentile young men, he having a longing for a Gentile son-in-law, but he found no takers. Had he been less discriminating in his choice, and been satisfied with a Jew son-in-law, he could doubtless have married the girl off in twenty-four hours. What slip in maidenly virtue, what dishonor, would not the Jew gladly hug to his breast for the sake of a hundred thousand dollars? A hundred thousand dollars! Joost t'ink of it, Moses!

In many of the factories operated by the Jews throughout the country, the life of an honest girl therein employed is made simply a hell, by reason of the Jews' predominant lechery. Instances in support of this assertion have turned up by scores within the past ten years. In Newark, N.J., some time ago, a number of factory girls demanded the discharge of a certain foreman, upon the ground that he was in the habit of systematically insulting them by indecent proposals and actions. The Jew employers refused to discharge the Jew employee, whereupon the girls struck. As they were preparing to leave, this Jew foreman came into a room where a number of the girls were putting together their effects. The sight of him evoked quite a storm of indignation and rage; and seizing upon him, the girls forced him to the window and, disregarding his shrieks, threw him out headlong.

In Paterson, N.J., similar charges were preferred against another Jew foreman; and not long ago, in New York, the officers of the Society for the Prevention of Cruelty to Children neatly trapped a Jew employer who was in the habit of inducing little girls under fourteen to remain after work-hours, and debauching them. Similar instances of the workings of Jew lechery might be quoted from all over the country, at tedious length.

The Jew drummer is one of the most assiduous patrons of houses of prostitution throughout the country. Without the Jew clientele, it is safe to say that fully sixty per cent of the houses of ill-fame in the various cities of the United States, excepting, for obvious reasons, New York and Chicago, would be compelled to go out of existence. Not only is the Jew a liberal patron of these houses of prostitution; but such is the insatiability of his carnal appetites, and to such an extent does he give rein to his lasciviousness, that his debauches only too frequently exceed the ordinary limits of lust. Those certain hideous and abhorrent forms of vice, which have their origin in countries of the East, and which have in recent years sprung into existence in this country, have been taught to the abandoned creatures who practice them, and fostered, elaborated, and encouraged, by the lecherous Jew!

> Anon., *The American Jew* (New York, 1888), Chapter 9.

Quite apart from his alleged criminality, the Jew was viewed by anti-Semites as a disgusting and revolting specimen of humanity, with whom one would want to avoid coming into any social contact. The Jew, as Henry Adams expressed it with his customary facility for language, "makes me creep."[3]

The Jew "Makes Me Creep" (1901).

We arrived here [Warsaw] yesterday afternoon, after a tiresome night and day in what they call an express, through a country flatter than Florida, and less varied. But we had the pleasure of seeing at last the Polish Jew, and he was a startling revelation even to me, who have seen *pas mal de Jew*. The country is not bad; on the contrary, it is a good deal like our plains, more or less sandy, but well-watered. It is the people that make one tired. You would gratify all your worst instincts if you see a dozen women reaping the grain, and one big, clumsy man standing over them, superintending and doing nothing. With what pleasure should I have called your attention to it, knowing your ferocious and evil nature in regard to my sex! While Sister Anne is really so indifferent to masculine crime, wrapped up as she is in the passion for her two hulking boys! I can get very little fun out of her on that account, and she seems to grow worse always. She bore the journey well—better than I expected, for I found it fatiguing; but we've a worse one tomorrow to Moscow, and I shall be glad to see her well over it. Warsaw is a big, bustling city, like all other cities, only mostly Jew, in which it is peculiar to

Poland. I see little to remark in the streets; nothing in the shops. The people are uglier than on Pennsylvania Avenue which is otherwise my lowest standard. Like all other cities and places, it is evidently flattened out, and has lost most of its characteristics. The Jews and I are the only curious antiquities in it. My only merit as a curio is antiquity, but the Jew is also a curiosity. He makes me creep.

> W. C. Ford, ed., *Letters of Henry Adams, 1892–1918* (Boston and New York, 1938), p. 338.

It was both easy and natural, for those whom the Jew made "creep," to seek to isolate them from all social contact. As early as 1872 an instance of social discrimination against Jews was brought to the public's attention by one B. F. Waterman who had been denied membership in a company of the New York State militia.[4] Commenting on the prevalence of such behavior almost twenty years later, the *Evening Post* remarked, "The 'Christian Place' or the Jew-free club, is a prejudice which in the main keeps Jews and Christians socially apart in nearly every city in the country, which excludes Jews from more or less all the leading summer hotels. . . . In fact, there is no social phenomenon more familiar to all New Yorkers, and particularly to the philosophers of journalism, than this prejudice. . . ."[5] The following extracts would seem to mirror with some precision the sentiments of those who sought to avoid social intercourse with Jews.

"We Do Not Like the Jews as a Class" (1879).

Several days ago a rumor was circulated to the effect that Austin Corbin, the President of the Manhattan Beach Company, had taken an open stand against admitting Jews to the beach or hotel. This report was on Sunday strengthened by a statement from Mr. P. S. Gilmore, the leader of the Manhattan Beach band, who said that Mr. Corbin told him he was going to oppose the Jews, and that he would rather "sink" the two millions invested in the railway and hotel than have a single Israelite take advantage of its attractions. A representative of the *Herald* called upon Mr. Corbin at his banking establishment in the new Trinity building, No. 115 Broadway, yesterday, to ascertain what foundation there was for these most extraordinary rumors. Mr. Corbin at first exhibited some timidity about talking on the subject, but finally invited the reporter into his private office, where he was joined by his brother and partner, Daniel C. Corbin.

"You see," he began, "I don't want to speak too strongly, as it might be mistaken for something entirely different from its intended sense. Personally I am opposed to Jews. They are a pretentious class, who expect three times as much for their money as other people. They give us more trouble on our road and in our hotel than we can stand. Another thing is, that they are driving away the class of people who are beginning to make Coney Island the most fashionable and magnificent watering place in the world."

"Of course, this must affect business?"

"Why, they are hurting us in every way, and we do not want them. We cannot bring the highest social element to Manhattan Beach if the Jews persist in coming. They won't associate with Jews, and that's all there is about it."

"Do you intend to make an open stand against them?"

"Yes, I do. They are contemptible as a class, and I never knew but one 'white' Jew in my life. The rest I found were not safe people to deal with in business. Now, I feel pretty warm over this matter, and I will write a statement which you can publish."

Mr. Corbin sat down at his desk and wrote a few sentences on a slip of paper, as follows:—

"We do not like the Jews as a class. There are some well-behaved people among them, but as a rule they make themselves offensive to the kind of people who principally patronize our road and hotel, and I am satisfied we should be better off without than with their custom."

"There," said he, handing the statement to the reporter, "that is my opinion, and I am prepared to follow up the matter. It is a question that has to be handled without gloves. It stands this way:—We must have a good place for society to patronize. I say that we cannot do so and have Jews. They are a destestable and vulgar people. What do you say, eh, Dan?"

This last sentence was addressed to his brother, Mr. Daniel Corbin, who had taken an active part in the conversation. "Dan" said, with great emphasis, "Vulgar? I can only find one term for them, and that is nasty. It describes the Jews perfectly."

Mr. Austin Corbin then spoke warmly of the loss sustained by the Manhattan Beach Company in consequence of Israelitish patronage.

"Do you mean, Mr. Corbin, that the presence of Jews attracts the element of ruffianism?" asked the reporter.

"Not always. But the thing is this. The Jews drive off the people whose places are filled by a less particular class. The latter are not rich enough to have any preference in the matter. Even they, in my opinion, bear with them only because they can't help it. It is not the Jew's religion I object to; it is the offensiveness which they possess as a sect or nationality. I would not oppose any man because of his creed."

"Will the other members of the Manhattan Beach Company support you in your position?"

"I expect them to. They know just as much about it as I do, and no reasonable man can deny that the Jews will creep in a place just as it is about to become a grand success and spoil everything. They are not wanted at the Beach, and that settles it."

"Have you spoken to any other members about it?"

"No; but I guess they know my opinions."

Mr. Corbin rose from the chair he had been sitting in and paced the floor. "I'll tell you," said he, running his fingers through his hair, "if I had had my way and there was no one to consult in the matter but myself, I would have stopped the Jews from coming long ago. You just publish my statement. It covers the whole ground, and I mean every word of it."

Mr. Corbin concluded the conversation by telling the reporter to be sure and not give the impression that he was warring against the Jewish religion, but he stigmatized the Jews as having no place in first-class society.

New York Herald, July 22, 1879.

The Jew at the Summer Resort (1888).

The general detestation, abhorrence, and contempt with which the American Jew is regarded socially, is, perhaps, nowhere more strongly exemplified than at the summer-resort hotel. Nearly every hotel-keeper at the summer resorts throughout the country is anxious to exclude the Jew from his house, and keeps a sharp and constant watch to bar him out. Owing to the Jew's characteristic lack of delicacy, his obtrusiveness and impudence, this is a somewhat difficult matter; but the summer hotel-keeper, who by dint of long practice and experience is enabled to smell a descendant of the tribe a long way off, succeeds fairly well.

Whenever a Jew nose casts its sinister shadow over the register, the hotel-keeper suddenly discovers that his hostelry is full to overflowing, and profoundly, but firmly, regrets his inability to receive any more guests. Whenever a Moses, or a Jacobs, or a Blumenstein writes asking for accommodation, a reply is hastily rushed off to him to the effect that every room in the house has been engaged three months ahead.

Often the Jew, surmising how he is detested and abhorred, but determined to thrust his nose where it is not wanted, contrives, in applying by letter, to conceal his nefarious identity. In this way he at times succeeds in slipping in. Then the hotel-keeper's silent wrath is terrible to witness; his days and nights are passed in fear and trembling of some infamous *faux pas* on the part of his unbidden guests; and he feels himself in constant danger of his Christian guests sending down for their bills and deserting the house. Only too often in such cases are his worst fears realized.

And yet, Heaven knows! the summer hotel-keeper is not

wont to be any too particular as to the character of his guests. What with the shortness of the season and the heavy expenses that he is under, it is not so much quality *as* quantity of guests that he is after. But the Jew is so objectionable in general manners, habits, and bearing, so obnoxious to good morals, good manners, and good taste, that he is sure to drive other guests away from the house. Hence, by reason of his general vileness, he is a source of pecuniary loss to the hotel-keeper; and therefore the latter, liberal-minded or indifferent as he may be, keeps him out.

But, to come right down to details, what are the particular objectionable qualities in the Jew guest? Well, they are almost too numerous to enumerate. In the first place, the Jew is loud, vulgar, and intrusive. He is loud in his speech and in his dress; he is vulgar in his deportment in the hotel corridors and on the verandas; his table manners are execrable, not to say disgusting; and he is intrusive in forcing his company, with a brazen impudence that knows no check, upon people who do not desire to suffer the infliction and contamination of his acquaintance.

As for the fat Jewesses, as they waddle across the hotel veranda, their gross paunches quivering, and their coarse, pudgy fingers covered with diamonds, they are objects offensive to the sight, blotches on the summer landscape, veritable eyesores. They, in their way, are quite as objectionable as the men.

Then, too, another reason why the Jew and the Jewess are objectionable to the hotel-keeper is that the Israelite is ever haunted by the feeling that he is not getting enough for his money. He is paying high terms; he feels that he never can eat up enough and use up enough to make an equivalent for the outlay he is undertaking. The thought that the hotel-keeper may be making too much profit out of him causes cold shudders to run down his spine, no matter how high in the nineties the thermometer may stand. These curious feelings lead him into wasting food which he cannot eat, and subjecting the furniture and carpets to unnecessarily rough usage,

as if to thereby get the more for his money. Singular, is it not?
. . . Never, probably, were the reasons why the summer
hotel-keeper bars out the Jew from his house more energetically and more forcibly expressed than by a certain wealthy
and prominent citizen, whose action in publicly shutting the
Jews out from his hotel at the most fashionable of all the New
York summering places created a tremendous sensation
some years ago. On the day when the edict of exclusion was
issued, this gentleman, upon being hard-pressed for his reasons, thus expressed himself to an interviewer of the *New
York Times*: "You presume that I had good reasons for shutting the Jews out from the Grand Union? Good reasons, eh?
Well, I should say I had! After screwing and scraping and
hoarding all winter, these Jews come to the Grand Union for
a couple of weeks, bent on cutting a shine. Not content with
obtruding their offensive personalities on the verandas of the
hotel, and monopolizing the chairs to the exclusion of Christian guests, they cock their ungainly feet high in the air, and
talk 'shop' in voices to be heard a mile away. They come
down to the dining room, gorge themselves to bursting, and,
fearing that they will not get enough for their money, they
go upstairs again, and vomit over the furniture. Descending
again to the dining room, they gorge themselves once more,
and then swagger out upon the veranda, and protrude their
ill-shaped bellies in Christian faces. Rather would I shut up
the hotel forever than again admit another Jew!"

Pretty forcible! But on the whole, a very accurate description of the true state of affairs.

Yet another reason why the hotel-keeper excludes the Jew
is the latter's personal uncleanliness. The Jews, as a race, are
undoubtedly the dirtiest people on the face of the earth.
They seem to have a profound aversion to soap and cold
water, and to the maxim that cleanliness is next to godliness.
All the many rules laid down for their guidance in this connection, in Holy Writ, seem to have gone for naught. Even
in the ears of the wealthiest Jewesses, laden down as they
may be with gigantic diamond solitaires, you will often see
great deposits of dirt nestling in the lobes. The men and the

women alike are so subject to body-lice that it is not safe to occupy a bed in which they have slept, or even to bathe on the same seashore as that upon which they have disported.

Last season a certain millionaire manufacturer of New York, a representative business man, and a prince of good fellows, whose name is known from Maine to California, went down to the West End at Long Branch, taking with him his family, his grooms, his fast trotters, and all the paraphernalia of a swell establishment. Having established himself comfortably in one of the finest cottages at the West End, he set about enjoying himself, one of his favorite forms of amusement being to go bathing. It so happened that a short distance to the north of him was a cottage which was used as a Jew boarding house, and there Israel was gathered in force. The weather was very warm; and, garbed in heavy bathing-dresses of outlandish pattern, the Jews used to go bathing at times when the Christian manufacturer was in the water.

The manufacturer had not been at the Branch many days, when he found himself afflicted with a most peculiar and violent itching in various parts of the body. He washed and scratched, and still he continued to itch with increasing intensity. At last, when he had almost worked himself into a state of nervous collapse, he came to the conclusion that he must be suffering from some strange skin malady; and he hurried off to a doctor.

The doctor looked him over and laughed. "My dear Mr. _____," he said, "you are suffering from body-lice. Let me see: you are staying at the _____ cottage, and near you is that Jewish boarding house. You have caught these little inflictions while bathing in the water at the same time as they. I have known of similar cases here before. Remember, wherever these Jews are around, to look out for lice in the very air."

Within twenty-four hours later the snug cottage by the sea was dismantled, the swell establishment was broken up, and the fast trotters, the grooms, and their millionaire master were speeding away from the Branch. They were fleeing from the Jews as one flees from the pestilence.

Can it be wondered at that the summer hotel-keeper sternly waves away the Jew, and refuses to take him within his doors?

Anon., *The American Jew* (New York, 1888), Chapter 3.

As distaste for immigrants in general, and for Jewish immigrants in particular, grew, and pressure for imposing restrictions on immigration mounted, racism in America sought to justify itself with a scientific rationale. A number of prominent social scientists showed themselves willing to provide it, and to "prove" that certain national groups were intrinsically inferior to others and should therefore be denied access to the United States. A notable contribution to this endeavor was made by Edward Alsworth Ross, a professor of sociology at the University of Wisconsin, in a book entitled *The Old World in the New*.[6] First published in 1914, the book attracted widespread interest and much favorable comment. "From ten to twenty per cent" of immigrants in general, Ross declared, "are hirsute, low-browed, big-faced persons of obviously low mentality," "ox-like men" who "clearly belong in skins, in wattled huts at the close of the Great Ice Age."[7] Immigrants are "ugly" and are "bound to lessen good looks among us"[8]; the Mediterranean peoples among them "are morally below the races of northern Europe."[9] These and other equally scientific observations led Ross to conclude that for America to continue to permit free immigration was tantamount to national suicide. "A people that has no more respect for its ancestors and no more pride of race than this deserves the extinction that surely awaits it," he pronounced at the conclusion of his study.[10] The Jews, of course, were by no means excluded from these pejorative judgments, and indeed Ross devoted an entire chapter of his book to an evaluation of them. Nevertheless, it is interesting to note that Ross did not despair utterly of the ability of the Jews to improve themselves. "It will be long before they produce the stoical type who blithely fares forth into the wilderness, portaging his canoe, poling it against the current, wading in torrents, living on bacon [*sic!*] and beans, and sleeping on the ground, all for 'fun' or 'to keep hard,' " he ventured to predict,[11] but eventually they would probably succeed in acquiring these exemplarily American virtues.

The East European Hebrews (1914).

In his defense of Flaccus, a Roman governor who had "squeezed" his Jewish subjects, Cicero lowers his voice when he comes to speak of the Jews, for, as he explains to the judges, there are persons who might excite against him this numerous, clannish, and powerful element. With much greater reason might an American lower his voice today in discussing two million Hebrew immigrants united by a strong race consciousness and already ably represented at every level of wealth, power, and influence in the United States.

At the time of the Revolution there were perhaps 700 Jewish families in the colonies. In 1826 the number of Jews in the United States was estimated at 6,000; in 1840, at 15,000; in 1848 at 50,000. The immigration from Germany brought great numbers, and at the outbreak of the Civil War there were probably 150,000 Jews in this country. In 1888, after the first wave from Russia, they were estimated at 400,000. Since the beginning of 1899, one and one-third millions of Hebrews have settled in this country.

Easily one-fifth of the Hebrews in the world are with us, and the freshet shows no signs of subsiding. America is coming to be hailed as the "promised land," and Zionist dreams are yielding to the conviction that it will be much easier for the keen-witted Russian Jews to prosper here as a free component in a nation of a hundred millions than to grub a living out of the baked hillsides of Palestine. With Mr. Zangwill they exult that: "America has ample room for all the six millions of the Pale; any one of her 48 states could absorb them. And next to being in a country of their own, there could be no better fate for them than to be together in a land of civil and religious liberty, of whose Constitution Christianity forms no part and where their collective votes would practically guarantee them against future persecution."

Hence the endeavor of the Jews to control the immigration policy of the United States. Although theirs is but a seventh of our net immigration, they led the fight on the Immigration

Commission's bill. The power of the million Jews in the metropolis lined up the Congressional delegation from New York in solid opposition to the literacy test. The systematic campaign in newspapers and magazines to break down all arguments for restriction and to calm nativist fears is waged by and for one race. Hebrew money is behind the National Liberal Immigration League and its numerous publications. From the paper before the commercial body or the scientific association to the heavy treatise produced with the aid of the Baron de Hirsch Fund, the literature that proves the blessings of immigration to all classes in America emanates from subtle Hebrew brains. In order to admit their brethren from the Pale the brightest of the Semites are keeping our doors open to the dullest of the Aryans!

Migrating as families the Hebrews from eastern Europe are pretty evenly divided between the sexes. Their illiteracy is 26 per cent, about the average. Artisans and professional men are rather numerous among them. They come from cities and settle in cities—half of them in New York. Centuries of enforced Ghetto life seem to have bred in them a herding instinct. No other physiques can so well withstand the toxins of urban congestion. Save the Italians, more Jews will crowd upon a given space than any other nationality. As they prosper they do not proportionately enlarge their quarters. Of Boston tenement-house Jews Dr. Bushee testifies: "Their inborn love of money-making leads them to crowd into the smallest quarters. Families having very respectable bank accounts have been known to occupy cellar rooms where damp and cold streaked the walls." "There are actually streets in the West End where, while Jews are moving in, negro housewives are gathering up their skirts and seeking a more spotless environment."

The first stream of Russo-Hebrew immigrants started flowing in 1882 in consequence of the reactionary policy of Alexander III. It contained many students and members of scholarly families, who stimulated intellectual activity among their fellows here and were leaders in radical thought. These idealists established newspapers in the

Jewish-German Jargon and thus made Yiddish *(Jüdisch)* a literary language. The second stream reached us after 1890 and brought immigrants who were not steeped in modern ideas but held to Talmudic traditions and the learning of the rabbis. The more recent flow taps lower social strata and is prompted by economic motives. These later arrivals lack both the idealism of the first stream and the religious culture of the second.

Besides the Russian Jews we are receiving large numbers from Galicia, Hungary, and Roumania. The last are said to be of a high type, whereas the Galician Jews are the lowest. It is these whom Joseph Pennell, the illustrator, found to be "people who, despite their poverty, never work with their hands; whose town . . . is but a hideous nightmare of dirt, disease, and poverty" and its misery and ugliness "the outcome of their own habits and way of life and not, as is usually supposed, forced upon them by Christian persecutors."

The Hebrew immigrants rarely lay their hands to basic production. In tilling the soil, in food growing, in extracting minerals, in building, construction, and transportation, they have little part. Sometimes they direct these operations, often they finance them, but even in direst poverty they contrive to avoid hard muscular labor. Under pressure the Jew takes to the pack as the Italian takes to the pick.

In the '80s numerous rural colonies of Hebrews were planted, but, despite much help from the outside, all except the colonies near Vineland, New Jersey, utterly failed. In New York and New England there are more than a thousand Hebrew farmers, but most of them speculate in real estate, keep summer boarders, or depend on some side enterprise —peddling, cattle trading, or junk buying—for a material part of their income. The Hebrew farmers, said to number 6,000, maintain a federation, and are provided with a farmers' journal. New colonies are launched at brief intervals, and Jewish city boys are being trained for country life. Still, not over one Hebrew family in a hundred is on the land and the rural trend is but a trickle compared with the huge inflow.

Perhaps two-fifths of the Hebrew immigrants gain their

living from garment-making. Naturally the greater part of the clothing and dry goods trade, the country over, is in their hands. They make eighty-five per cent of the cigars and most of the domestic cigarettes. They purchase all but an insignificant part of the leaf tobacco from the farmers and sell it to the manufacturers. They are prominent in the retailing of spirits, and the Jewish distiller is almost as typical as the German brewer.

None can beat the Jew at a bargain, for through all the intricacies of commerce he can scent his profit. The peddler, junk dealer, or pawn broker is on the first rung of the ladder. The more capable rise in a few years to be theatrical managers, bankers, or heads of department stores. Moreover great numbers are clerks and salesmen and thousands are municipal and building contractors. Many of the second generation enter the civil service and the professions. Already in several of the largest municipalities and in the Federal bureaus a large proportion of the positions are held by keen-witted Jews. Twenty years ago under the spoils system the Irish held most of the city jobs in New York. Now under the test system the Jews are driving them out. Among the school teachers of the city Jewesses outnumber the women of any other nationality. Owing to their aversion to "blind-alley" occupations Jewish girls shun housework and crowd into the factories, while those who can get training become stenographers, bookkeepers, accountants, and private secretaries. One-thirteenth of the students in our seventy-seven leading universities and colleges are of Hebrew parentage. The young Jews take eagerly to medicine and it is said that from seven hundred to nine hundred of the physicians in New York are of their race. More noticeable is the influx into dentistry and especially into pharmacy. Their trend into the legal profession has been pronounced, and of late there is a movement of Jewish students into engineering, agriculture, and forestry.

The Jewish immigrants cherish a pure, close-knit family life, and the position of the woman in the home is one of dignity. More than any other immigrants they are ready to assume the support of distant needy relatives. They care for their own poor, and the spirit of cooperation among them is very noticeable. Their temper is sensitive and humane; very rarely is a Jew charged with any form of brutality. There is among them a fine *elite* which responds to the appeal of the ideal and is found in every kind of ameliorative work.

Nevertheless, fair-minded observers agree that certain bad qualities crop out all too often among these eastern Europeans. A school principal remarks that his Jewish pupils are more importunate to get a mark changed than his other pupils. A settlement warden who during the summer entertains hundreds of nursing slum mothers at a country "home" says: "The Jewish mothers are always asking for *something extra* over the regular kit we provide each guest for her stay." "The last thing the son of Jacob wants," observes an eminent sociologist, "is a square deal." A veteran New York social worker cannot forgive the Ghetto its littering and defiling of the parks. "Look at Tompkins Square," he exclaims hotly, "and compare it to what it was twenty-five years ago amid a German population!" As for the caretakers of the parks their comment on this matter is unprintable. Genial settlement residents, who never tire of praising Italian or Greek, testify that no other immigrants are so noisy, pushing, and disdainful of the rights of others as the Hebrews. That the worst exploiters of these immigrants are sweaters, landlords, employers, and "white slavers" of their own race no one gainsays.

The authorities complain that the East European Hebrews feel no reverence for law as such and are willing to break any ordinance they find in their way. The fact that pleasure-loving Jewish business men spare Jewesses but pursue Gentile girls excites bitter comment. The insurance companies scan a Jewish fire risk more closely than any other. Credit men say the Jewish merchant is often "slippery" and will "fail" in order to get rid of his debts. For lying the immigrant has a very bad reputation. In the North End of Boston "the readiness of the Jews to commit perjury has passed into a proverb." Conscientious immigration officials become very sore over the incessant fire of false accusations to which they are subjected by the Jewish press and societies. United States senators complain that during the close of the struggle over the immigration bill they were overwhelmed with a torrent of crooked statistics and misrepresentations by the Hebrews fighting the literacy test.

Graver yet is the charge that these East European immigrants lower standards wherever they enter. In the boot and shoe trade some Hebrew jobbers who, after sending in an order to the manufacturer, find the market taking an unexpected downward turn, will reject a consignment on some pretext in order to evade a loss. Says Dr. Bushee: "The shame of a variety of underhanded methods in trade not easily punishable by law must be laid at the door of a certain type of Jew." It is charged that for personal gain the Jewish dealer wilfully disregards the customs of the trade and thereby throws trade ethics into confusion. Physicians and lawyers complain that their Jewish colleagues tend to break down the ethics of their professions. It is certain that Jews have commercialized the social evil, commercialized the theater, and done much to commercialize the newspaper.

The Jewish leaders admit much truth in the impeachment. One accounts for the bad reputation of his race in the legal profession by pointing out that they had entered the tricky branches of it, viz., commercial law and criminal law. Says a high-minded lawyer; "If the average American entered law as we have to, without money, connections, or adequate professional education, he would be a shyster too." Another observes that the sharp practice of the Russo-Jewish lawyer belongs to the earlier part of his career when he must succeed or starve. As he prospers, his sense of responsibility grows. For example, some years ago the Bar Association of New York opposed the promotion of a certain Hebrew lawyer to the bench on the grounds of his unprofessional practices. But this same lawyer made one of the best judges the city ever had, and when he retired he was banquetted by the Association.

The truth seems to be that the lower class of Jews of eastern Europe reach here moral cripples, their souls warped and dwarfed by iron circumstance. The experience of Russian repression has made them haters of government and corrupters of the police. Life amid a bigotted and hostile population has left them aloof and thick-skinned. A tribal spirit intensified by social isolation prompts them to rush to the rescue of the caught rascal of their own race. Pent within the Talmud and the Pale of Settlement, their interests have become few, and many of them have developed a monstrous and repulsive love of gain. When now they use their Old World shove and wile and lie in a society like ours, as unprotected as a snail out of its shell, they rapidly push up into a position of prosperous parasitism, leaving scorn and curses in their wake.

Gradually, however, it dawns upon this twisted soul that there is no need to be weasel or hedgehog. He finds himself in a new game, the rules of which are made by *all* the players. He himself is a part of the state that is weakened by his law-breaking, a member of the profession that is degraded by his sharp practices. So smirk and cringe and trick presently fall away from him and he stands erect. This is why, in the same profession at the same time, those most active in breaking down standards are Jews and those most active in raising standards are Jews—of an earlier coming or a later generation. "On the average," says a Jewish leader, "only the third generation feels perfectly at home in American society." This explains the frequent statement that the Jews are "the limit"—among the worst of the worst and among the best of the best.

The Hebrew immigrants usually commit their crimes for gain; and among gainful crimes they lean to gambling, larceny, and the receiving of stolen goods rather than to the more daring crimes of robbery and burglary. The fewness of the Hebrews in prison has been used to spread the impression that they are uncommonly law-abiding. The fact is it is harder to catch and convict criminals of cunning than criminals of violence. The chief of police of any large city will bear emphatic testimony as to the trouble Hebrew law-breakers cause him. Most alarming is the great increase of criminality among Jewish young men and the growth of prostitution among Jewish girls. Says a Jewish ex-assistant attorney-general of the United States in an address before the B'nai B'rith: "Suddenly we find appearing in the life of the large cities the scarlet woman of Jewish birth." "In the women's night court of New York City and on gilded Broadway the majority of street walkers bear Jewish names." "This sudden break in Jewish morality was not natural. It was a product of cold, calculating, mercenary methods, devised and handled by men of Jewish birth." Says the president of the Conference of American Rabbis: "The Jewish world has been stirred from center to circumference by the recent disclosures of the part Jews have played in the pursuance of the white slave traffic." On May 14, 1911, a Yiddish paper in New York said, editorially:

"It is almost impossible to comprehend the indifference with which the large New York Jewish population hears and reads, day after day, about the thefts and murders that are perpetrated every day by Jewish gangs—real bands of robbers—and no one raises a voice of protest, and no demand is made for the protection of the reputation of the Jews of America and for the life and property of the Jewish citizens.

"A few years ago when Commissioner Bingham came out with a statement about Jewish thieves, the Jews raised a cry of protest that reached the heavens. The main cry was that Bingham exaggerated and overestimated the number of Jewish criminals. But when we hear of the murders, hold-ups, and burglaries committed in the Jewish section by Jewish criminals, we must, with heartache, justify Mr. Bingham."

Two weeks later the same paper said: "How much more will Jewish hearts bleed when the English press comes out with descriptions of gambling houses packed with Jewish gamblers, of the blind cigar stores where Jewish thieves and murderers are reared, of the gangs that work systematically and fasten like vampires among the peaceable Jewish population, and of all the other nests of theft, robbery, murder, and lawlessness that have multiplied in our midst."

This startling growth reflects the moral crisis through

which many immigrants are passing. Enveloped in the husks of medievalism, the religion of many a Jew perishes in the American environment. The immigrant who loses his religion is worse than the religionless American because his early standards are dropped along with his faith. With his clear brain sharpened in the American school, the egoistic, conscienceless young Jew constitutes a menace. As a Jewish labor leader said to me, "The non-morality of the young Jewish business men is fearful. Socialism inspires an ethics in the heart of the Jewish workingman, but there are many without either the old religion or the new. I am aghast at the consciencelessness of the *Luft-proletariat* without feeling for place, community, or nationality."

If the Hebrews are a race certainly one of their traits is *intellectuality.* In Boston the milk station nurse gets far more results from her explanations to Jewish mothers than from her talks to Irish or Italian mothers. The Jewish parent, however grasping, rarely exploits his children, for he appreciates how schooling will add to their earning capacity. The young Jews have the foresight to avoid "blind alley" occupations. Between the years of fourteen and seventeen the Irish and Italian boys earn more than the Jewish lads; but after eighteen the Jewish boys will be earning more, for they have selected occupations in which you can work up. The Jew is the easiest man to sell life insurance to, for he catches the idea sooner than any other immigrant. As philanthropist he is the first to appreciate scientific charity. As voter he is the first to repudiate the political leader and rise to a broad outlook. As exploited worker he is the first to find his way to a theory of his hard lot, viz., capitalism. As employer he is quick to respond to the idea of "welfare work." The Jewish patrons of the libraries welcome guidance in their reading and they want always the best; in fiction, Dickens, Tolstoi, Zola; in philosophy, Darwin, Spencer, Haeckel. No other readers are so ready to tackle the heavyweights in economics and sociology.

From many school principals comes the observation that their Jewish pupils are either very bright or distinctly dull.

Among the Russo-Jewish children many fall behind but some distinguish themselves in their studies. The proportion of backward pupils is about the average for school children of non-English-speaking parentage; but the brilliant pupils indicate the presence in Hebrew immigration of a gifted element which scarcely shows itself in other streams of immigration. Teachers report that their Jewish pupils "seem to have hungry minds." They "grasp information as they do everything else, recognizing it as the requisite for success." Says a principal: "Their progress in studies is simply another manifestation of the acquisitiveness of the race." Another thinks their school successes are won more by intense application than by natural superiority, and judges his Irish pupils would do still better if only they would work as many hours.

The Jewish gift for mathematics and chess is well known. They have great imagination, but it is the "combinative" imagination rather than the free poetic fancy of the Celt. They analyze out the factors of a process and mentally put them together in new ways. Their talent for anticipating the course of the market, making fresh combinations in business, diagnosing diseases, and suggesting scientific hypotheses is not questioned. On the other hand, an eminent savant thinks the best Jewish minds are not strong in generalization and deems them clever, acute, and industrious rather than able in the highest sense. On the whole, the Russo-Jewish immigration is richer in gray matter than any other recent stream, and it may be richer than any large inflow since the colonial era.

Perhaps *abstractness* is another trait of the Jewish mind. To the Hebrew things present themselves not softened by an atmosphere of sentiment, but with the sharp outlines of that desert landscape in which his ancestors wandered. As farmer he is slovenly and does not root in the soil like the German. As poet he shows little feeling for nature. Unlike the German artisan who becomes fond of what he creates, the Jew does not love the concrete for its own sake. What he cares for is the *value* in it. Hence he is rarely a good artisan, and perhaps the reason why he makes his craft a mere stepping-stone to business is that he does not relish his work. The Jew shines in literature, music, and acting—the arts of expression—but not often is he an artist in the manipulation of materials. In theology, law, and diplomacy—which involve the abstract— the Jewish mind has distinguished itself more than in technology or the study of nature.

The Jew has *little feeling for the particular.* He cares little for pets. He loves man rather than men, and from Isaiah to Karl Marx he holds the record in projects of social amelioration. The Jew loves without romance and fights without hatred. He is loyal to his purposes rather than to persons. He finds general principles for whatever he wants to do. As circumstances change he will make up with his worst enemy or part company with his closest ally. Hence his wonderful adaptability. Flexible and rational the Jewish mind cannot be bound by conventions. The good will of a Southern gentleman takes set forms such as courtesy and attentions, while the kindly Jew is ready with any form of help that may be needed. So the South looked askance at the Jews as "no gentlemen." Nor have the Irish with their strong personal loyalty or hostility liked the Jews. On the other hand the Yankees have for the Jews a cousinly feeling. Puritanism was a kind of Hebraism and throve most in the parts of England where, centuries before, the Jews had been thickest. With this rationalism, his shrewdness, his inquisitiveness and acquisitiveness, the Yankee can meet the Jew on his own ground.

Like all races that survive the sepsis of civilization, the Hebrews show great *tenacity of purpose.* Their constancy has worn out their persecutors and won them the epithet of "stiff-necked." In their religious ideas our Jewish immigrants are so stubborn that the Protestant churches despair of making proselytes among them. The sky-rocket careers leading from the peddler's pack to the banker's desk or the professor's chair testify to rare singleness of purpose. Whatever his goal—money, scholarship, or recognition—the true Israelite never loses sight of it, cannot be distracted, presses steadily on, and in the end masters circumstance instead of being dominated by it. As strikers the Jewish wage earners will starve rather than yield. The Jewish reader in the libraries sticks indomitably to the course of reading he has entered on. No other policy holder is so reliable as the Jew in keeping up his premiums. The Jewish canvasser, bill collector, insurance solicitor, or commercial traveler takes no rebuff, returns brazenly again and again, and will risk being kicked down stairs rather than lose his man. During the Civil War General Grant wrote to the war department regarding the Jewish cotton traders who pressed into the South with the northern armies: "I have instructed the commanding officer to refuse all permits to Jews to come South, and I have frequently had them expelled from the department, but they come in with their carpet-sacks in spite of all that can be done to prevent it." Charity agents say that although their Hebrew cases are few, they cost them more than other cases in the end because of the unblushing persistence of the applicant. Some chiefs of police will not tolerate the Hebrew prostitute in their city because they find it impossible to subject her to any regulations.

In New York the line is drawn against the Jews in hotels, resorts, clubs, and private schools, and constantly this line hardens and extends. They cry "Bigotry," but bigotry has little or nothing to do with it. What is disliked in the Jews is not their religion but certain ways and manners. Moreover, the Gentile resents being obliged to engage in a humiliating and undignified scramble in order to keep his trade or his clients against the Jewish invaders. The line is not yet rigid, for the genial editor of *Vorwaerts*, Mr. Abram Cahan, tells me that he and his literary brethren from the Pale have never encountered anti-Semitism in the Americans they meet. Not the socialist Jews but the vulgar upstart parvenus are made to feel the discrimination.

This cruel prejudice—for all lump condemnations are cruel—is no importation, no hangover from the past. It appears to spring out of contemporary experiences and is invading circle after circle of the broad-minded. People who give their lives to befriending immigrants shake their heads over the Galician Jews. It is astonishing how much of the sympathy that twenty years ago went out to the fugitives from Russian massacres has turned sour. Through fear of retaliation little criticism gets into print; in the open the Philo-Semites have it all their way. The situation is: Honey above, gall beneath. If the Czar, by keeping up the pressure which has already rid him of two million undesired subjects, should succeed in driving out the bulk of his six million Jews to the United States, we shall see the rise of a Jewish question here, perhaps riots and anti-Jewish legislation. No doubt thirty or forty thousand Hebrews from eastern Europe could be absorbed by this country each year without any marked growth of race prejudice; but when they come in two or three or even four times as fast, the lump outgrows the leaven, and there will be trouble.

America is probably the strongest solvent Jewish separatism has ever encountered. It is not only that here the Jew finds himself a free man and a citizen. That has occurred before, without causing the Jew to merge into the general population. It is that here more than anywhere else in the world *the future is expected to be in all respects better than the past.* No civilized people ever so belittled the past in the face of the future as we do. This is why tradition withers and dies in our air; and the dogma that the Jews are a "peculiar people" and must shun intermarriage with the Gentiles is only a tradition. The Jewish dietary laws are rapidly going. In New York only one-fourth of the two hundred thousand Jewish workmen keep their Sabbath and only one-fifth of the Jews belong to the synagogue. The neglect of the synagogue is as marked as the falling away of non-Jews from the church. Mixed marriages, although by no means numerous in the centers, are on the increase, and in 1909 the Central Conference of Jewish Rabbis resolved that such marriages "are contrary to the tradition of the Jewish religion and should therefore be discouraged by the American Rabbinate." Certainly every mixed marriage is, as one rabbi puts it, "a nail in the coffin of Judaism," and free mixing would in time end the Jews as a distinct ethnic strain.

The "hard shell" leaders are urging the Jews in America to cherish their distinctive traditions and to refrain from mingling their blood with Gentiles. But the liberal and radical leaders insist that in this new, ultra-modern environment nothing is gained by holding the Jews within the wall of Orthodox Judaism. As a prominent Hebrew leader said to me: "By blending with the American the Jew will gain in physique, and this, with its attendant participation in normal labor, sports, athletics, outdoor life, and the like, will lessen the hypersensibility and the sensuality of the Jew and make him less vain, unscrupulous, and pleasure-loving."

It is too soon yet to foretell whether or not this vast and growing body of Jews from eastern Europe is to melt and disappear in the American population just as numbers of Portuguese, Dutch, English, and French Jews in our early days became blent with the rest of the people. In any case, the immigrant Jews are being assimilated outwardly. The long coat, the side curls, beard and fringes, the "Wandering Jew" figure, and the martyr air disappear as if by magic after a brief taste of American life. It would seem as if the experience of Russia and America in assimilating the Jews is happily illustrated by the old story of the rivalry of the wind and the sun in trying to strip the traveler of his cloak.

> E. A. Ross, *The Old World in the New*
> (New York, 1914), Chapter 7.

Far more influential than Ross's *The Old World in the New* was the magnum opus of Madison Grant, *The Passing of the Great Race*. A member of an old and wealthy family, Grant played a prominent role in New York society, and was a friend of Theodore Roosevelt.[12] "The Catholic Church under Jewish leadership, the Jews, and the Communist Labor Party are all international organizations and as such are hopelessly irreconcilable to the principles of nationalism upon which modern Christendom is founded," Grant believed.[13] To this paranoia he brought the pseudo-scientific rationales derived from his active membership in such organizations as the American Breeders Association and the Eugenics Research Association.

After the First World War, he played an important role in framing the legislation which restricted immigration to the United States.

The Passing of the Great Race (1916).

There exists today a widespread and fatuous belief in the power of environment, as well as of education and opportunity, to alter heredity, which arises from the dogma of the brotherhood of man, derived in turn from the loose thinkers of the French Revolution and their American mimics. Such beliefs have done much damage in the past, and if allowed to go uncontradicted, may do much more serious damage in the future. Thus the view that the negro slave was an unfortunate cousin of the white man, deeply tanned by the tropic sun, and denied the blessings of Christianity and civilization, played no small part with the sentimentalists of the Civil War period, and it has taken us fifty years to learn that speaking English, wearing good clothes, and going to school and to church does not transform a negro into a white man. Nor was a Syrian or Egyptian freedman transformed into a Roman by wearing a toga and applauding his favorite gladiator in the amphitheater. We shall have a similar experience with the Polish Jew, whose dwarf stature, peculiar mentality, and ruthless concentration on self-interest are being engrafted upon the stock of the nation.

Recent attempts have been made in the interest of inferior races among our immigrants to show that the shape of the skull does change, not merely in a century, but in a single generation. In 1910, the report of the anthropological expert of the Congressional Immigration Commission gravely declared that a round-skull Jew on his way across the Atlantic might and did have a round-skull child, but that a few years later, in response to the subtle elixir of American institutions, as exemplified in an East Side tenement, might and did have a child whose skull was appreciably longer; and that a long-skull south Italian, breeding freely, would have precisely the same experience in the reverse direction. In other words, the

Melting Pot was acting instantly under the influence of a changed environment.

What the Melting Pot actually does in practice can be seen in Mexico, where the absorption of the blood of the original Spanish conquerors by the native Indian population has produced the racial mixture which we call Mexican, and which is now engaged in demonstrating its incapacity for self-government. The world has seen many such mixtures of races, and the character of a mongrel race is only just beginning to be understood at its true value.

It must be borne in mind that the specializations which characterize the higher races are of relatively recent development, are highly unstable, and, when mixed with generalized or primitive characters, tend to disappear. Whether we like to admit it or not, the result of the mixture of two races, in the long run, gives us a race reverting to the more ancient, generalized, and lower type. The cross between a white man and an Indian is an Indian; the cross between a white man and a negro is a negro; and the cross between any of the three European races and a Jew is a Jew.

. . . The prosperity that followed the [Civil War] attracted hordes of newcomers who were welcomed by the native Americans to operate factories, build railroads, and fill up the waste spaces—"developing the country," it was called.

These new immigrants were no longer exclusively members of the Nordic races as were the earlier ones who came of their own impulse to improve their social conditions. The transportation lines advertised America as a land flowing with milk and honey, and the European governments took the opportunity to unload upon careless, wealthy, and hospitable America the sweepings of their jails and asylums. The result was that the new immigration, while it still included many strong elements from the north of Europe, contained a large and increasing number of the weak, the broken, and the mentally crippled of all races drawn from the lowest stratum of the Mediterranean basin and the Balkans, together with hordes of the wretched, submerged populations of the Polish Ghettos.

With a pathetic and fatuous belief in the efficacy of American institutions and environment to reverse or obliterate immemorial hereditary tendencies, these newcomers were welcomed and given a share in our land and prosperity. The American taxed himself to sanitate and educate these poor helots, and as soon as they could speak English, encouraged them to enter into the political life, first of municipalities and then of the nation.

The result is showing plainly in the rapid decline in the birth-rate of native Americans because the poorer classes of Colonial stock, where they still exist, will not bring children into the world to compete in the labor market with the Slovak, the Italian, the Syrian, and the Jew. The native American is too proud to mix socially with them, and is gradually withdrawing from the scene, abandoning to these aliens the land which he conquered and developed. The man of the old stock is being crowded out of many country districts by these foreigners, just as he is today being literally driven off the streets of New York City by the swarms of Polish Jews. These immigrants adopt the language of the native American; they wear his clothes; they steal his name, and they are beginning to take his women, but they seldom adopt his religion or understand his ideals, and while he is being elbowed out of his own home the American looks calmly abroad and urges on others the suicidal ethics which are exterminating his own race.

As to what the future mixture will be, it is evident that in large sections of the country the native American will entirely disappear. He will not intermarry with inferior races, and he cannot compete in the sweatshop and in the street trench with the newcomers. Large cities from the days of Rome, Alexandria, and Byzantium have always been gathering points of diverse races, but New York is becoming a *cloaca gentium* which will produce many amazing racial hybrids and some ethnic horrors that will be beyond the powers of future anthropologists to unravel.

One thing is certain: in any such mixture, the surviving traits will be determined by competition between the lowest

and most primitive elements and the specialized traits of
Nordic man; his stature, his light-colored eyes, his fair skin,
his blond hair, his straight nose, and his splendid fighting and
moral qualities will have little part in the resultant mixture.

Madison Grant, *The Passing of the
Great Race* (New York, 1916), pp. 14–16,
80–82.

The view of Jews as crime-ridden, as social undesirables, and
as racially peculiar (if not always as racially inferior) was perni-
cious enough to cause widespread unease among Jews and
anti-Semites alike. But this catalog of accusations was evidently
not considered sufficient; the Jew was held guilty of still further
monstrosities. The most significant of these was the charge that
he was, in a subtle but terrible and purposeful way, undermining the very foundations, economic, social, and cultural, on
which Western civilization rested. The Jews were infiltrating
everywhere. "The atmosphere" in Washington, Henry Adams
reported, "really has become a Jew atmosphere"; his age was
infested by "infernal Jewry"; the economy was "in the hands
of the Jews," who were ruining it. So acute was the challenge
to Christian virtue that another writer was led to cry, "Who
shall redeem our liberty, who shall restore to us our country?"

The "Jew Atmosphere" of Washington (1914).

The winter is nearly over, I am seventy-six years old, and
nearly over too. As I go, my thoughts turn to you and I want
to know how you are. Of myself, I have almost nothing to tell.
It is quite astonishing how the circle narrows. I think that in
reality as many people pass by, and I hear as much as I ever
did, but it is no longer a part of me. I am inclined to think
it not wholly my fault. The atmosphere really has become a
Jew atmosphere. It is curious and evidently good for some
people, but it isolates me. I do not know the language, and
my friends are as ignorant as I. We are still in power, after
a fashion. Our sway over what we call society is undisputed.
We keep Jews far away, and the anti-Jew feeling is quite
rabid. We are anti-everything and we are will up-lifters; yet

we somehow seem to be more Jewish every day. This is not my own diagnosis. I make none. I care not a straw what happens provided the fabric lasts a few months more; but will it do so? I am uneasy about you. I judge you to be worse than we. At least you are making almost as much howl about it.

W. C. Ford, ed., *Letters of Henry Adams, 1892–1918* (Boston and New York, 1938), p. 620.

"Infernal Jewry" (1894).

I am myself more than ever at odds with my time. I detest it, and everything that belongs to it, and live only in the wish to see the end of it, with all its infernal Jewry. I want to put every money-lender to death, and to sink Lombard Street and Wall Street under the ocean. Then, perhaps, men of our kind might have some chance of being honorably killed in battle and eaten by our enemies. I want to go to India, and be a Brahmin, and worship a monkey.

W. C. Ford, ed., *Letters of Henry Adams, 1892–1918* (Boston and New York, 1938), p. 35.

"We Are in the Hands of the Jews" (1896).

You ask me a business question, which I had better answer at once, in case it may be of immediate interest.

If the silver question were a simple matter of money-standard in America, I should advise anyone to buy, of course not bonds but stock, on a silver basis; for, unless the world ends, America is the safest of all now-existing countries; but the money standard is for the present a very secondary consideration. America is horribly in debt to Europe. The smallest estimate of European capital invested there is £600,000,000 (six hundred million pounds). The common estimate is one thousand millions. A large portion of this—no one can ever guess how large—is floating capital, all practically Jew money, and lent practically on call. The owners of this capital have repeatedly and energetically declared that it would be withdrawn if there was even a danger of free coinage of silver. Now, no one doubts—and every Jew in London has acted on the belief—that America cannot anyway maintain the gold standard. She is insolvent on the gold standard, and must be driven either on to paper or on to silver. The rise in gold has doubled the burden of her debt, and gold is still rising. Therefore, since she must anyway, within a few years, go into insolvency, and since indubitably a very large political party prefers to throw her at once into bankruptcy on the gold basis rather than to make things worse by increasing the debt, the chances are very great that Europe, partly in self-defense and partly in a wish to punish and make a terrible example of her, will withdraw capital enough to make a very severe crisis. Already, stocks have been let down to the level of the panic of '93. In fact, the drop was too fast, and the Jew bankers had to try to check it the other day by helping J. P. Morgan to lend the market some £20,000,000 of exchange; in other words, they increased our debt on call, or rather on three months' credit, to that amount. Twenty millions, however, will go a very short way if Europe really calls her loans; and she may do so any day.

In this situation, an investment is sheer gambling. We are in the hands of the Jews. They can do what they please with our values.

But, mind—when I say that an American investment is a gamble, I by no means intend to say that European investments are any better. On the contrary, after the utmost study that I can give to the subject, I have been able to discover no possible grounds for the values now nominally quoted on the European bourses. Certainly, Turkish, Spanish, and Italian credit is worse than a gamble; it is a certain loss to the investor, even at half the present prices. A sweeping repudiation of French debt is a mere question of time. A war, which can, only with the greatest difficulty, be avoided, would bankrupt England in two or three years. The price of English consols today is at least 25 per cent too high on any theory of politics or economy. The same may be said of every stock quoted on any exchange in Europe. Taking the admitted inflation, and the political chances, I should be inclined to say that a loss of fifty per cent was more likely, on any investment, than a gain of ten. As for the situation in England, it is the rottenest of all. The proof of it is the idle deposits in the banks.

For three years I have told you that in my opinion there was only one safe and surely profitable investment, and that is gold, locked up in one's private safe. There you have no risk but the burlgar. In any other form you have the burglar, the Jew, the Czar, the socialist, and, above all, the total, irremediable, radical rottenness of our whole social, industrial, financial, and political system.

W. C. Ford, ed., *Letters of Henry Adams, 1892–1918* (Boston and New York, 1938), pp. 110–111.

"The Original Mr. Jacobs" (1888).

It must not be supposed that the Jews as a class are an intelligent race. Assurance is often mistaken for intelligence. I admit that there have been eminent men among the Jews, as, for instance, their renowned lawgiver and leader in ancient times, Moses. But a careful examination of this anomaly (it is not an exception) will show that the great men among the Jews have drunk copious drafts of Aryan civilization, and have quickly either renounced Judaism or adopted a nominal, sometimes a real, Christianity. Thus their famous men— Heinrich Heine, Ludwig Börne, Edward Gans, Moses Mendelssohn, Disraeli, and Johann Neander—cannot be fairly called Jews; for they either became rank infidels, or they carefully tried to conceal their origin by a change of name, a practice followed to the present day.

What a difference between the Aryan and the Jew! The one is the child of light, and the other of darkness. See how the Aryan raises his head and looks toward the sky; while the

Jew constantly looks on the ground, always thinking, always meditating, always contriving, always plotting, plotting, plotting. By the term Aryan we designate the superior family of the white race. The word is a kin to a certain word meaning *best* or *noblest,* which enters into the formation of many English words, as for instance, aristocrat, etc.

"Nobody," says Littré, "can deny to the Romans their Aryan character." Modern erudition recognizes the common parentage of the Latin and the Greek with the Persian and the Sanskrit, and has drawn together all these scattered brothers into one and the same fold. There is, therefore, a brotherhood existing among all the superior white nations. A misfortune to the one, like an electric shock, reaches the heart of all. These different nations of Aryan origin fraternize easily with one another, amalgamate, and in time become one, and to such an extent that it is difficult when so amalgamated to separate or to distinguish them. The Jew alone, ever since his first appearance upon the earth, has remained separate and distinct, and will to the end remain as alien in the great family of nations.

No race of men excepting, perhaps, the negroes, have a physiognomy so characteristic; no race has preserved more faithfully the original type. "It is our own ideas," says Edward Drumont, "which are in the way of our thoroughly understanding the Jew, and clearly depicting him—ideas due mainly to the atmosphere in which we live, an atmosphere absolutely distinct from that breathed by the Jew."

"The Jew is a coward" is a common expression. Eighteen centuries of persecution supported with incredible endurance testify that if the Jew lacks combativeness, he has that other form of courage called persistence.

Can we seriously treat as cowards people who have suffered everything rather than renounce their faith?

"The Jew is a worshiper of money." This affirmation is rather a declamatory phrase than a thoughtful or serious utterance.

How often do we see men and women with time-honored names offer their greetings to a Seligman, an Oppenheimer, or a Rothschild, every one of whom regards Christ, whom the Christians adore, as the greatest of impostors. What prompts them to do that? Has the Jew who attracts them superior intelligence? Is he an incomparable entertainer? Has he rendered service to the Government? By no means. He is an alien, a German or a Pole, a Jew in faith, little given to conversation, a vain fellow, who often repays the hospitality that he gives to his guest with vulgarities; a hospitality that he extends only through vanity and ostentation.

What motives bring together these eminent men? The love of money. Why do they go there? To kneel before the golden calf.

"Would you know what is the voice of the blood," said to one of his friends a French duke, who, despite the tears of his mother, had married a Rothschild of Frankfort. "See!" He called his little boy, took out a louis from his pocket, and showed it to him. The eyes of the child almost started from their sockets. It was the Semitic instinct manifesting itself.

It has already been stated that nearly all Christian nations are linked together by the closest ties by reason of their common descent from the Aryan race, which has given to the world its greatest civilizations.

Sidon, Carthage, and Tyre no doubt attained, in times gone by, a high degree of commercial prosperity. Tradition has it that the Hebrews had connections with certain of the old, half-Arab inhabitants of the Sinatic peninsula, and the Arabian empire in ancient times attained a passing splendor. But this ephemeral prosperity in no wise resembled the fertile and enduring civilizations of Greece or Rome, or even the Christian society of the Middle Ages.

The Aryan alone possesses the idea of justice, the sentiment of liberty, the conception of the beautiful.

Gellion-Danglar, in his admirable work, *Les Semites et le Semitisme*, says: "The Semitic civilizations, however brilliant they may appear, are only vain images, more or less vulgar parodies, paper edifices, which certain people have the complacency to display as enduring works made of marble and bronze. The bizarre, the monstrous, hold in it the place of the beautiful; while profusion and ostentation have banished from art both taste and decency."

From the earliest times we find the Aryan in conflict with the Jew. Troy was a city peopled by Jews, and the conflict between these two races explains the peculiar vibration emanating from the Trojan War. Louis Benloew says, "Paris was one of those ambulatory Jews who wandered about the coast of Greece. Not content with carrying off the beautiful Helen, which an Aryan might have done in the blindness of passion, he also carried away the treasure of his host. Herodotus, the historian, describes him as having been forced by a tempest to land in Egypt, and being denounced to Pharaoh not only for having dishonored the host who welcomed him, but also for having stolen his treasures, was ordered by the Egyptian king immediately to depart from his dominion, for Pharaoh was unwilling to violate the laws of hospitality which Paris had so little respected."

From the earliest dawn of history, the dream of the Semite, in fact his fixed thought and purpose, has been to reduce the Aryan to servitude, to put him to the severest straits. He sought to reach that point by war. Hannibal, who pitched his camp under the walls of Rome, well-nigh succeeded. But the ruins of Carthage and the bleaching bones of the Saracens, record the lessons given to these presumptuous devils.

Judaism, however, is still confident of success. But it is no longer the Carthaginian or the Saracen who conducts the movement. It is the Jew of today who has replaced violence with treachery and fraud. Silent, progressive, serpent-like, slow encroachment has succeeded the boisterous invasion of old. No more armed hordes announce their arrival with cries, but separate companies wind their way slowly, group by group, and take possession without noise, of all places, of all functions of a country, from the lowest to the highest.

In the environs of Wilna, that hot-bed of Judaism, has been organized many an exodus which has brought misfortune to Germany, France, and England, and now threatens to do likewise in the United States.

Previously to the year 1825 there were hardly any Jews in

America. Today the Jewish societies in New York city alone own real estate valued at nearly thirty million dollars. There are now more than nine hundred thousand Israelites in the United States. Let the reader stroll down Broadway, or down any of the leading streets of New York city, and he will find Jewish names plenty as the locusts of Egypt. By far the greatest number of these Jews come from Wilna, and these Wilna Jews during the Franco-Prussian war assassinated the wounded French soldiers lying upon the field of battle. Thiers relates this episode in his *Histoire du Consulat et de l'Empire*. "Horrible thing to be told," he says, "the miserable Polish Jew, as soon as they saw the enemy in retreat, began to throw our wounded soldiers out of the windows, and, sometimes even to strangle them, thus getting rid of them, after having despoiled them of everything. A sad home offered to the Russians, the partisans of whom they were."

The Jew is a born trafficker, a born liar, full of cunning and intrigue. The Aryan is enthusiastic, heroic, chivalrous, frank, and confident. The Jew sees nothing beyond the present. The Aryan is the child of Heaven, constantly preoccupied with superior aspirations. The one lives in the real, the other in the ideal.

The Jew is mercenary by instinct. He has the bent for everything pertaining to business and for everything that gives him the opportunity to cheat his fellow men. The Aryan is an agriculturist, poet, and above all else, a soldier. War is his element. He goes merrily to face danger and he despises death.

The Jew has no creative faculty. On the other hand, the Aryan invents. Not one invention was ever made by a Jew. There is not a word of truth in the stereotyped phrase that the Jews invented the letter of credit. The letter of credit, the check, was in use in Athens four centuries before the Christian era. In Isocrates this fact is plainly told. The Aryan organizes, creates, while the Jew derives all the resulting advantages which he naturally keeps for himself. The Aryan undertakes voyages and adventure and discovers unknown regions. The Jew waits until all has been explored, until the country has been opened, to enrich himself at the expense of others. In a word—everything pertaining to daring deeds, everything tending to enlarge the terrestrial domain, is absolutely beyond the Jew. He can exist only in the midst of a civilization he has not created. The Aryan is hail, fellow, well met. He is happy provided one relates to him by one of those legends for which his imagination longs, being wholly enwrapped in the marvelous. What pleases him is not one of those Semitic adventures contained in the "Thousand and One Nights," in which singers discover untold treasures, and fishermen cast their nets in the sea and draw them out full of diamonds. To move the Aryan there should be heroic deeds full of devotion, a hero who scorns danger, like Gilbert de Roussilon, for instance, who, after having refused to wed the daughter of a Sultan, pierced five thousand miscreants with a single blow of his unerring lance.

However perspicacious the intelligence of the Jew may appear, it is in reality limited. He has neither the faculty to foresee events, nor of looking beyond his hooked nose; nor the gift of understanding delicate shades of thought and character, for which the Aryan exposes his life without regret.

Renan has thus described many of these points: "The Semitic race is recognized in a unique manner by negative characters. It has neither mythology nor epopee, neither science nor philosophy, neither fiction, plastic arts, nor civil life; in a word, absence of complexity of shade—exclusive sentiment of unity—is its characteristic. Morality has itself always been understood by that race in a manner different from ours. The Jew recognizes duties peculiar to himself. To carry out his vengeance, avenge that which he believes to be his right, is, with him, a sort of obligation. On the other hand, to ask him to keep his word, render justice in a disinterested manner, is to ask him to do the impossible. There is nothing that takes the place in those passionate souls of the indomitable sentiment of *I*. Besides, religion is, with the Jew, a sort of special duty, which has but a distant tie with everyday morality."

Elsewhere he adds: "The spirit of the Jew lacks delicacy and breadth. Interest is never banished from his morality. The ideal woman, depicted in the Book of Proverbs, is an economical housekeeper, profitable to her husband, but, withal, of a very limited morality. Jewish poetry offers scarcely a page embellished with the charm of sentimentality. Love enters into it only in the form of a lascivious and burning voluptuousness."

Gustave Tridon, in his book *Le Molochisme Juif*, calls the Jew, "The stain in the picture of civilization, the bad genius of the earth. His gifts are pests. To fight the Semitic ideas is the duty of the Aryan race."

Renan wrote the above before the unheard-of successes of Judaism during recent years. Nothing is more curious than to study the manner with which Renan, so wonderfully endowed with a scholarly point of view, yet so low in respect to character, kneels before his victors. Renan, after having asserted that the supposed services rendered to civilization by the Jews amount to nothing, suddenly declares, in a lecture delivered before the Society for the Promotion of Jewish Studies, that the Jews are our benefactors. But Alphonse de Rothschild presided over the society, which fact explains the lies uttered by Renan. The Jew banker smiled on the orator prostrated before him, with a smile at once patronizing and scornful. "What a valet!" he seems to say; "what a miserable fellow." We, on our part, would say, how much he is to be pitied. You, both great and small; you, who defend as well as you can the victim of Calvary, the God whom your fathers have prayed to, do you not feel a thousand times happier than this apostate, who kisses the hand of the executioner of Christ for a handful of gold thrown at him with disgust? Do you not believe that the poor missionary, who offers his prayer before a piece of bread, has a more tranquil soul than this rich academician of princely income, and friend of the Rothschilds?

The Jews yearn for whatever flatters their vanity. They seek with grotesque eagerness military titles, titles of baron and count, which look as well on those manipulators of money as the hat of a woman upon a monkey. "There is no trickster," says Edward Drumont, "no matter of how low degree, no dealer in cast-off clothing, no special partner in a pawn shop, who is not a member of the Legion of Honor."

The right of the Jew to oppress others is a part of his religion. It is for him an article of faith. It is repeated in every line of the Bible and the Talmud.

"Thou shalt break him with a rod of iron. Thou shalt dash him in pieces like a potter's vessel." All means are good, provided that they are directed against the Christian—the *Goy* (singular *Goy*, plural *Goyim*).

"One can and must kill the head of the *Goyim*." "The money of the *Goyim* belongs to the Jews. Hence it is permitted to rob and deceive them."

The social evolution itself of the Jew is absolutely different from ours. The type of the Aryan family in the state of civilization is that of the Roman *gens*, which gave rise to the feudal family. During many generations the vital force and the genius are, so to speak, limited, but at once, and unexpectedly, there appears an illustrious representative who has the sum total of the qualities of his manly race. This predestined being often takes a century to make his appearance, but from the lowest extractions there sometimes rises one of those complete figures, at once charming and valorous, heroic and lettered, just and great, such as are to be met with so often in the pages of history.

In the Semitic race things occur differently. In the East a camel-driver, a water-carrier, a barber, is often raised to the highest honors by a whim of the sovereign. He suddenly becomes a pasha, a vizier, a confidant of the prince, like Mustapha-ben-Ismael, who introduced himself to be bardo by selling small cakes and who, according to the suggestive expression of M. Dauphin, "rendered to his master services both day and night."

The same case applies to the Jew. Beyond the sacerdotal families, which constitute a veritable nobility, distinction of rank does not exist. There are no illustrious families among the Jews. Glory is never left as a legacy. In less than twenty years, if circumstances are favorable, the Jew attains his full development. He is born in the bosom of a Judengasse, earns a little money in a successful operation, gravitates to a great city, buys the title of a baron, assumes the manners of one who has always been reared in velvet. The transition is instantaneous. He experiences no astonishment, he ignores all the delicacies of modesty.

Take a Russian Jew as he is in his native place, clad in dirty garments that beggar description, wearing ear-rings as long as corkscrews, and after a month of baths, he will install himself in a box at the opera with the *aplomb* of a Seligman or a Wormser.

We know, here in the United States, of two Jew brothers who in Germany were itinerant venders of notions and who, from village to village, their pack on their shoulders, sold cheap wares. They made a little money, came to New York, engaged a gentleman to write a book in German for them, the elder put his name on it as the author, opened a school, gave to himself the title of professor, engaged two or three teachers of foreign languages, had them write as many books in their native tongue, repeated the same effrontery as in the case of the German work, except that now he appeared as co-author, and today the ignorant suspender dealers of Germany enrich themselves by selling at a high price their assurance to the easily gulled Americans.

On the other hand an honest Gentile of the middle or even of the lowest class who has enriched himself in an honorable way will always have an embarrassed air and will avoid the elegant centers of society. His son, reared in the midst of better conditions, will with greater ease of manner enter the refined circles of the world. The grandchild will, in the course of time, if the family continues to live in easy circumstances, live honestly, and in the true Christian spirit represent the picture of the true gentleman so common in our American society. He will be endowed with a delicacy of thought and a refinement of sentiment that the Jew never possesses.

If the Jew suddenly reaches the extreme of assurance, he

never attains distinction. Excepting in the case of a few Portuguese Jews who in youth have beautiful and expressive eyes, and in old age a certain Oriental majesty, one can never find among the Jews that indescribable calm, courtesy, and dignity which distinguish the American, the Englishman, the Frenchman, or any other Christian gentleman, though clothed in threadbare garments.

The Jew is insolent, never proud. He never gets beyond what is termed "cheek." The Rothschilds, and others of the same class, notwithstanding their millions, appear little better than dealers in cast-off clothing. Their women with all their diamonds always look like venders of toilet articles, clothed in gaudy garments. Equality, the first condition of social intercourse, is lacking among the Jews. The Jew—let this remark be well kept in mind—will never be the equal of the Gentile. He either cringes before you or seeks to crush you. He is either above you or below you, never your equal.

Let the reader only refresh his memory, and he will acknowledge that even in a few minutes' conversation this phenomenon clearly manifests itself. As soon as you enter into conversation with a Jew at all familiarly he will seek to overwhelm you. It is necessary continually to remind him who you are and what he is.

The monotony of type is the striking peculiarity of the Jewish race. The Jew lacks that refined culture, that sparkling cleverness which is the very salt of conversation. One rarely meets with those piquant observations and witty remarks which many a conversationalist sows by hazard in the intimacy of the social circle. Were the Jew equipped with these advantages, he would turn them to his own pecuniary benefit.

The Jew is a monochord, and the longest conversation offers no surprises to him.

It is necessary to become acquainted with the native, the Oriental Jew, in order to understand fully the Jew of civilization. The Presburg Jew, particularly, gives an idea of the intermediate state between the sordid Jew of Galicia and the opulent Jew of the capitals.

Picture to yourself a road that creeps up dry, dusty, almost whitish. To the right and left are small, singly little shops, or small houses like those in the Orient, furnished with bars and not unlike those in the Middle Ages. In the public highway exists pell-mell—in the midst of dirt of all kinds, bits of iron, broken pieces of odds and ends, heaps of garbage—a population of seven or eight thousand Jews. Yonder swelter the old men remarkable for their ugly features, and by their side lie young girls of wondrous beauty, clothed in tatters. The long coat dominates among men, who mark the present by the greasy tall hat they wear, and recall the past with their dirty feet, which are always bare, and with their never-combed hair. One seems everywhere to recognize faces of familiar acquaintances, and this corner of the Ghetto has the air of a little Paris or New York. These two dirty Jews yonder, revolting in their general aspect, do they not resemble Dreyfus, Lockroy, or better still, are they not the striking picture of many well-known Jews here in New York? Notice this young bony girl who walks bare-footed, dressed in a dirty *camisole* and a skirt that reaches to her knees. Is she not the very type of Sarah Bernhardt when a child? In fine, put on diamonds, new garments, on all these people, on all these dealers in second-hand articles, receivers of stolen goods, keepers of pawn-shops, money lenders on wages, and you will have the upper class of the New York Jews.

These Jews, however, are not in the least dissatisfied with their condition, for they wait patiently for the time of full tide which will carry them into a city, and shortly afterward to fortune.

At the end of the hill one finds himself before the castle of Schlossberg, the four walls of which alone remain standing, but where once were crowned the kings of Hungary. This castle stands like a motionless giant with a strange relief looking at space. At its feet slowly flows the Danube, sleepy and morose, and seeming to oppose itself with a dogged resistance to the steamboats that with difficulty ply their way up the stream. To the left lies the island of Au, with its small country seats. At your feet stretch banks of sand, and in the far distance are to be seen large islands called "The Garden of Gold." This spot, once the seat of royalty, has today a profoundly melancholy aspect. The feudal world, with all its glories, its heroic recollections, its triumphant pomp, is in ruins, like yonder deserted castle. The new world moves and agitates itself a few steps distant in yonder Jewish colony, from which will rise, until the hour of Christian regeneration strikes, the Jew millionaires, worshiped by a servile society, the Jew traders who delight in glaring advertisements, in fact, all those who, with Jewish effrontery, pose before an imbecile and easily guiled public.

One must not judge of the artistic or literary ability of the Jews by what they publish today. The Jew is incapable of rising above a very limited height. They have no men of genius to compare with Dante, Shakespeare, Bossuet, Victor Hugo, Emerson, Longfellow, Newton. The man of genius is a superior being, ready to sacrifice himself for the good of humanity. It is the nature of the Jew to sacrifice nothing at all. Their Shakespeare is Adolph D'Ennery, and their Raphael is Worms. What more striking example of the utter lack of creative power among the Semitic races could we have than a Carthage, which, though she was for a time mistress of the world, has not left behind a single work of art? The excavations made there have brought to light only a few insignificant objects, while the humblest town of Greece yields every day new treasures. . . . In art the Jews have created nothing original, powerful, or touching. They produce only low, vulgar works. They busy themselves with what enables them to make "moneys"; with what flatters the vulgar appetites of the multitude; with what satisfies their Jewish venom and hatred. They often accomplish this by turning into ridicule the pious recollections, heroic deeds, august traditions of the Christians, at whose expense they live.

"Note well," says Edward Drumont, "the manner in which the Jew carries out his work. If called upon to ridicule the army at a time when a terrible war is about to break forth, the Jew Ludovic Halevy produces the disgraceful composition known as the General Boum. If heroism, honest love, or any immortal masterpiece is to be ridiculed, the Jew, Offenbach, is at hand. Is it necessary to hold up to scorn the works of Shakespeare, of Racine, or of Molière? The Jew Busnach is ready to perform the task. In a word, the Jew corrupts everything that exists. The innocent and mirth-provoking old French dance, the *bonne enfant,* is turned by the Jew into the ignoble can-can. From the light, airy, joyous songs of old he constructs those obscene, rude, and lascivious airs and, at times, cutting journalism of old he has converted into blackmail. From the attractive photographs of the eighteenth century he develops the most obscene pictures to be thought of. From the innocent and amusing caricatures of Daumier, he makes the infamous, impure pictures of Strauss, a worthy parent of the musician of the same name.

"The dancing halls, where the youth of bygone days amused themselves in an honest way, have degenerated into a place of prostitution, thanks to the Jew Markowski and the androgynous Wolff. Thus while these low creatures commit these infamous acts in France and elsewhere, they have the effrontery to screen themselves by declaring, 'Behold, how low France has fallen! Behold her literature! Behold what she is producing!' "

When have the ancestors of these men prayed with our own? In what corner of the village or of the city are their family tombs? In what parish registry does one find the names of these newcomers, who, less than a century ago, had not the right to live on the earth from which they now seek to drive us away. By what right do they attach themselves to the traditions of our race?

The Jew acquires easily the slang of a language, but never its purity and finish. In order to speak a language one must first of all think in the language. There is, between the expression and the thought, the closest connection. One must not expect a Jew to naturalize his style as he does his person. One must have sucked, at one's own birth, of the native beverage, have truly arisen from the native soil. Then one can defend, like Henry Clay or Daniel Webster; write like Hawthorne and Shakespeare, who hated and despised the Jew; attack like Voltaire; defend like Choate. As I am writing the above, I recall the account given by the Rabbi Benjamin de Tudèle who, while visiting Greece during the Middle Ages, met a horde of Jews encamped upon Mount Parnassus. What a lamentable spectacle! Hordes of these servile circumcised dogs, whom Aristophenes so despised, installed among those laurels where, during the glorious times of Hellas, the God with the Silver Bow guided the sacred choir of the sister muses.

This inability to acquire a foreign language extends even to its pronunciation. The Jew who so easily speaks slang always retains a guttural sound that never fails to manifest itself. Richard Andrée has affirmed this fact in his book entitled *Interesting Observations Respecting the Jews.* "Most of the Jews," he says, "even the educated, have a peculiar accent that causes them easily to be recognized. It is a mark of race common among the Jews of all nations."

The Jew, being thus incapable of entering into the domains of creative art, has also failed to penetrate into the unexplored regions of science. He sells eyeglasses and telescopes, but never discovers new stars in the immensity of the heavens, like Leverrier. He does not discover a new continent like Columbus; he does not divine the laws of attraction, like Newton. The claim of the Jews, that they kept the depot of science during the Middle Ages, and transmitted to us the discoveries of the Arabs, is not true. The Jews have made themselves appear learned by picking up some crumbs from the books of Aristotle. They have simply played the role of the ass in the fable, who put on the skin of a dead lion. During centuries they have monopolized the profession of medicine, which rendered espionage easy by permitting them to enter everywhere, but never for a minute did they think of the circulation of the blood. The Jew doctors of that period were a thousand times more ignorant in a scientific point of view than their contemporaries. They believed that the heavens were solid; that the firmament was pierced with holes from which rain fell. They formulated axioms of this sort: "A little wine and bread taken on an empty stomach preserve the liver from sixty maladies"; "It is a sign of too much blood when one dreams of a cock."

It is to the Aryan that we owe all discoveries, both great and small. It is to him that is due the art of printing, the discovery of gunpowder, of steam, of electricity, of the circulation of the blood, of the laws of attraction. All progress has been evolved from the natural development of Christian civilization. The Jew, one must never weary of repeating, only exploits that which Christians genius and work have achieved.

The true emblem of the Jew is that hideous bird that installs itself in the nest constructed by another. We know of a Jew abroad whose like would make an interesting subject for a novel. A few years ago he gave himself the title of general, and recently posed before the world as an archaeologist. He palmed off before a board of mummified directors a large number of objects, many of them of more than doubtful authenticity, and pocketed for his worthless collection a princely fortune.

Having indicated the principal traits common to all Jews, let us now examine more closely the race and the species. The principal signs by which the Jews can be recognized are the following: The famous hooked nose, the restless eye, the close-set teeth, the elongated ears, the square nails (instead of being tapered in the shape of an almond), the flat foot, the round knees, the soft hand almost melting with the hypocrisy of the traitor. Often they have one arm longer than the other. Lavater observes: "Physical degradation closely follows upon moral degradation. This is strongly remarked among the Jews, who, of all races of men, are the most depraved."

Anon., The Original Mr. Jacobs (New York, 1888), pp. 3–17.

A View of the Jewish Immigrant (1888).

Toward the close of the year 1825 a band of Polish Jews, about one hundred in number, landed in New York. Previously there were hardly any Jews in this country. This band was under the leadership of one Gugenheim; and as they traveled through Europe to the land of their destination, they reminded one of those patriarchal families so often mentioned in the Old Testament. They were bound together, not only by the ties of common religion, but by those of common misfortune; for they had suffered persecution at the hands of the Russians, which persecution, however, they fully merited.

These Jews, when first seen by the people of this country, presented a type different from any of the other immigrants that ever have landed upon our hospitable shores. They attracted unusual attention by their hooked noses, restless eyes, elongated ears, square nails, flat feet, round knees, and soft hands.

Myriads of parasites could be seen by the naked eye, nestling upon their dirty heads. They wore long coats dripping with filth, while their faces and beards looked suety with sluttishness.

The above description of this batch of Jew emigrants is not in the least exaggerated.

Not one among them had with him any other wearing apparel than the scanty garments he wore. When they landed they had no friends to welcome them; they had no resources; they were ignorant of the language of the country; and it was doubtful whether one among them had sufficient money to pay for a night's rest in the cheapest Bowery lodging-house of today. But within a few years after their arrival we find the greater part of these Jews occupying prominent positions in the financial world of the metropolis. Later on we find their descendants prominent as bankers in New York, prominent as bankers in Chicago, in St. Louis, and in other leading cities in the United States. It is the descendants of the above-described Jew immigrants who today display with vul-

gar effrontery their wealth, who control the clothing business, the tobacco business, the sugar business, of this great
country, and who establish newspapers that cast a stigma
upon American journalism, and who seek to direct and mold
public opinion.

How have these Jews accomplished all this? Is it by their
surpassing intelligence? No. There is no race of men more
intelligent than the Aryan. Is it by any useful invention of
their part, or by devoting themselves to mechanical pursuits?
No, certainly not.

Again, the most diligent inquiry fails to discover any considerable number of Jew farmers throughout the territory of
the United States. One will look long before he finds a Jew
laborer among the workmen who build our railroads, work
our mines, or develop the resources of this country.

The Jew's soft hands and curved fingers grasp only the
values that others have produced. Wherever the Jew is allowed to establish himself, dishonesty takes the place of
honesty; immorality, of virtue; disease, of health; sluttishness,
of cleanliness; anarchy, of order. One has but to study the
social and political history of the different nations in Europe,
during the last fifty years, to discover the poisonous work of
the Jew. He has sapped the foundation of every government.
He has reduced France from a nation of first rank to a second-
class power. He has made Russia to writhe under incessant
internal revolutions. He has ruined Turkey. He has so
thoroughly impregnated England with his own Jewish cow-
ardice that England's martial spirit has sadly deteriorated.
He is now carrying out his work of deterioration and destruction in the United States. From the time when the Jew first
appeared upon the face of the earth, to this day, history does
not record a single invention that can be claimed by the Jews.

They have never founded a state of any magnitude, though
they have always been more numerous than the Romans,
who conquered the world, and now exceed in numbers any
of the minor peoples in Europe. With a momentary exception in Moorish Spain, they have never dominated any people, or conciliated any people, even in the East, where they

have had fair chances, or founded any great city. They have never produced a great soldier, and we cannot yet credit them with a statesman of the first class. Lord Beaconsfield was hardly more than a great party leader in politics, though he had a certain genius for apprehending the passing waves of emotion in the British people. Herr Lasker has never over-thrown a government; M. Fould was only a clear-headed banker; and Sir H. Drummond Wolff has scarcely made a mark.

The peculiar way the Jew has of accomplishing his diaboli-cal work, or of "getting along," to use his own expression, can best be illustrated by studying the early history of the little band of Jew immigrants above referred to.

They began life in the New World as itinerant venders of cheap notions. For their petty stock in trade, consisting of pencils, pens, stockings, pocketbooks, and of all manner of odds and ends, they were trusted; but every night they were obliged to make returns of sales made to the one who had supplied them with the goods. Gradually they increased their little capital, and next they became receivers of stolen goods; and, to this day, it is the Jews who control this particu-lar industry in all our cities. They established pawnshops, made advances for which an exorbitant rate of interest was charged, exercised every manner of usury, and introduced crookedness and theft in all transactions. They established petty stores, stocked them with an insignificant amount of cheap goods, insured them far beyond their actual value, and shortly afterward set fire to them, collected the insurance, and repeated this crime from time to time throughout the country. Thus they grew rich.

This crime of incendiarism, previous to the advent of the Jews, was with us, comparatively speaking, unknown. The Jews mulcted the insurance companies of vast sums of money before the companies became aware of the fraud practiced upon them. It is a matter of record that many of the leading insurance companies today hesitate, and often refuse, to in-sure the stock of anyone having a Jewish countenance or a Jewish name. Recently the president of a large insurance company telegraphed to his agent in Chicago, "Look carefully before taking any risks offered by men whose names end in *ein, ky* or *kie."* Good advice, indeed!

It has been said that the Jews despise manual labor. Who has ever heard of a Jew miner? Still, no sooner is the mining-camp established than it is followed by Jew vampires, who rob the sturdy miner of his hard-earned wages, by every kind of deceit. The Irishmen, the Germans, the Italians, in a word, the immigrant from every part of the world, has contributed and still contributes, more or less, to the prosperity of our country. The Jew, we repeat it, has never done anything tending to increase the national prosperity. He only seeks the fat of the land. He only thrives upon what others produce.

We have been accused of being Jew-baiters, of wishing "to create a revolution" against the Jews. This is not true. We despise only villainy, and our aim is to direct the attention of Americans to the danger that lurks in the Jews.

Anon., *The American Jew* (New York, 1888), Chapter 1.

"Who Shall Restore to Us Our Liberty?" (1879).

Type is the conservator of race and the security of government. The disintegration of the European principalities began with the introduction of foreign elements. War, with its consequent admixture of the conquerors with the nations conquered, the blending of races, of ideas and customs, the contact with barbarians, all proved fruitful germs of agitation and disorder.

There is in the organization of man an element more powerful than reason. It is instinct. Until the maxims of reason are adopted, and by long practice become an integral part of the moral constitution, in short, acquire the force of instinct, there occurs a conflict which lends to subversion of order. This truth is exemplified in both the political and religious history of the world, and especially in the war of the Crusades. The nations of Europe were not in their infancy, for, surrounded by old institutions, they still preserved the memory of her ancient civilization. But while far removed from the crudities and imperfections which attest adolescence, they had not yet attained that degree of development which lends to maturity its greatest charm. With society, as with individuals, education, temperament, and a thousand influences conspire to produce qualities the most conflicting and contradictory.

In the war of the Crusades the principles of Christianity and those of barbarism met face to face in the arena with no barrier between them. Here you witness the holiest maxims constantly proclaimed—legitimacy, law, reason, justice invoked; the tribunal of Jehovah appealed to, and his authority declared. This was the influence of Christianity. But at the same time we are shocked by the numberless acts of violence, of cruelties practiced—pillage, rape, murder, and other atrocities. This was the influence of barbarism. Grand ideas, vast plans, noble inspirations, social and political views of a high order agitated the minds of men, while their hearts were filled with a holy enthusiasm which lifted them out of themselves into regions that give birth to martyrs. Here again we witness the influence of Christianity. But look at the execution! You will find disorder, improvidence, violence, lack of discipline; you will find nowhere concert of action, united though they were in one common cause. Thus the instincts of barbarism came in conflict with their higher and more exalted conceptions of life born of aspirations evoked by the new religion.

Youths thirsting for knowledge crowd the halls of philosophy. Eloquent and powerful voices call them to the realms of science. A noble enthusiasm fires heart and brain, animates and inspires the mind to new labors and research after truth. But we see these same youths who exhibit such noble dispositions, who inspire such exalted hopes, and whose destiny prefigures as the leaders of the van of a new and glorious civilization, we see them turbulent, licentious, committing the most deplorable acts of violence, fighting in the streets and forming in the midst of cities an unruly faction, amenable neither to law nor order.

Thus briefly we see illustrated the ever contending forces

of hereditary instinct against the evolution of moral sentiments not yet become congenital—not yet crystallized into
a Type. Type isolates, strengthens, and preserves. It erects a
barrier against the encroachment of innovations whose tendency is to weaken and destroy. We say of certain old families, "they are clannish," but fail to recognize the fact that
their preservation is due to this very element.

Coming down to modern times, we find two races which
illustrate most forcibly the immutability of clanship or type.
These are the Jews and the Gypsies, between whom there
exist strong resemblances. Neither race has national existence, nor do they owe allegiance to any Government in the
world. They have preserved their peculiar customs and religion through ages of wanderings, and though inhabiting every country on the globe, preserve their ancient Type. . . .

The Jews, in one essential unlike the Gypsies, have not only
made history but have a history. Their earliest historians
present them as a nomadic tribe of Asia, wandering from
place to place, driving their flocks and herds before them.
Again, unlike the Gypsies, they are a warlike race. The love
of conquest and of gain are their dominant characteristics.
Like the Gypsies, their origin is obscure, and we have no
record save that which the Jews themselves furnish. Arabic
tradition, however, and especially the Koran, fixes the fact
that Abraham, an Arab patriarch, lived with his tribes and his
herds in Arabia, and laid the foundation of the holy Raaba
[*sic;* the reference is presumably to the Kaaba—Ed.]—the
temple in Mecca which has at all times been the seat of
monotheistic worship, and where, to this day, prayers are
offered up to the God of Abraham, Ishmael, and Mahomed.

The Arab excels all other nomadic tribes in mental endowments. He is energetic, fiery, quick to plan, and ready of
execution, with an unparalleled craftiness and cunning.
These faculties are also inherent in the Jew; but they possess
certain other qualities which give them an additional advantage. The Arab is quick and energetic, but lacks patience and
perseverance; whereas the Jew combines with a fiery temperament an obstinacy so inflexible that it is well said, a Jew

never yields, and knows neither forgetting nor forgiving. Major Osman Bey, an officer in the Turkish Army, has published a work entitled *The Conquest of the World by the Jew,* to which I am largely indebted for the facts which I present. A race endowed with natural gifts of such extraordinary character naturally excites expectations of remarkable achievements. With temperament and mental endowment so irresistible, stimulated by a passion of gain so deeply rooted as to extinguish all other desires, the Jew, even in his nomadic state, comprehended a principle of ethics which other races learned later, viz: "that wealth constitutes power."

While the Jew possessed no theoretical ideas of political economy, he was the first to adopt and practice its principles. He observed that it is not he who acquires, but he who saves, that acquires wealth; and he who saves obtains supremacy over him who squanders. Furthermore, he observes that, in general, men in their desire to obtain that which they do not possess place little value on that which they have already obtained. From these observations the Jew derived those principles which, to this day, are the foundation of his social, political, and commercial acumen.

He ceased to act upon old modes of warfare, but formulated a new principle which has made him the "conqueror of the world." This new principle of conquest, which demonstrates the rare genius of the race, led him to seize only the movable property of the enemy—their gold and silver, and such valuables as he could carry away—destroying no life and leaving their field and vineyard. Said the Jew: "If we can make their riches our own they become our slaves. . . ."

When forced to abdicate a conquered country, they not only carried off their plunder, but obtained as well a moral victory over the enemy by attaching the blame to them, and representing themselves to be the persecuted people. This policy, a masterpiece of Machiavellianism, has never been excelled by any other race or sect, and constitutes to this day the soul and spirit of Judaism.

The Mosaic period witnessed a revolution of this policy, the result of a reaction in the minds of the leaders, who were shocked at the spectacle of the "chosen people of the Lord" given up to a system of highway robbery and usury. "A people who belong to the foremost of nations must enter openly and honestly upon a career that leads to prosperity and civilization," and, in consequence, the principle of armed conquest again assumed the ascendant. However, with the fall of Judah, its stay and support, the principle of armed conquest fell also.

At this period in the history of this remarkable race, they developed a religious phase, and the prophecies became the central idea around which all others revolved. With that instinctive shrewdness which had thus far served him so well, the Jew realized that only through the policy indicated by Abraham, Isaac, and Jacob could the prophecies receive fulfillment, which promised to the sons of Israel the conquest of the world. "Of what use is it to us," said he, "that we possess a country of our own, a kingdom, fortresses and armies, which a single storm may destroy, making us the slaves of the conquerer? No! The Mosaic idea is only a chimera, though it may be beautiful. Our riches, our power, must not be concentrated at one point, but scattered over the face of the world. With no fixed habitation, we shall be ever ready to invade the land where the harvest is most bountiful."

The conquest of Judea, by the Romans, gave a decisive direction to the cosmopolitan tendencies of the Jews, and they soon penetrated into all the eastern and western provinces of the Roman Empire. History records the sequel. Their system of usury and intolerant spirit aroused the Romans, and Titus made war upon them, but through a mistaken policy, directed the campaign against the citadel of the Jews, instead of seeking to destroy and uproot their political machinations.

At a later period we find the race established in all the chief commercial centers of Europe. One body settled in France, another in Genoa, while at the same time colonies arose in all the chief cities of Spain, the Netherlands, Germany, and Poland. With the Christian Church and the feudal power opposing hostile measures to their advance—subject to the most cruel persecution—no power could stem the tide of Jewish conquest, which slowly, gradually gained advantage. There is but one kind of hostility which the Jew fears, viz: that which assumes the form of competition, and meeting them in their own vantage ground, attacks their principle of *finesse* and of financial polity.

The assertion that the dispersed Jews form a powerful and most dangerous league that threatens the destruction of our country is by no means a chimera. The universal belief that the Jews have been scattered over the face of the world because of their refusal to recognize the divine mission of Christ is not supported by history. Innumerable proofs may be cited to establish the fact that the dispersion of the Jews has been a voluntary and organized emigration. From Kamt-schatka to San Francisco, in the midst of Europe, throughout Asia, we find the scattered people bound firmly together by the same religious and historical traditions, animated by one single idea, one faith, that they are the chosen people of Jehovah, and that the treasures of the world are their inheri-tance. The Jewish marauder, traveling the steppes of Tar-tary, the stockbroker of Vienna, of India, of Paris, of New York: among all you will find the same faith, and the same confidence in their future autocracy.

Jewish solidarity is so great that if you attack one Jew, all the Jews of the five continents arise as one man. This fact was illustrated in our own history. When General Grant was fac-ing opposing forces in Tennessee, he was greatly annoyed by the number of Jews who followed the army, preying upon the soldiers, and he issued an order banishing them from the camp. It was followed by an appeal from the Jews of all the large cities, who sent a delegation to Washington to remon-strate with President Lincoln upon the injustice done them, and in consequence General Grant was forced to rescind the order.

Throughout the Middle Ages the Jews quietly laid stone upon stone in the structure of their projected dynasty. Re-gardless of the movements of the Gentile world, they planned the battle of usury throughout Europe, a spy in every camp, and waited patiently for the hour of victory. It came.

The French Revolution sounded the tocsin of liberty, and the Jews leaped forth like birds of prey to the carrion. With the atheist, the Jacobin, the Carbonnaire, they cried, *"Vive la Republique"* or *"Vive le Roi,"* as interest dictated. But while these cries in the mouths of others signified imperative demand for new measures of administration, to the Jew, loyal to his nation's policy, it meant power.

Side by side with the extraordinary financial system, which spreads like a network over Europe and America, we witness the gradual social emancipation of this remarkable race. Proud England today, with a monarchy, a House of Lords and Commons, is governed by a Jew. Lord Macaulay declared, to make a Jew the privy councillor to a Christian sovereign would be a standing disgrace to the nation. "But the Chancellor of the Exchequer is ever in doubt until he confers with the Jew. He controls the money, and consequently the policy, of the nation. The scrawl of the Jew on the back of a piece of paper has more power than the sovereign decree of kings, or of three republics as the United States of America."

Within a short period the world witnessed the strange anomaly of a Christian sovereign interposing to protect a nation of "infidels" against the encroachment of another Christian power. What motive could thus actuate her most Christian Majesty? Was it the chivalry of giving protection to the weak, of justice rebuking wrong? No! What then? It was the Jewish shekel behind the Christian throne.

"I hold two hundred million pounds sterling of Turkish bonds," said the English Jew. "Turkey must be preserved! Millions for Turkey!" Russia, with a population of four million of Jews, pleads in vain for a loan. Not a sliver for Russia. But peace restored, the Jew from his hoarded millions proffers a loan at exorbitant interest to restore her commerce.

Deprived of that prestige which a recognized nationality confers, the Jews realized the necessity of a federal head, and this distinction was ultimately conferred upon Nathan Meyer de Rothschild, who found the English branch of the Jewish alliance in 1806, and who subsequently bought with his gold admission to the English peerage. Upon his death in 1826, the chieftainship was conferred upon his nephew Lionel who, dying last June, bequeathed the honor to his son, who has thus become absolute sovereign of the Jewish dynasty. We find his representative in every country and in every commercial center wielding an influence that controls the financial policy of the world. As king of finance, Rothschild commands the masses of Jewish capital as absolutely as does the Russian Emperor his armies. The power of this autocrat outmeasures that of any potentate on the globe. No measures of national policy can be arranged without his sanction. The nations of Europe are but pieces on a chessboard which he moves at will. At his mandate war rears her ghastly head, or peace smiles a benison.

Conversing with an English gentleman a few weeks since, he declared that England "dare not go to war without the consent of the Rothschilds." His power in the United States is established by the fact of the conversion of the silver bonds, payable, principal and interest, in gold. The demonetization of silver was effected by one Siegel, a Jew of London. With a fund of $500,000 he came to Washington. What followed? We are all familiar with the trickery practiced by which the demonetization of silver was effected. What became of the $500,000? The London *Banker's Magazine* stated that "the mission of Mr. Siegel to Washington has been successful in its purpose of demonetizing silver."

Since 1864 the United States bonds have been a most prolific source of speculation and profit to the Jews. In one single transaction the Rothschilds invested $143,000,000, realizing a clear profit of $333,000,000. How many United States bonds do they hold today, to be paid in gold? Judge Warwick Martin informed me that in a recent visit to England, on board from New York to Liverpool, were three agents of the Rothschilds, who admitted that they carried bonds to the amount of $10,000,000. It is known that this is but an insignificant part of his real investment. The wealth of the Rothschilds is fabulous.

THE "NEW TRANS-ATLANTIC HEBREW LINE"

FOR THE EXCLUSIVE USE OF "THE PERSECUTED."

A HINT TO THE HEBREWS.

HOW THEY MAY MAKE THEMSELVES INDEPENDENT OF THE WATERING PLACE HOTELS.

Our peaceful rural districts as they are liable to be infested if this Russian exodus of the persecuted Hebrews continues much longer.

MR. IPSENSCHNEID.— Sells you nice diamont shtud sheap, mine frent, Don'd gif it avay! It vas shmuggled!

MR. HERSOOT.—Thanks; I've got one!

Talkative old gent.—"DO YOU KNOW, SIR, A FORTNIGHT AGO, IN A LEADING HOTEL IN BERLIN, I WAS HOOTED BECAUSE THEY SAID I WAS AN ENGLISHMAN."

German Jew.—"IT VAS ZE SAME MIT ME."

Whoever assists the Jew in his work, is bound to become besmirched.

The "Kosher Xmas" Spirit

Keep Christmas Christian
Buy From Gentiles Only!

ROOSEVELT'S IDEAL "NINE OLD MEN"

There IS a Jewish World Plot

JEWS SAY SO!

NATIONAL RENAISSANCE BULLETIN

EDITORIAL STAFF
Editor, James H. Madole
Secretary, Joseph Rudden
Circulation, Edward Cassidy

May-June, 1963
Vol. 14, Nos. 5 & 6
Published in New York, N.Y.
$2.00 per 12 issues

Official Organ of the NATIONAL RENAISSANCE PARTY devoted to a restoration of the American Republic, the preservation of American sovereignty, and the establishment of an American regime based on the principles of racial nationalism and social justice.

JEWISH WAR VETERANS INCITE MAJOR RIOT IN YORKVILLE
James H. Madole

On May 25, 1963, a day that will live forever in the hearts and minds of every American patriot throughout the continental United States, a mere handful of dedicated young fighters from the NRP Security Echelon risked their lives and freedom in the streets of Yorkville against hundreds of well-organized, hate-filled Jewish fanatics. While the local press and radio sought to depict these screaming maniacs as "aroused citizens of Yorkville fighting a "neo-Nazi" invasion" IT WAS A WELL KNOWN FACT THAT THESE JEWISH GOON SQUADS HAD BEEN CARRIED INTO NEW YORK CITY BY CHARTERED BUSES FROM JERSEY CITY, PHILADELPHIA, AND CHICAGO. These buses were parked conspicuously on East 84th Street during the course of the two hour rally. Jewish thugs stalked menacingly through the crowd of 5000 spectators seeking to beat up or intimidate any onlookers who dared

Corbin's "White Jew" and Whiter Jewess.

Kinky hair must positively be straightened out.

"And the Lord hardened Corbin's heart

HINTS FOR THE JEWS.—SEVERAL W

GETTING TO MANHATTAN BEACH.

THE NEW JERUSAL

FORMERLY NEW YORK.

MOSES.

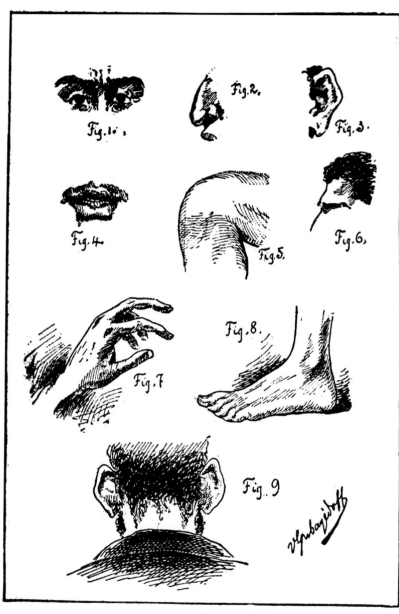

HOW WE MAY KNOW HIM.

Fig. 1. Restless suspicious eyes.	**Fig. 5.** Round knees.
Fig. 2. Curved nose and nostrils.	**Fig. 6.** Low brow.
Fig. 3. Ill-shapen ears of great size like those of a bat.	**Fig. 7.** Long clammy fingers.
	Fig. 8. Flat feet.
Fig. 4. Thick lips and sharp rat's teeth.	**Fig 9.** Repulsive rear view.

Three members of the family each possess $3,000,000,000. When we reflect that this immense wealth is the fruit of the labor of thousands of beings who are virtually his subjects, and who labor incessantly to support his power and splendor, one almost doubts one's sanity.

In the year 1840 the Jews called a council at Cracow. Their object was to consult upon proper methods to extend their dynasty. "All methods are vain," pronounced one, "while the press is not in our hands." Today they own the London *Times*, the London *Daily Telegraph* with its circulation of 100,000 copies, and journals in every commercial city of Europe, 12 journals in the United States, including the New York *Tribune*, all of which advocate the supremacy of gold as the basis of all finance. In 1848 the Jews came into conflict with the Roumanians, a conflict not yet terminated. Such was their power even at that time the Roumanians could with difficulty find two or three journals to undertake their defense. The Jews put in motion such an overwhelming mass of journals that the Roumanians found themselves excommunicated by the whole civilized world as fanatics. . . .

The necessity of restraining the cupidity of the Jews was the foundation of the Spanish Inquisition. The greater part of the wealth of the Christians had passed into the hands of the Jews. Everywhere, the Christian found himself his debtor. Hence the hatred of the Jew; thence the troubles and tumults, which on many occasions caused the shedding of blood.

Some thirty years ago, an association was formed in Paris called the "Universal Israelite Association," to which belong the prominent Jews of all countries. This conclave has at its disposal a large staff of officers, composed of newspaper writers, secret agents, spies, couriers, all men of high intellectual endowments, speaking all languages, and occupying important positions on every continent. Belonging to this association are four Jews, who represent the United States officially at foreign courts.

In this lengthy and yet greatly abridged sketch of Jewish history, we read our national warning. We find here the confirmation of the statement of Osman Bey, "that the Jew is the ruler of the world, and that he has obtained its conquest without the firing of a gun." Without a country, with no national existence, owing allegiance to no government, yet by his *finesse* and masterly statesmanship, he today controls the money power of the world. Gold ever has been to the Jew the symbol and representative of wealth. Today, with all his vast resources, his power over the dynasties of Europe and our own Republic, he is striving to enforce a money system based upon a superstitious and a false philosophy. From the height of their immense capital, the weight whereof threatens to crush all other nations, they command the world of finance and industry. All the colossal enterprises of modern times are Jewish monopolies—the Sutrian Southern Railway, the mines of Brazil, the Union Pacific Railway—these are but a few of the many.

To what extent are we ourselves, our children, mortgaged to the Jew? The national debt to be paid in gold! Do we fully comprehend that this is equivalent to saying that it is never to be paid? Could we command the gold coin of the whole civilized world we could only discharge the interest. When shall we, then, pay either the principal or the interest? Today there is not a Gentile who is free from Jewish thraldom.

We observe one prevalent characteristic of the Jew—he never engages in agriculture, the opening of mines, or laboring in mechanical arts. But wherever on the globe commerce exists there hovers the Jew with his bag of gold. Wherever he goes he carries with him the curse of usury. "A curse," says Gibbon, "that ruins nations and peoples; that feeds the blindest and most besotted appetites of man's vilest nature; condemned by pagan sage and Christian morality."

The Jew has extended his network of finance from one end of the world to the other. Concealed behind his desk, the counter, ten millions of this race prey uninterruptedly upon the vitals of mankind. In this remarkable preservation of the Jewish race we see operating the same factor that has preserved the Gypsies from extermination. With that wonderful sagacity and prescience which constitutes the genius of this race, they have preserved unvitiated the Type. In spite of their worldwide Dispersion; in spite of the persecutions of 1,800 years, we find in them the same mental and physical characteristics which, under the theocratic rule of Abraham, led their hosts to victory. The Jew may well be pardoned the superstition that he is "the chosen of the Lord." We turn the pages of Christian history in vain to find a record of the self-abnegation—the sacrifices to which for centuries the Jews submitted. Persecuted and despised, wrapped in rags, he fought with bitter misery, sustained by a sublime faith that the "Lion of the tribe of Judah" should yet wave its banner above the battlements of the world, conqueror of its regions.

Preserving the integrity of Type, the race may still bid defiance to the world. It is invincible. No calamity, save that of pestilence decimating the earth, can destroy it. For three hundred years the state of modern society has been such that all events have acquired a character of generalization and, consequently, an importance which distinguishes them from other events of a similar character occurring at other periods and under different social conditions. Perusing the history of antiquity, we find the events recorded there were isolated, to a greater or less degree; consequently, their benefactions were less widely spread, and in the same ratio, their evils were more confined. Carthage, Rome, Sparta, all these nations were more or less advanced in the career of civilization, each following its own path, and progressing in a different direction. Political constitution, ideas, usages, and customs rendered each independent of the influence of the other, nor do we find evidence of a tendency to bring nations to one common center. We find, unless forced to intermix, ancient nations lived for long periods in close proximity without losing their distinctive characteristics.

But the political aspect of the modern world is vastly different. In spite of geographical boundaries, we are all fast growing into one large family, in which no event of importance can occur to one member without materially affecting all others. Even the ideas of a faction agitate nations, and affect governments. Nothing remains isolated. All things assume a character of universality, and acquire by expansion a terrible force.

Do we undertake the study of the history of one nation, we find ourselves inevitably involved in the history of other nations. Even in the study of science and art we find a thousand vital links connecting them with objects apparently widely separated. Thus nations are connected. Objects become assimilated and relations multiply. For this reason, non-intervention in politics has become an impossibility. We may not interfere directly, but that mighty fulcrum, the press, disseminates opinions which must necessarily have an influence in determining issues. No reflecting mind can be blind to the results which this condition imposes. The tendency of the day is toward the destruction of Types. Nations are losing their individuality. Governments are becoming assimilated, and with this assimilation thrones are becoming less stable and republics less republic.

The problem of Europe is today, "How sovereign power may be restricted without being destroyed."

The problem of America is, "How may our Republic be preserved."

We call ourselves Americans. But the typical American is he whom we term a savage. He alone possesses a generic name. Civilized America is but a conglomerate of opposing nationalities. Every ship from Europe introduces a disorganizing element. Monarchist instincts born of hereditary conditions make us a people of factions, of fanatics. Here are blended all nationalities under the sun; races between whom there exists constitutional antagonism here meet, here unite to frame laws antagonistic to their own instincts. The legitimate result of such legislation must tend to disintegration. Time, you answer, "will blend distinctions, modify and assimilate differences." Not while each day, each year, adds thousands to our foreign element.

To preserve our Republic we must stop emigration; we must breed a Type, a people that has existed under no other form of government; a people in whom republican principles are inherent, whose mental and physical organization is in harmony with the genius of our institutions. Do not mistake me and infer that this is a measure which I approve and advise. I am not so presumptuous. I present facts and their legitimate deductions. But I think no one will dispute the truth of the axiom with which I started, that "Type is the conservator of race, and of governments."

We see its wonderful efficacy in the preservation of two races standing isolated and alone for centuries amid elements whose force was directed to their annihilation. But admitting the truth of this axiom, we recognize another fact of greater vital importance at this crisis of our national history, the existence of an enemy in our midst working silently and with a subtlety that surprises only when we peruse the record upon the page of history, the insidious undermining of American liberty by the Jew.

We say we have a country. Where? The soil we press with our feet, the roof that shelters our children, the broad expanse of unclaimed prairie, our rivers rolling their surging tides to the sea, our majestic mountains whose crests kiss the sky, all, all are mortgaged to the Jew. Who shall redeem our liberty, who shall restore to us our country, our homes, our hearthstones? Where is our redeemer? Who shall liberate us from these—*bonds?*

> Elizabeth Bryant, "Types of Mankind as Affecting the Financial History of the World; Delivered Before the Greenback Labor Club of the District of Columbia, October 7, 1879" (Washington, D.C., 1879), pp. 1–8.

4. Jew-Hatred in the 1920s

In the 1920s anti-Semitic prejudices were openly voiced in some of the highest circles in the land, whether political, economic, or literary. The move to suspend mass immigration from Europe, for example, was in large part prompted by an anti-Semitic desire to keep Jews out of the United States.

While much of the agitation in this connection seems to have been inspired by the notion that the Jews are, generally speaking, a repulsive collection of people (a notion which was given expression in a variety of literary forms), the still more sinister and dangerous image of the Jew as a conspirator was also prevalent at this time. The Bolshevik menace was seen as a

Jewish plot to overthrow civilization, or at least to capture it for the Jewish conspiracy. These paranoic views received their most notable expression with the dissemination of the notorious forgery, the *Protocols of the Elders of Zion*, whose chief proponent was no less influential a personage than Henry Ford.[1]

The fear that the United States was threatened with an inundation of squalid, filthy, and mentally deficient Jews from Europe is clearly expressed in the report submitted to the House of Representatives by its Committee on Immigration and Naturalization in 1920.

"Temporary Suspension of Immigration" (1920).

Mr. Johnson of Washington, from the Committee on Immigration and Naturalization, submitted the following Report. (To accompany H.R. 14461.)

The Committee on Immigration and Naturalization reports H.R. 14461, a bill for the temporary suspension of immigration, and recommends its passage.

During the third session of the Sixty-fifth Congress [December 1, 1918, to March 4, 1919], the Committee on Immigration and Naturalization gave thorough consideration to the question of immigration restriction. Several bills were introduced and extended hearings were held. The then chairman of this committee, the late Hon. John L. Burnett, introduced a bill, H.R. 15302, which was reported favorably by the committee January 29, 1919. This bill provided for the prohibition of immigration for a period of four years. The committee was practically unanimously in favor of such a prohibition, and at that time it was thought such a bill could be passed if time for its consideration could be given on the floor of the House. But the House calendars were so congested that the bill did not receive a hearing and therefore failed of enactment. . . .

. . . Since Mr. Burnett's bill . . . was reported, January 29, 1919, almost two years have passed. The flood of immigration which was expected when Mr. Burnett's bill was under consideration did not set in until the summer of 1920. This committee is informed that had steamship accommodations been available, this flood of immigration would have set in more than a year ago. But steamship accommodatioms were not available, due to the necessities of demobilization of the armies, and it was not until the spring and summer of 1920 that the real effects of unsettled conditions in Europe began to evidence themselves in a stream of emigration from European countries.

It is impossible today to estimate the effect which the Burnett bill would have produced had it become a law during the Sixty-fifth Congress. But of this much we can be certain: That countless numbers of persons now coming to the United States would not have left their homes in Europe during the past year. Half of the four-year suspension period proposed in the Burnett bill has elapsed. The flow of immigration to the United States is now in full flood. The need for restrictive legislation is apparent. The accommodations at Ellis Island are not sufficient for the avalanche of new arrivals; larger cities have not houses for them; work cannot be found for them; and, further, the bulk of the newer arrivals are of the dependent rather than the working class. . . .

Members of your committee, as a result of personal investigation at Ellis Island, discovered that on one Sunday, November 15, 1920, more than 16,600 aliens were either at Ellis Island or on ships in New York Harbor awaiting examination. This number included about 4,000 seamen. To make this great number of examinations there was a maximum number of 85 inspectors available. In order to follow the law exactly, this pitiful number of Federal inspectors would have to examine each alien as to a passport, ability to read 30 or 40 words in his native tongue or dialect, also as to his political belief, and as to his capacity to sustain himself, as well as inquiry concerning all of the provisions of the immigration laws. Medical examinations are made by officials of the Public Health Service.

Some years ago, before the passport law and the literacy test law, 5,000 aliens could be examined in the time now needed for examination of 3,000 aliens.

Members of the commitee found the new immigration at
Ellis Island to consist practically of all nationalities except
Orientals. It found by far the largest percentage of immigrants to be peoples of Jewish extraction. On the steamship
New Amsterdam, sailing from Rotterdam, the committee
found that 80 per cent of the steerage passengers were from
Galicia, practically all of Jewish extraction. On the *New Ro-
chelle,* arriving from Danzig, the committee estimated that
more than 90 per cent were of the Semitic race. The committee is confirmed in the belief that the major portions of recent arrivals come without funds. It was apparent to the
committee that a large percentage of those arriving were
incapable of earning a livelihood. These are temporarily de-
tained, causing great congestion, much delay, and pitiful distress, until relatives or others arrive to give bonds that the
newcomers will not become public charges.

On one day the committee found in the special inquiry
room at Ellis Island, which could not conveniently accommo-
date 300, 1,200 people were obliged to stand and await attention in stifling atmosphere.

A visit to the room for temporary detention revealed very
crowded conditions and stifling atmosphere. A frail young
woman appealed to the committee to help her out of this
bedlam of foreigners of all nationalities, 795 in one comparatively small room, stating that she had been waiting there,
with two small children, for two days and had nearly reached
the limit of her endurance. . . .

. . . While considering this subject of immigration it might
be well to study also conditions of emigration on the other
side. . . .

. . . The committee has confirmed the published statements
of a commissioner of the Hebrew Sheltering and Aid Society
of America made after his personal investigation in Poland,
to the effect that "If there were in existence a ship that could
hold 3,000,000 human beings, the 3,000,000 Jews of Poland
would board it to escape to America."

In the preparation and presentation of this legislation to

the House of Representatives the Committee on Immigration and Naturalization has disregarded the statements of a Polish labor commissioner to the effect that 225,000 Hebrews have been furnished this year with funds for passage to the United States. The committee has disregarded all statements that might give a religious bias of any kind to the matter under consideration. It is fair to state, however, that the largest number of Jews coming to the United States before the war in a single year was 153,748 (1906); while during the one month of October 1920, it is estimated that of the 74,665 immigrants arriving at Ellis Island, more than 75 per cent were of the Semitic race.

Figures available for the fiscal year ending June 30, 1920, show that a very small number of these peoples gave as their reason for coming to the United States the desire to escape religious or political persecution.

The committee did not investigate charges of extensive funds from America passing through agencies in Warsaw and elsewhere. The committee does believe, however, that these funds, whether large or small, together with generous contributions made both by government and individuals for the relief of distress in central Europe, combined with the reports which have spread everywhere concerning prospects for certain prosperity and immediate wealth in the United States, all combine to play a part in encouraging the downtrodden of all the war-wrecked countries to sell everything and to pay in their depreciated monies $120 to $130 for steerage passage to the United States in addition to $10 for United States consular visa and registration. . . .

The committee is satisfied that fraudulent passports are being issued, fraudulent visas being charged for by unscrupulous aliens, and that even fraudulent steamship tickets are being sold by the hundreds to the desperate population of many European countries.

The committee has a report from one man, lately returned from central Europe, who says that the situation is as if every person there was walking through heavy muck with two to three hundred pounds weight on his back, striving to reach some seaport where he might board a ship to the United States. Enough are coming to verify this simile, and already the cries of distress are coming to the Committee on Immigration and Naturalization from the housing committees of several of the great cities, who contend that the newest arrivals from Europe are forced to pile in on unnaturalized alien residents of already crowded and unhealthy tenement houses. . . .

APPENDIX A.

Department of State,
Consular Service,
Washington
December 4, 1920.

My Dear Mr. Johnson: In accordance with your request of this morning it gives me great pleasure to send you herewith paraphrases of statements in regard to immigration received from officers of this Government who have visited the countries mentioned. I hope you will find the data of value in connection with the presentation of your bill to Congress.

Very sincerely yours,

Wilbur J. Carr

Hon. Albert Johnson,
    Chairman Committee on Immigration,
        House of Representatives.

AUSTRIA

Vienna.—Sixty per cent of the present emigrants are of the Jewish race, 20 per cent are of the German race, and 20 per cent of other races. The favorite occupation of these emigrants is merchant or clerk.

GERMANY

Berlin.—It is estimated that 2,000,000 Germans desire to emigrate to the United States if passport restrictions are removed.

The Germans who proceed to the United States are not of the most desirable class, due to the fact that military service is at present in most cases an absolute bar. Most of those who receive permission to leave for the United States are the aged parents of American citizens or minor children. Th wives of declarants who are now permitted to proceed are almost always of the lower classes. The Poles, Austrians, and nationals of the different Russian States who apply for visas are as a rule of the most undesirable type of emigrant. They are usually traders who only increase the number of middlemen or if they work they usually go into sweatshops.

NETHERLANDS

Rotterdam.—The great mass of aliens passing through Rotterdam at the present time are Russian Poles or Polish Jews of the usual ghetto type. Most of them are more or less directly and frankly getting out of Poland to avoid war conditions. They are filthy, un-American and often dangerous in their habits.

POLAND

Warsaw.—Concerning the general characteristics of aliens emigrating to the United States from Poland and the occupation or trade followed by them, reports indicate such to be substantially as follows:

(a) Physically deficient:
    (1) Wasted by disease and lack of food supplies.
    (2) Reduced to an unprecedented state of life during the period of the war, as the result of oppression and want.
    (3) Present existence in squalor and filth.

(b) Mentally deficient:
    (1) Illy educated, if not illiterate, and too frequently with minds so stultified as to admit of little betterment.

(2) Abnormally twisted because of (a) reaction from war strain, (b) shock of revolutionary disorders, (c) the dullness and stultification resulting from past years of oppression and abuse.

(c) Economically undesirable:

   (1) Twenty per cent is given as a round and generous estimate of productive laborers among present applicants for visas. This estimate is meant to include workers or those who may be expected to become workers, from both sexes. The remaining percentage may be expected to be a drain on the resources of America for years.

   (2) Of the 50 per cent of emigrants from Poland who may be termed efficients, 40 per cent—of the total number of emigrants—will enter a trade as a middleman, not a producer. These will thrive on the efforts of their associates.

   (3) The productive labor, small percentage as it is, will be found in America, in the sweatshops in the large centers of population. It is decidedly not agricultural, but urban in character. In this report female applicants as housewives, etc., are of course termed as efficients.

(d) Socially undesirable:

   (1) Eighty-five to ninety per cent lack any conception of patriotic or national spirit. And the majority of this percentage is mentally incapable of acquiring it.

   (2) Seventy-five per cent or upward will congregate in the large urban centers, such as New York or Baltimore, and add to undesirable congestion, already a grave civic problem.

   (3) Immigrants of similar class are to be found already in the United States who, taken as a class and not individually, have proved unassimilable.

   (4) All Europe is experiencing in the reaction from the war a corruption of moral standards. This may even be least noticeable in Germany. The introduction of these lowered standards can not fail but have its evil influence in the United States.

(e) At the moment, 90 per cent may be regarded as a low estimate of the proportion representing the Jewish race among emigrants to America from Poland.

(f) The unassimilability of these classes politically is a fact too often proved in the past to bear any argument.

EXTRACTS FROM REPORTS OF OFFICERS
WHO HAVE VISITED POLAND

Report of March 3.—A large number of people are endeavoring to proceed to the United States regardless of travel and other difficulties. The majority of these people belong to the undesirable classes; that is, those who are prone to congregate in the large cities, and from whom the present type of political and labor agitators are drawn. These do not belong to the good classes of agricultural and factory workers.

Report of April 6.—Approximately 100,000 persons are desirous of immediately leaving Poland for the purpose of coming to the United States. Ninety-five per cent of these persons are of the very lowest classes of the country and are considered to be thoroughly undesirable. Many of these persons have trachoma and other quarantinable diseases and come from typhus-infected areas. They are filthy and ignorant and the majority are verminous. Persons who come in contact with these prospective emigrants are obliged, owing to their insanitary conditions, to take the greatest precautions to avoid contamination. There is a grave menace to other parts of Europe because persons from typhus-infected areas travel to European ports. The strictest quarantine regulations should be observed for emigrants from Poland. To permit large numbers of such persons with such characteristics to enter the United States is believed to be a dangerous policy, inasmuch as it is impossible to determine the attitude of these persons toward orderly government owing to the present political and social unrest in this part of Europe. There appears to be under the present serious circumstances no adequate reason for the voyage to the United States of other than commercial men and of wives with or without young children whose husbands are already in this country.

Report of April 10.—Outbreak of cholera this spring and summer anticipated. Typhus situation is a menace to travel.

Report of May 15.—Typhus conditions have shown little, if any, improvement. Some organizations interested in sending certain classes of Polish citizens to United States are objecting to quarantine restrictions, and are endeavoring to avoid these regulations through transshipment through other countries. Some emigrants are objecting to certain sanitary provisions, such as removal of beards and clipping of hair.

Report of May 17.—One immigrant aid society, which has offices in Poland, is said to be planning to send 250,000 emigrants of one race alone, the Jewish, to the United States within the next three years. The increase of emigration from Poland raises two important questions for the United States —first, public health, and, second, public safety. Many Bolshevik sympathizers are in Poland. It is difficult through visa control to keep out the undesirables.

Report of June 28.—Reports indicate 34,538 cases of typhus in Galicia and Poland in 1916, 43,480 in 1917, 97,082 in 1918, 232,206 in 1919, and the first two months of 1920, 46,500. Typhus situation in Poland shows little improvement despite active campaign against it. Refugees from infected areas in Russia are constantly pouring into Poland. Unconfirmed reports show that 8 per cent of the population of the city of Zhitomir, Ukraine, died of typhus between January and April 1920.

Report of July 11.—All emigrants who pass through Danzig are decidedly inferior type, physically, mentally, and morally, and because of their insanitary habits constitute a menace to the health of all with whom they come in contact.

Report of July 11.—Crowds collecting in Warsaw for the purpose of procuring necessary papers to enable them to emigrate are alleged to be a menace to the health of Warsaw. It is alleged that one of the reasons for the remarkable increase in the number of intending emigrants from Poland to the

United States may be found in the activities of representatives at Warsaw of American immigrant aid societies, who are reported to have aided the emigrants to obtain passports, to have arranged for special care on trains to ports of departure, to have negotiated with steamship companies for ships to intermediate ports, and special trains to connect with the trans-Atlantic liners.

Report of October 1.—It is estimated that 350,000 Polish subjects of the Hebrew race alone are anxious to proceed to the United States for the purpose of joining relatives or for other reasons. Another estimate places the figure of those who will attempt to reach the United States during the next three years at 5,000,000. Crowds estimated at 6,000 have at times waited before the Warsaw consulate to obtain visas. It is impossible to overestimate the peril of the class of emigrants coming from this part of the world, and every possible care and safeguard should be used to keep out the undesirables.

RUMANIA

Bucharest.—Possibly 10 per cent are Rumanians from Transylvania or the Old Kingdom. The remainder are Jews, mostly from Bessarabia and Bukovina, practically all, except women and children, being petty merchants or salesmen. It should be noted that the proportion of men emigrating is increasing and that now a few are probably fugitives from Ukrania who have managed to obtain Rumanian passports. Ninety per cent of applicants are Jews of both sexes and all ages.

> *Temporary Suspension of Immigration,* 66th. Congress, 3rd. Session, House of Representatives, Report No. 1109, December 6, 1920.

Poetic expression—albeit of an extraordinarily crude kind—of the sentiments contained in the Immigration and Naturalization Committee report, was made available to the American public by John Jay Chapman through the courtesy of the *Ku Klux Kourier:*[2]

The Nation-Wreckers (1922).

How restful it is to survey the sea
From some low, windswept, silvery, sandy dune,
And watch the eternal climbing of the moon
Full-orbed above the shore's complacency;
Wondering the while if Asian plains there be,
Or rock-walled valleys, never shined upon,
Save by the perpendicular sun at noon,
So safe, so guarded, so remote as we.

But see, a sail!—nay more—from every land
They cloud the ocean, conveyed by a crew
Of Master Pirates who have work in hand:
Old Europe's nation-wreckers heave in view!
And lo, to aid them, on our margin stand
Our citizens—the Jesuit and the Jew.

> Richard B. Hovey, *John Jay Chapman,
> An American Mind* (New York, 1959),
> p. 132.

The paranoiac fear of a purposeful conspiracy aimed at "wrecking" America contained in Chapman's poem was widely echoed. A short-lived publication with the curious title of *The Brooklyn Anti-Bolshevist*, for example, was committed to the belief that Bolshevism, a tool of the Jewish conspiracy, had placed America in danger of imminent collapse.

"Jewish Traitors Hastened Our Advent into the War, Ruined Russia's Armies, and Saved Germany from Defeat in 1917" (1918).

Ever since the sinking of the *Lusitania*, Socialist leaders have charged that certain Wall Street interests, allied with British capitalists, were using that disaster as a lever to drag this country into the war. When war was actually declared on April 6, 1917, they proceeded to saddle the full responsibility upon J. P. Morgan . . . and the two old political parties. Morris Hillquit exploited this charge in his speeches during the Mayoralty campaign last year. Mr. Hillquit did not produce any evidence to sustain the charge. It was not necessary. He was addressing audiences made up of Bolshevists like himself, and what he said against Christians was accepted as gospel.

It is the purpose of this article to answer Mr. Hillquit by showing that it was his own Bolshevist party, financed and directed by the German-Jewish end of Wall Street, that are the real criminals in the matter. Furthermore, it will be shown that after hastening this country into the war, they deliberately plotted to bring about the defeat of our armies by destroying the Russian army of five million soldiers, thus preventing an allied victory over Germany in 1917.

From the time of its formation in Paris in 1860, the United Israelitisch Alliance has been scheming to force the Russian government to allow the Jews to have greater freedom in exploiting the native population. The first part of the scheme was to introduce Socialism, Nihilism, Anarchism, Terrorism, and other doctrines in order to breed distrust and hatred against the bourgeoisie, the upper classes, and the government. As a result of this propaganda there followed a campaign of malignant lies, and cold-blooded murders, on a scale unparalleled in the history of any country. The first notable victim of this fiendish campaign was Alexander II, the Liberator Czar (1881), one of the noblest monarchs that ever reigned. Twenty years before he had freed fifty million serfs, and made provision for their future welfare. He was murdered because he refused to allow the Jews to swarm over Russia to exploit the newly liberated peasants.

Three years before the Czar's murder, in 1878, while Russia was battling on distant fields to save wretched Armenians from the Turkish butcher, the Nihilists, as they were then called, made their first attempt to overturn the government. The attempt hardly got beyond the first stage before it was defeated. Another attempt made in 1905 came very near being successful. It was defeated by the courage and loyalty of the officers of the Russian army.

The opening of the world war and the absence of the armies from the capital gave the traitors another opportunity to gain the success which they had almost won nine years before. In a book on Russia published in 1905 Carl Joubert gives the inside facts, showing how the traitors of that period carried out their plans for intercepting supplies sent from Russia to the armies in Manchuria. It was doubtless this method of starving and crippling the troops that brought on the defeat of Russia in her war with Japan. And it is quite likely too that the same tactics have been employed to cripple the Russian armies in the present war.

It required immense sums of money to carry out their plans for crippling the army, and in employing vast numbers of spies and propagandists to poison the minds of the soldiers against the government. And now that the Revolution has succeeded, we are beginning to get more detailed information as to who financed that undertaking.

At a meeting held in New York to glorify the birth of the new republic, George D. Kennan told how the gospel of revolution had been spread among Russian officers and soldiers, prisoners of war, with the financial assistance of Jacob H. Schiff of New York, and with the consent of the Japanese government at the time of the Russo-Japanese war. In addressing the House Judiciary Committee on the Espionage Bill, Mr. John D. Moore, secretary of the Friends of Irish Freedom, stated that "the revolution in Russia was fostered, engineered and made possible by the influence of American citizens." Mr. Moore further stated that Jacob H. Schiff, the New York banker, had greatly aided the cause of Russian freedom. Mr. Kennan's account of the methods by which Russian soldiers were seduced by Schiff's money goes far to explain the treason of General Korniloff, the Cossack leader, in 1917. There is no doubt that, while a prisoner in Austria, he was approached by Jewish agents and converted to their plans. He was permitted to escape by the Austrian government and, after making his way back to Russia, was restored to his old command. In March 1917, he was in Petrograd and under his direction the Cossack regiments took the leading part in forcing the abdication of the Czar, and in making the revolution a success.

Most of the funds needed to carry on the propaganda of the

revolution undoubtedly came from the Jews in the United States. There are more rich Jews and more Jewish working people earning high wages in this country than in any other.

It was reported at the time that fifteen thousand Jews went from New York to Russia with Trotsky and that their expenses were paid out of the revolutionary funds. The fact that there was no such return movement of Russian exiles from any other country goes far to confirm John D. Moore's statement that the revolution was fostered, engineered, and made possible by the influence of American citizens. Mr. Moore failed to state, however, that practically all of these American citizens were Bolshevist Jews posing as internationalists—followers of Morris Hillquit and Leon Trotsky. They furnished the money, the men, and the brains of the whole movement. . . .

Although the activities of these traitors has been a matter of common knowledge ever since we entered into the war, not one of them has yet been arrested and placed on trial. If any such parties were found in Germany conspiring to cripple the governments of Austria, Turkey, or Bulgaria, we may be sure that the Kaiser would make very short work of them. And he would be within his rights. There is no canon of national or international punishment on such criminals. What is it then that paralyzes the arm of our Government in this matter? Why is it that so much time and money is spent in hunting out and prosecuting little offenders, while these —the greatest of all criminals—whose freedom is a positive menace to our success in this awful conflict, are not even arrested?

> *The Anti-Bolshevist, A Monthly Magazine Devoted to the Defense of the American Institutions Against the Jewish Bolshevist Doctrines of Morris Hillquist and Leon Trotsky* (Brooklyn, New York), vol. 1, September 1918.

By far the most notable expression of the fear of a Jewish conspiracy directed against America was that propounded under the auspices of Henry Ford's *Dearborn Independent*. Although at least two editions of the *Protocols of the Elders of Zion* had already been published—in Boston and in New York[3] —the dubious honor of having propagated their wicked fantasies most effectively belongs to the *Dearborn Independent* which, from May to October of 1920, published a lengthy series of articles purporting to indicate the extent to which the program laid out in the *Protocols* had already been implemented. In November 1920 these articles appeared in book form, in four volumes, under the title of *The International Jew: the World's Foremost Problem*. Half a million copies of this book were put into circulation in the United States alone, and it was subsequently translated into German, Russian, and Spanish; *The International Jew*, Norman Cohn remarks, "probably did more than any other work to make the *Protocols* world-famous."[4] The lunatic ravings of this book are almost beyond imagination —the First World War was a Jewish plot, as is the decay of American life evinced by "sport clothes," the seizure of baseball, the movie industry, etc., by the Jewish conspiracy; Bolshevism, of course, is also a tool of the Jewish conspiracy, and although Lenin and his wife had not a drop of Jewish blood in their veins, and were childless, we are given a cozy picture of them chatting away at home in Yiddish with their little ones: proof that the Jewish conspiracy is on the verge of achieving final success lies in the fact that the Bolshevik Star has one point less than the Star of David. When the World Program of the Protocols is complete, the final point will be added.[5] It is to Ford's credit that, in 1927, he announced his unqualified retraction of all the charges contained in *The International Jew*.[6] The retraction did not, however, impede the progress of the book, particularly in Europe, as the chief statement of the alleged Jewish danger; while anti-Semites in the United States saw in Ford's apology merely further proof of the insidious power of the Jewish conspiracy.[7]

The Jew in Character and Business (1920).

The Jew is again being singled out for critical attention throughout the world. His emergence in the financial, political, and social spheres has been so complete and spectacular since the war, that his place, power, and purpose in the world

are being given a new scrutiny, much of it unfriendly. Persecution is not a new experience to the Jew, but intensive
scrutiny of his nature and super-nationality is. He has suffered for more than 2,000 years from what may be called the
instinctive anti-Semitism of the other races, but this antagonism has never been intelligent nor has it been able to make
itself intelligible. Nowadays, however, the Jew is being
placed, as it were, under the microscope of economic observation that the reasons for his power, the reasons for his
separateness, the reasons for his suffering may be defined and
understood.

In Russia he is charged with being the source of Bolshevism, an accusation which is serious or not, according to the
circle in which it is made; we in America, hearing the fervid
eloquence and perceiving the prophetic ardor of young Jewish apostles of social and industrial reform, can calmly estimate how it may be. In Germany he is charged with being
the cause of the Empire's collapse and a very considerable
literature has sprung up, bearing with it a mass of circum-
stantial evidence that gives the thinker pause. In England he
is charged with being the real world ruler, who rules as a
super-nation over the nations, rules by the power of gold, and
who plays nation against nation for his own purposes, remaining himself discreetly in the background. In America it is
pointed out to what extent the elder Jews of wealth and the
younger Jews of ambition swarmed through the war organizations—principally those departments which dealt with the
commercial and industrial business of war, and also the extent to which they have clung to the advantage which their
experience as agents of the government gave them.

In simple words, the question of the Jews has come to the
fore, but like other questions which lend themselves to prejudice, efforts will be made to hush it up as impolitic for open
discussion. If, however, experience has taught us anything it
is that questions thus suppressed will sooner or later break
out in undesirable and unprofitable forms.

The Jew is the world's enigma. Poor in his masses, he yet
controls the world's finances. Scattered abroad without coun-

try or government, he yet presents a unity of race continuity which no other people has achieved. Living under legal disabilities in almost every land, he has become the power behind many a throne. There are ancient prophecies to the effect that the Jew will return to his own land and from that center rule the world, though not until he has undergone an assault by the united nations of mankind.

The single description which will include a larger percentage of Jews than members of any other race is this: he is in business. It may be only gathering rags and selling them, but he is in business. From the sale of old clothes to the control of international trade and finance, the Jew is supremely gifted for business. More than any other race he exhibits a decided aversion to industrial employment, which he balances by an equally decided adaptability to trade. The Gentile boy works his way up, taking employment in the productive or technical departments; but the Jewish boy prefers to begin as messenger, salesman or clerk—anything—so long as it is connected with the commercial side of the business. An early Prussian census illustrates this characteristic: of a total population of 269,400, the Jews comprised six per cent or 16,164. Of these, 12,000 were traders and 4,164 were workmen. Of the Gentile population, the other 94 per cent, or 253,236 people, there were only 17,000 traders.

A modern census would show a large professional and literary class added to the traders, but no diminution of the percentage of traders and not much if any increase in the number of wage toilers. In America alone most of the big business, the trusts and the banks, the natural resources and the chief agricultural products, especially tobacco, cotton, and sugar, are in the control of Jewish financiers or their agents. Jewish journalists are a large and powerful group here. "Large numbers of department stores are held by Jewish firms," says the *Jewish Encyclopedia,* and many if not most of them are run under Gentile names. Jews are the largest and most numerous landlords of residence property in the country. They are supreme in the theatrical world. They absolutely control the circulation of publications throughout the country. Fewer than any race whose presence among us is noticeable, they receive daily an amount of favorable publicity which would be impossible did they not have the facilities for creating and distributing it themselves. Werner Sombart, in his *Jew and Modern Capitalism,* says, "If the conditions in America continue to develop along the same lines as in the last generation, if the immigration statistics and the proportion of births among all the nationalities remain the same, our imagination may picture the United States of fifty or a hundred years hence as a land inhabited only by Slavs, Negroes, and Jews, wherein the Jews will naturally occupy the position of economic leadership." Sombart is a pro-Jewish writer.

The question is, If the Jew is in control, how did it happen? This is a free country. The Jew comprises only about three per cent of the population; to every Jew there are 97 Gentiles; to the 3,000,000 Jews in the United States there are 97,000,000 Gentiles. If the Jew is in control, is it because of his superior ability, or is it because of the inferiority and don't-care attitude of the Gentiles?

It would be very simple to answer that the Jews came to America, took their chances like other people, and proved more successful in the competitive struggle. But that would not include all the facts. And before a more adequate answer can be given, two points should be made clear. The first is this: all Jews are not rich controllers of wealth. There are poor Jews aplenty, though most of them even in their poverty are their own masters. While it may be true that the chief financial controllers of the country are Jews, it is not true that every Jew is one of the financial controllers of the country. The classes must be kept distinct for a reason which will appear when the methods of the rich Jews and the methods of the poor Jews to gain power are differentiated. Secondly, the fact of Jewish solidarity renders it difficult to measure Gentile and Jewish achievements by the same standard. When a great block of wealth in America was made possible by the lavish use of another block of wealth from across the seas; that is to say, when certain Jewish immigrants came to the United States with the financial backing of European Jewry behind them, it would be unfair to explain the rise of that class of immigration by the same rules which account for the rise of, say, the Germans or the Poles who came here with no resource but their ambition and strength. To be sure, many individual Jews come in that way, too, with no dependence but themselves, but it would not be true to say that that massive control of affairs which is exercised by Jewish wealth was won by individual initiative; it was rather the extension of financial control across the sea.

That, indeed, is where any explanation of Jewish control must begin. Here is a race whose entire period of national history saw them peasants on the land, whose ancient genius was spiritual rather than material, bucolic rather than commercial, yet today, when they have no country, no government, and are persecuted in one way or another everywhere they go, they are declared to be the principal though unofficial rulers of the earth. How does so strange a charge arise, and why do so many circumstances seem to justify it?

Begin at the beginning. During the formative period of their national character the Jews lived under a law which made plutocracy and pauperism equally impossible among them. Modern reformers who are constructing model social systems on paper would do well to look into the social system under which the early Jews were organized. The Law of Moses made a "money aristocracy," such as Jewish financiers form today, impossible because it forbade the taking of interest. It made impossible also the continuous enjoyment of profit wrung out of another's distress. Profiteering and sheer speculation were not favored under the Jewish system. There could be no land-hogging; the land was apportioned among the people, and though it might be lost by debt or sold under stress, it was returned every 50 years to its original family ownership, at which time, called "The Year of Jubilee," there was practically a new social beginning. The rise of great landlords and a moneyed class was impossible under such a system, although the interim of 50 years gave ample scope for individual initiative to assert itself under fair competitive conditions.

If, therefore, the Jews had retained their status as a nation, and had remained in Palestine under the Law of Moses, they would hardly have achieved the financial distinction which they have since won. Jews never got rich out of one another. Even in modern times they have not become rich out of each other but out of the nations among whom they dwelt. Jewish law permitted the Jew to do business with a Gentile on a different basis than that on which he did business with a brother Jew. What is called "the Law of the Stranger" was defined thus: "unto a stranger thou mayest lend upon usury; but unto thy brother thou shalt not lend upon usury."

Being dispersed among the nations, but never merging themselves with the nations and never losing a very distinctive identity, the Jew has had the opportunity to practice "the ethics of the stranger" for many centuries. Being strangers among strangers, and often among cruelly hostile strangers, they have found this law a compensating advantage. Still, this alone would not account for the Jew's preeminence in finance. The explanation of that must be sought in the Jew himself, his vigor, resourcefulness, and special proclivities.

Very early in the Jewish story we discover the tendency of Israel to be a master nation, with other nations as its vassals. Notwithstanding the fact that the whole prophetic purpose wih reference to Israel seems to have been the moral enlightenment of the world through its agency, Israel's "will to mastery" apparently hindered that purpose. At least such would seem to be the tone of the Old Testament. Divinely ordered to drive out the Canaanites that their corrupt ideas might not contaminate Israel, the Jews did not obey, according to the old record. They looked over the Canaanitish people and perceived what great amount of manpower would be wasted if they were expelled, and so Israel enslaved them— "And it came to pass, when Israel was strong, that they put the Canaanites to tribute, and did not utterly drive them out." It was this form of disobedience, this preference of material mastery over spiritual leadership, that marked the beginning of Israel's age-long disciplinary distress.

The Jews' dispersion among the nations temporarily (that is, for more than 25 centuries now) changed the program which their scriptures declare was divinely planned, and that dispersion continues until today. There are spiritual leaders in modern Judaism who still claim that Israel's mission to the nations is spiritual, but their assertions that Israel is today fulfilling that mission are not as convincing as they might be if accompanied by more evidence. Israel throughout the modern centuries is still looking at the Gentile world and estimating what its manpower can be made to yield. But the discipline upon Israel still holds; he is an exile from his own land, condemned to be discriminated against wherever he goes, until the time when exile and homelessness shall end in a reestablished Palestine, and Jerusalem again become the moral center of the earth, even as the elder prophets have declared.

Had the Jew become an employee, a worker for other men, his dispersion would not probably have been so wide. But becoming a trader, his instincts drew him round the habitable earth. There were Jews in China at an early date. They appeared as traders in England at the time of the Saxons. Jewish traders were in South America 100 years before the Pilgrim Fathers landed at Plymouth Rock. Jews established the sugar industry in the Island of St. Thomas in 1492. They were well established in Brazil when only a few villages dotted the eastern coast of what is now the United States. And how far they penetrated when once they came here is indicated by the fact that the first white child born in Georgia was a Jew—Isaac Minis. The Jew's presence round the earth, his clannishness with his own people, made him a nation scattered among the nations, a corporation with agents everywhere.

Another talent, however, contributed greatly to his rise in financial power—his ability to invent new devices for doing business. Until the Jew was pitted against the world, business was very crudely done. And when we trace the origins of many of the business methods which simplify and facilitate trade today, more likely than not we find a Jewish name at the end of the clue. Many of the indispensable instruments of credit and exchange were thought out by Jewish merchants, not only for use between themselves, but to check and hold the Gentiles with whom they dealt. The oldest bill of exchange extant was drawn by a Jew—one Simon Rubens. The promissory note was a Jewish invention, as was also the check "payable to bearer."

An interesting bit of history attaches to the "payable to bearer" instrument. The Jews' enemies were always stripping them of their last ounce of wealth, yet strangely, the Jews recovered very quickly and were soon rich again. How this sudden recovery from looting and poverty? Their assets were concealed under "bearer" and so a goodly portion was always saved. In an age when it was lawful for any pirate to seize goods consigned to Jews, the Jews were able to protect themselves by consigning goods on policies that bore no names.

The influence of the Jew was to center business around goods instead of persons. Previously all claims had been against persons; the Jew knew that the goods were more reliable than the persons with whom he dealt, and so he contrived to have claims laid against goods. Besides, this device enabled him to keep himself out of sight as much as possible. This introduced an element of hardness into business, inasmuch as it was goods which were being dealt in rather than men being dealt with, and this hardness remains. Another tendency which survives and which is of advantage in veiling the very large control which Jews have attained, is of the same origin as "bearer" bills; it permits a business dominated by Jewish capital to appear under a name that gives no hint of Jewish control.

The Jew is the only and original international capitalist, but as a rule he prefers not to emblazon that fact upon the skies; he prefers to use Gentile banks and trust companies as his agents and instruments. The suggestive term "Gentile front" often appears in connection with this practice.

The invention of the stock exchange is also credited to

Jewish financial talent. In Berlin, Paris, London, Frankfort, and Hamburg, Jews were in control of the first stock exchanges, while Venice and Genoa were openly referred to in the talk of the day as "Jew cities" where great trading and banking facilities might be found. The Bank of England was established upon the counsel and assistance of Jewish emigrants from Holland. The Bank of Amsterdam and the Bank of Hamburg both arose through Jewish influence.

There is a curious fact to be noted in connection with the persecution and consequent wanderings of the Jews about Europe and that is: wherever they wandered, the center of business seemed to go with them. When the Jews were free in Spain, there was the world's gold center. When Spain drove out the Jews, Spain lost financial leadership and has never regained it. Students of the economic history of Europe have always been puzzled to discover why the center of trade should have shifted from Spain, Portugal, and Italy, up to the northern countries of Holland, Germany, and England. They have sought for the cause in many things, but none has proved completely explanatory. When, however, it is known that the change was coincident with the expulsion of the Jews from the South and their flight to the North, when it is known that upon the Jews' arrival the northern countries began a commercial life which has flourished until our day, the explanation does not seem difficult. Time and again it has proved to be the fact that when the Jews were forced to move, the center of the world's precious metals moved with them.

This distribution of the Jews over Europe and the world, each Jewish community linked in a fellowship of blood, faith, and suffering with every other group, made it possible for the Jew to be international in the sense that no other race or group of merchants could be at that time. Not only were they everywhere (Americans and Russians are everywhere, too) but they were in touch. They were organized before the days of conscious international commercial organizations, they were bound together by the sinews of a common life. It was observed by many writers in the Middle Ages that the Jews knew more of what was transpiring in Europe than the governments did. They also had better knowledge of what was likely to occur. They knew more about conditions than the statesmen did. This information they imparted by letter from group to group, country to country. Indeed, they may be said thus to have originated unconsciously the financial newsletter. Certainly the information they were able to obtain and thus distribute was invaluable to them in their speculative enterprises. Advance knowledge was an immense advantage in days when news was scarce, slow, and unreliable.

This enabled Jewish financiers to become the agents of national loans, a form of business which they encouraged wherever possible. The Jew has always desired to have nations for his customers. National loans were facilitated by the presence of members of the same family of financiers in various countries, thus making an interlocking directorate by which king could be played against king, government against government, and the shrewdest use made of national prejudices and fears, all to the no small profit of the fiscal agent.

One of the charges most commonly made against Jewish financiers today is that they still favor this larger field of finance. Indeed, in all the criticism that is heard regarding the Jew as a business man, there is comparatively little said against him as an individual merchant serving individual customers. Thousands of small Jewish merchants are highly respected by their trade, just as tens of thousands of Jewish families are respected as our neighbors. The criticism, insofar as it respects the more important financiers, is not racial at all. Unfortunately the element of race, which so easily lends itself to misinterpretation as racial prejudice, is injected into the question by the mere fact that the chain of international finance as it is traced around the world discloses at every link a Jewish capitalist, financial family, or a Jewish-controlled banking system. Many have professed to see in this circumstance a conscious organization of Jewish power for Gentile control, while others have attributed the circumstance to Jewish racial sympathies, to the continuity of their family affairs down the line of descent, and to the increase of collateral branches. In the old Scriptural phrase, Israel grows as the vine grows, ever shooting out new branches and deepening old roots, but always part of the one vine.

The Jew's aptitude for dealing with governments may also be traced to the years of his persecution. He early learned the power of gold in dealing with mercenary enemies. Wherever he went there followed him like a curse the aroused antipathy of other peoples. The Jew was never popular as a race; even the most fervid Jew will not deny that, howsoever he may explain it. Individuals have been popular, of course; many phases of Jewish nature are found to be very lovable when known; but nevertheless one of the burdens the Jews have had to bear as a race is this burden of racial unpopularity. Even in modern times, in civilized countries, in conditions which render persecution absolutely impossible, this unpopularity exists. And what is more, the Jew has not seemed to care to cultivate the friendship of the Gentile masses, due perhaps to the failures of experience, but due more likely to his inborn persuasion that he belongs to a superior race. Whatever the true reason, he has always placed his main dependence on cultivating friendship with kings and nobles. What cared the Jew if the people gnashed their teeth against him, so long as the king and the court were his friends? Thus there was always, even through most of the severely trying times, "a court Jew," one who had bought by loans and held by the stranglehold of debt an entrance to the king's chamber. The policy of the Jews has always been to "go to headquarters." They never tried to placate the Russian people, but they did endeavor to enlist the Russian court. They never tried to placate the German people, but they did succeed in permeating the German court. In England they shrug their shoulders at the outspoken anti-Jew reactions of the British populace—what care they? Have they not all of lorddom at their heels, do they not hold the strings of Britain's purse?

Through this ability of theirs to "go to headquarters" it is possible to account for the stronghold they got upon various governments and nations. Added to this ability was, of course, the ability to produce what the governments wanted.

If a government wanted a loan, the Jew at court could arrange it through Jews at other financial centers and political capitals. If one government wanted to pay another government a debt without risking the precious metal to a mule train through a robber-infested country, the Jew at court arranged that too. He transferred a piece of paper and the debt was paid by the banking house at the foreign capital. The first time an army was ever fed in the modern commissary way, it was done by a Jew—he had the capital and he had the system; moreover he had the delight of having a nation for his customer.

And this tendency, which served the race so well throughout the troublous centuries, shows no sign of abatement. Certainly, seeing to what an extent a race numerically so unimportant influences the various governments of the world today, the Jew who reflects upon the disparity between his people's number and their power may be pardoned if he sees in that fact a proof of their racial superiority.

It may be said also that Jewish inventiveness in business devices continues to the present time, as well as Jewish adaptability to changing conditions. The Jew is credited with being the first to establish branch houses in foreign countries in order that responsible representatives of the home office might be on the ground taking instant advantage of every opening. During the war a great deal was said about the "peaceful penetration" which the "German Government" had effected in the United States by establishing here branch offices and factories of German firms. The fact that there were many German branch houses here is unquestionable. It should be known, however, that they were not the evidence of German enterprise but of Jewish enterprise. The old German business houses were too conservative to "run after customers" even in the hustling United States, but the Jewish firms were not, and they came straight to America and hustled. In due time the competition forced the more conservative German firms to follow suit. But the idea was Jewish in its origin, not German.

Another modern business method whose origin is credited

to Jewish financiers is that by which related industries are brought together, as for example, if an electrical power company is acquired, then the street railway company using the electricity would be acquired too, one purpose being in this way to conserve all the profit accruing along the line, from the origination of the power down to the delivery of the street car ride; but perhaps the main purpose being that, by the control of the power house the price of current could be increased to the car company, and by the control of the car company the cost of a ride could be increased to the public, the controllers thus receiving an additional profit all down the line. There is much of this going on in the world today, and in the United States particularly. The portion of the business immediately next to the ultimate consumer explains that its costs have risen, but it does not explain that the costs were increased by the owners and not by outsiders who were forced to do so by economic pressure.

There is apparently in the world today a central financial force which is playing a vast and closely organized game, with the world for its table and universal control for its stakes. The people of civilized countries have lost all confidence in the explanation that "economic conditions" are responsible for all the changes that occur. Under the camouflage of "economic law" a great many phenomena have been accounted for which were not due to any law whatever except the law of the selfish human will as operated by a few men who have the purpose and the power to work on a wide scale with nations as their vassals.

Whatever else may be national, no one today believes that finance is national. Finance is international. Nobody today believes that international finance is in any way competitive. There are some independent banking houses, but few strong independent ones. The great masters, the few whose minds see clearly the entire play of the plan, control numerous banking houses and trust companies, and one is used for this while another is used for that, but there is no disharmony between them, no correction of each other's methods, no competition in the interests of the business world. There is as much unity of policy between the principal banking houses of every country as there is between the various branches of the United States Post Office—and for the same reason, namely, they are all operated from the same source and for the same purpose.

Just before the war Germany bought very heavily in American cotton and had huge quantities of it tied up here for export. When war came, the ownership of that mountainous mass of cotton wealth changed in one night from Jewish names in Hamburg to Jewish names in London. At this writing cotton is selling in England for less than it is selling in the United States, and the effect of that is to lower the American price. When the price lowers sufficiently, the market is cleared of cotton by buyers previously prepared, and then the price soars to high figures again. In the meantime, the same powers that have engineered the apparently causeless strengthening and weakening of the cotton market have seized upon stricken Germany to be the sweatshop of the world. Certain groups control the cotton, lend it to Germany to be manufactured, leave a pittance of it there in payment for the labor that was used, and then profiteer the length and breadth of the world on the lie that "cotton is scarce." And when, tracing all these antisocial and colossally unfair methods to their source, it is found that the responsible parties all have a common characteristic, is it any wonder that the warning which comes across the sea—"Wait until America becomes awake to the Jew!"—has a new meaning?

Certainly, economic reasons no longer explain the condition in which the world finds itself today. Neither does the ordinary explanation of "the heartlessness of capital." Capital has endeavored as never before to meet the demands of labor, and labor has gone to extremes in leading capital to new concessions—but what has it advantaged either of them? Labor has heretofore thought that capital was the sky over it, and it made the sky yield, but behold, there was yet a higher sky which neither capital nor labor had seen in their struggles one with another. That sky is so far unyielding.

That which we call capital here in America is usually money used in production, and we mistakenly refer to the manufacturer, the manager of work, the provider of tools and jobs—we refer to him as the "capitalist." Oh, no. He is not the capitalist in the real sense. Why, he himself must go to capitalists for the money with which to finance his plans. There is a power yet above him—a power which treats him far more callously and holds him in a more ruthless hand than he would ever dare display to labor. That, indeed, is one of the tragedies of these times, that "labor" and "capital" are fighting each other, when the conditions against which each one of them protests, and from which each one of them suffers, is not within their power to remedy at all, unless they find a way to wrest world control from that group of international financiers who create and control both these conditions.

There is a super-capitalism which is supported wholly by the fiction that gold is wealth. There is a super-government which is allied to no government, which is free from them all, and yet which has its hand in them all. There is a race, a part of humanity, which has never yet been received as a welcome part, and which has succeeded in raising itself to a power that the proudest Gentile race has never claimed— not even Rome in the days of her proudest power. It is becoming more and more the conviction of men all over the world that the labor question, the wage question, the land question cannot be settled until first of all this matter of an international super-capitalistic government is settled.

"To the victor belongs the spoils" is an old saying. And in a sense it is true that if all this power of control has been gained and held by a few men of a long-despised race, then either they are super-men whom it is powerless to resist, or they are ordinary men whom the rest of the world has permitted to obtain an undue and unsafe degree of power. Unless the Jews are super-men, the Gentiles will have themselves to blame for what has transpired, and they can look for rectification in a new scrutiny of the situation and a candid examination of the experiences of other countries.

> *The International Jew: The World's Foremost Problem* (Dearborn, Illinois, 1920), Chapter 1.

"Jewish" Plan to Split Society by "Ideas" (1920).

The method by which the Protocols work for the breakdown of society should now be fairly evident to readers of these articles. An understanding of the *method* is necessary if one is to find the meaning of the currents and cross-currents which make so hopeless a hodge-podge of the present times. People who are confused and discouraged by the various voices and discordant theories of today, each seeming to be plausible and promising, may find a clear clue to the value of the voices and the meaning of the theories if they understand that their *confusion* and *discouragement* comprise the very objective which is sought. The uncertainty, hesitation, hopelessness, fear; the eagerness with which every promising plan and offered solution is grasped—these are the very reactions which the program outlined in the Protocols aims to produce. The condition is proof of the efficacy of the program.

It is a method that takes time, and the Protocols declare that it *has* taken time, indeed, centuries. Students of the matter find the identical program of the Protocols, announced and operated by the Jewish race, from the first century onward.

It has taken 1,900 years to bring Europe to its present degree of subjugation—violent subjugation in some countries, political subjugation in some, economic subjugation in all—but in America the same program, with almost the same degree of success, has required about 50 years. Certain mistaken *ideas* of liberalism, certain flabby *ideas* of tolerance, all of them originating at European sources which the Protocolists had completely polluted, were transported to America, and here under cover of the blindness and innocence of a false liberalism and tolerance, together with modern appliances for the swift acceleration of opinion, there has been worked a subjugation of our institutions and public thought which is the amazement of European observers. It is a fact that some of the important students of the Jewish Question, whom Jewish publicists are pleased to damn with the term "Anti-Semites," have been awakened to the existence of the Question not by what they have observed in Europe, but by what they have seen in the swift and distinct "close-up" which has been afforded in American affairs.

The center of Jewish power, the principal sponsors of the Jewish program, are resident in America, and the leverage which was used at the Peace Conference to fasten Jewish power more securely upon Europe was American leverage exercised at the behest of the strong Jewish pressure which was brought from the United States for that purpose. And these activities did not end with the Peace Conference.

The whole *method* of the Protocols may be described in one word, *Disintegration.* The undoing of what has been done, the creation of a long and hopeless interim in which attempts at reconstruction shall be baffled, and the gradual wearing down of public opinion and public confidence, until those who stand outside the created chaos shall insert their strong calm hand to seize control—that is the whole method of procedure.

Putting together the estimate of human nature which obtains in these Protocols, and their claims to a rather definite though as yet incomplete fulfillment of the World Program (these two comprising the themes of the previous two articles), some of the aspects of this propaganda of disintegration have become clear. But not all of them. There are yet other aspects of these methods, which will be dealt with in the present article, and there are yet future reaches of the program which will be considered later.

The first point of attack is Collective Opinion, that body of ideas which through men's agreement with them, holds large groups together in political, racial, religious, or social unity. Sometimes we call them "standard," sometimes we call them "ideals"; whatever they may be called, they are the invisible bonds of unity, they are the common faith, they are the great overarching reason for group unity and loyalty.

The Protocols assert that here the first attack has been made. The history of Jewish propaganda in the world shows that also.

The first wave of attack is to *corrupt* Collective Opinion. Now, to "corrupt" in the real sense does not mean anything unsavory or unclean. The whole power of every heresy is its attractiveness to the good mind. The whole explanation of the strong hold which untruth has gained upon the world of our day is that the untruth is reasonable, inspiring, and apparently good. It is only after a long discipline in false ideas —which are reasonable, inspiring, and good—that the evil fruits appear in acts and conditions which are unreasonable, destructive, and wholly evil. If you will trace the idea of Liberty as it has appeared in Russian history, from its philosophic beginning (a Jewish beginning, by the way) to its present ending (a Jewish ending also), you will see the process.

The Protocols claim that the Gentiles are not thinkers, that attractive ideas have been thrown at them so strategically and persistently that the power of thought is almost destroyed out of them. Fortunately this is a matter on which any Gentile may apply his own test. If he will segregate his ruling ideas, especially those that center round the thought of "democracy," he will discover that he is being ruled in his mind by a whole company of ideals into whose authority over him he has not inquired at all. He is ruled by "say so" whose origin he has not traced. And when, pursuing those ideas, he finds that they are not practicable, he is received by the explanation that "we are not yet sufficiently advanced." Yet when he does see men who are sufficiently "advanced" to put these very ideals into operation, he recoils from what he sees them do, because he knows that "advancement" such as that is deterioration—a form of disintegration. Yet every one of the ideas were "good," "reasonable," "inspiring," "humane," to begin with. And, if this Gentile will observe a little further, he will see that they are the most persistently preached ideas in the world; he will also see who the preachers are.

The Protocols distinctly declare that it is by means of the set of ideas which cluster around "democracy" that their first victory over public opinion was obtained. The *idea* is the weapon. And to be a weapon it must be an *idea* at variance with the natural trend of life. It must indeed be a theory opposed to the facts of life. And no theory so opposed can be expected to take root and become the ruling factor, unless it appeals to the mind as reasonable, inspiring, and good. The Truth frequently is depressing; the Truth sometimes seems to be evil; but it has this eternal advantage, it is the Truth, and what is built thereon neither brings nor yields to *confusion.*

This first step does not give the control of public opinion, but leads up to it. It is worthy of note that it is this sowing of "the poison of liberalism," as the Protocols name it, which comes first in order in those documents. Then, following upon that, the Protocols say:

> *To obtain control over public opinion it is first necessary to confuse it.*

Truth is one and cannot be confused, but this false, appealing liberalism which has been sown broadcast, and which is ripening faster under Jewish nurture in America than ever it did in Europe, is easily confused because it is not truth. It is error, and error has a thousand forms. Take a nation, a party, a city, an association in which "the poison of liberalism" has been sown, and you can split that up into as many factions as there are individuals simply by throwing among them certain modifications of the original idea. This is a piece of strategy well known to the forces that invisibly control mass-thought. Theodor Herzl, the arch-Jew, a man whose vision was wider than any stateman's and whose program paralleled the Protocols, knew this many years ago when he said that the Zionist (cryptic for "Jewish") state would come before the Socialist state could come; he knew with what endless divisions the "liberalism" which he and his predecessors had planted would be shackled and crippled.

The process of which all Gentiles have been the victims,

but never the Jews—never the Jews!—is just this—

First, to create an ideal of "broad-mindedness." That is the phrase which appears in every Jewish remonstrance against public mention of the Jew and his alleged World Program: "We thought you were too broad-minded a man to express such thoughts"; "we thought Mr. So-and-So was too broad-minded a man to suspect the Jews of this"; "we thought the daily or weekly or monthly such-and-such a paper was too broad-minded editorially to consider such material." It is a sort of keyword, indicative of the state of mind in which it is desired that the Gentiles be kept. It is a state of flabby tolerance. A state of mind which mouths meaningless phrases about Liberty, phrases which act as an opiate on the mind and conscience and which allow all sorts of things to be done under cover. The phrase, the slogan, is a very dependable Jewish weapon. ("In all times people have accepted words for acts."—Protocol 5.) The reality behind the phrase the Protocols frankly admit to be non-existent.

Nothing has served to create "broad-mindedness," a state of mind whose breadth indicates its lack of depth, so much as the ideas of liberalism which the Jews are constantly teaching to Gentiles and on which they never themselves act. We need a new sort of allegiance to the reality of life, to the facts as they are, which will enable us to stand up under all cajoling to "broad-mindedness" and assert a new intolerance of everything but truth. The terms "narrow" and "broad" as they are used today represent lies. The liberal man ought to believe more, he ought to be deep and wide in his beliefs in order to merit that name; but as a usual thing he believes nothing. He is not liberal at all. When you seek belief, belief with a foundation, belief with vitality, you must seek it among men who are sneered at, under this false Jewish-promoted notion of liberality, as "narrow men." Jewish propaganda, in common with the Protocols, is against men who have dug down to the rock; they want "broad-minded men" who can easily be shifted about the surface, and thus serve the invisible scheme in any manner desired. This type of men, on their part, never imagine but that their "broad-

mindedness" is a mark of their superiority and independence.

Now, see what follows. Men are born believers. For a time
they may believe in "broad-mindedness" and under the ter-
rific social pressure that has been set up in its favor they will
openly espouse it. But it is too shallow to satisfy any growing
roots of life. They must believe, deeply, something. For proof
of this, notice the undeniable strength of the negative beliefs
which are held by men who fancy that they believe nothing.
Therefore, some who are highly endowed with independence of spirit root down into those prohibited matters
which at some point touch Jewish concerns—these are the
"narrow" men. But others find it more convenient to cultivate those departments which promise a highway whereon
there shall be no clashes of vital opinion, no chance of the
charge of "intolerance"; in short they transfer all their con-
templative powers to the active life, even as it is written in
the Protocols:

> *To divert Gentile thought and observation, interest
> must be deflected to industry and commerce.*

It is amazing to look around and see the number of men
who have been actually browbeaten into committing their
whole lives to these secondary or even tertiary things, while
they look with great timidity and aversion at the vital things
which really rule the world and upon the issue of which the
world really depends.

But it is just this deflection to the materialistic base that
offers the Protocolists, and similarly Jewish propagandists,
their best hold. "Broad-mindedness" today consists in leaving vital matters severely alone. It descends quickly to
material-mindedness. Within this lower sphere all the discord which distresses the world today is to be found.

First, there is the ruin of the upper circles of industry and
commerce:

> *To make it possible for liberty definitely to disinte-
> grate and ruin Gentile society, industry must be placed
> on a speculative basis.*

No one needs to be told what this means. It means, as everything about us shouts, the prostitution of service to profits and the eventual disappearance of the profits. It means that the high art of management degenerates into exploitation. It means reckless confusion among the managers and dangerous unrest among the workmen.

But it means something worse: it means the split-up of Gentile society. Not a division between "Capital" and "Labor," but the division between the Gentiles at both ends of the working scheme. Gentile managers and manufacturers are not the "capitalists" of the United States. Most of them have to go to the "capitalists" for the funds with which they work—and the "capitalists" are Jewish, International Jews.

But with Jewish capital at one end of the Gentile working scheme putting the screws on the manufacturers, and with Jewish agitators and disruptionists and subversives at the other end of the Gentile working scheme putting the screws on the workmen, we have a condition at which the world-managers of the Protocol program must be immensely satisfied.

> *We might fear the combined strength of the Gentiles of vision with the blind strength of the masses, but we have taken all measures against such a possible contingency by raising a wall of mutual antagonism between these two forces. Thus, the blind force of the masses remains our support. We, and we alone, shall serve as their leaders. Naturally, we will direct their energy to achieve our end.*

—PROTOCOL 9

The indication that they are highly satisfied is that they are not only not doing anything to relieve the situation, but are apparently willing to have it made worse, and if it be at all possible for them to do so they would like to see this coming winter, and the privations which are scheduled for it (unless Gentile flabbiness before the Jewish power, high and low, receives a new backbone), bring the United States to the verge of, if not across the very line of, Bolshevism. They know the whole method of artificial scarcity and high prices.

It was practiced in the French Revolution and in Russia. All the signs of it are in this country too.

Industrial problems for their mental food and light amusement for their leisure hours, these are the Protocols' method with regard to the Gentile mind, and under cover of these the work is to be done—the work which is best expressed by the motto, "Divide and Rule."

Read this:

> *To divert over-restless people from discussing political questions, we shall now bring forward new problems apparently connected with them—problems of industry.*
>
> —PROTOCOL 13

Has not everyone been struck by the divorcement which exists in this country between the mass-thought which is almost exclusively devoted to industrial questions, and the party-thought which is endeavoring to keep the field of pure politics? And is it not a fact that our friends, the Jews, are strongly entrenched in both fields—in politics to keep it reactionary, and in industrial circles to keep it radical—and so widen the split? And what is this split but a split of the Gentiles?—for society is Gentile, and the disruptive influences are Jewish.

Read this:

> *We have included in the constitution rights for the people that are fictitious and not actual rights. All those so-called rights of the people can only exist in the abstract and can never be realized in practice * * * The proletarian gains no more from the constitution than the miserable crumbs thrown from our table in return for his votes to elect our agents and pass our measures. Republican rights are a bitter irony to the poor man, for the pressure of daily labor prevents him from using them, and at the same time, deprives him of the guaranty of a permanent and certain livelihood by making him dependent upon strikes organized either by his employers or his comrades.*
>
> —PROTOCOL 3

This remark about strikes is not at all puzzling to anyone who has studied the different types of strikes in this country. The number fomented from above the working class is astoundingly large.

Read this also:

> *We will force up wages which, however, will be of no benefit to the workers, for we will at the same time cause a rise in the prices of necessities, pretending that this is due to the decline of agriculture and of cattle raising. We will also artfully and deeply undermine the sources of production by instilling in the workmen ideas of anarchy.*
>
> —PROTOCOL 6

And this:

> *We will represent ourselves as the saviors of the working class who have come to liberate them from this oppression by suggesting that they join our army of socialists, anarchists, communists, to whom we always extend our help under the guise of the fraternal principles of universal human solidarity.*
>
> —PROTOCOL 3

"Broad-mindedness" again! In this connection it is always well to remember the words of Sir Eustace Percy, heretofore quoted, words which are sponsored by Jews themselves— "Not because the Jew cares for the positive side of radical philosophy, not because he desires to be a partaker in Gentile nationalism or Gentile democracy, but because no existing Gentile system of government is ever anything but distasteful to him."

Or, as the author of *The Conquering Jew* says: "He is democratic in his sentiments, but not in his nature. When he proclaims the common brotherhood of man, he is asking that the social gate now closed against him in so many quarters shall be open to him; not because he wants equality, but because he desires to be master in the social world, as he is showing himself in so many other spheres. Many an honorable Jew will, I doubt not, dispute the accuracy of this distinction; but if he does, it will be because he has lived so long in the atmosphere of the West that he is unconscious of what is bred in the bone of his Eastern race."

It is not difficult, therefore, to see the genealogy of the Jewish ideas of liberalism from their origin to their latest effects upon Gentile life. The *confusion* aimed for is here. There is not a reader of these lines who has not felt in his own life the burden of it. Bewilderment characterizes the whole mental climate of the people today. They do not know what to believe. First one set of facts is given to them, then another. First one explanation of conditions is given to them, and then another. The fact-shortage is acute. There is a whole market-full of explanations that explain nothing, but only deepen the *confusion*. The government itself seems to be hampered, and whenever it starts on a line of investigation finds itself mysteriously tangled up so that procedure is difficult. This governmental aspect is also set forth in the Protocols.

Add to this the onslaught on the human tendency toward religion, which is usually the last barrier to fall before violence and robbery unashamed stalk forth. In order to bring the condition about at which this World Program aims, the Fourth Protocol says:

> *It is for this reason that we must undermine faith, eradicate from the minds of the Gentiles the very principles of God and Soul, and replace these conceptions by mathematical calculations and material desires.*
>
> *When we deprived the masses of their belief in God, ruling authority was thrown into the gutter, where it became public property, and we seized it.*
>
> —PROTOCOL 4

> *We have taken good care long ago to discredit the Gentile clergy.*
>
> —PROTOCOL 17

> *When we become rulers we shall regard as undesirable the existence of any religion except our own, proclaiming One God with Whom our fate is tied as The*

> *Chosen People, and by Whom our fate has been made
> one with the fate of the world. For this reason we
> must destroy all other religions. If thereby should
> emerge contemporary atheists, then, as a transition
> step, this will not interfere with our aims.*
>
> —PROTOCOL 14

This will probably offer matter for reflection by the "broad-minded."

It is curious to note how this religious program has worked out in Russia where Trotsky (as loudly heralded in the American Jewish press) is said to have no religion, and where Jewish commissars tell dying Russians who ask for priests, "We have abolished the Almighty." Miss Katherine Dokoochief is reported, under a Philadelphia date, to have told the Near East Relief that Russian Christian churches have been subjected to the vilest indignities by the Bolsheviki, details of which she gives; but "the synagogues remain untouched, meeting with no damage."

All these lines of attack, whose object is the destruction of the natural rallying points of Gentile thought, and the substitution of other rallying points of an unwholesome and destructive nature, are assisted, as we saw in the last article, by the propaganda for luxury. Luxury is recognizedly one of the most enervating influences. Its course runs from ease, through softness, to flabbiness, to degeneracy, mental, physical, and moral. Its beginnings are attractive, its end is lasciviousness in some form, testifying to the complete breakdown of all the strong fiber of the life. It may make a theme for a more complete study some day, this lure to lasciviousness through luxury, and the identity of the forces that set the lure.

But now, to conclude this general view of the method, rather this part of the method, the confusion itself, which all these influences converge to produce, is expected to produce another more deeply helpless state. And that state is, *Exhaustion.*

It needs no imagination to see what this means. Exhaustion is today one of the conditions that menace the people. The recent political conventions and their effect upon the public fully illustrate it. Nobody seemed to care. Parties might make their declarations and candidates their promises—nobody cared. The war and its strain began the exhaustion; the "peace" and its confusion have about completed it. The people believe little and expect less. Confidence is gone. Initiative is nearly gone. The failure of movements falsely heralded as "people's movements" has gone far to make the people think that no people's movement is possible.

So say the Protocols:

> *To wear everyone out by dissensions, animosities, feuds, famine, inoculation of diseases, want, until the Gentiles see no other way of escape except an appeal to our money and power.*
>
> —PROTOCOL 10

> *We will so wear out and exhaust the Gentiles by all this that they will be compelled to offer us an international authority, which by its position will enable us to absorb without disturbance all the governmental forces of the world and thus form a super-government.*
>
> *We must so direct the education of Gentile society that its hands will drop in the weakness of discouragement in the face of any undertaking where initiative is needed.*
>
> —PROTOCOL 5

The Jews have never been worn out or exhausted. They have never been nonplused. This is the true psychic characteristic of those who have a clue to the maze. It is the unknown that exhausts the mind, the constant wandering around among tendencies and influences whose source is not known and whose purpose is not understood. Walking in the dark is wearing work. The Gentiles have been doing it for centuries. The others, having a pretty accurate idea what it was all about, have not succumbed. Even persecution is endurable if it is understandable, and the Jews of the world have always known just where it fitted in the scheme of things. Gentiles have suffered more from Jewish persecution than have the Jews, for after the persecutions were over, the Gentile was as much in the dark as ever; whereas Judaism simply took up again its century-long march toward a goal in which it implicitly believes, and which, some say who have deep knowledge of Jewish roots in the world and who too may be touched with exhaustion, they will achieve. However this may be, the revolution which would be necessary to unfasten the International Jewish system from its grip on the world, would probably have to be just as radical as any attempts the Jews have made to attain that grip. There are those who express serious doubts that the Gentiles are competent to do it at all. Maybe not. Let them at least know who their conquerors are.

> *The International Jew: The World's Foremost Problem* (Dearborn, Illinois, 1920), Chapter 13.

Compared with the almost cosmic evil of *The International Jew,* the following items seem practically benign—though of course they are anything but that. The potential for far greater mischief contained in the "mere" disliking of Jews is surely vividly illustrated in the letter which John Jay Chapman wrote while on vacation at Atlantic City in 1919. In this letter, Chapman finds the Jews "grotesque"—nothing more—and is able to make a reference to his former Jewish friend and associate in the anti-Tammany reform endeavor, Isaac Klein. Only three years later, however, Chapman was to write the poem reproduced on pages 124–25. Under certain circumstances, the "social" anti-Semite effortlessly slides into an infinitely more dangerous mood.

"They Look So Grotesque" (1919).

Judea—Israel—the Lost Tribes—lost no more! found— very much found, increased—multiplied—as the sands of the sea—upon the sands of the sea—Atlantic City—with cliff dwellings of 10,000 souls each—and regurgitating with Hebrews—only Hebrews. Families of tens and dozens—grave old plodders, gay young friskers—angel Jews, siren Jewesses

—puppy Jews—mastiff Jews—bulging matrons—spectacled backfish—golden-haired Jewish Dianas—sable-eyed Jewish Pucks, Jewish Mirandas—Romeos and Juliets. Jew Caesars— only no Shylock. It is a heathen menagerie of Israel. Only one Christian—a big Scottish YMCA-looking man who is starter of the facade of elevators—and is out of his real job just now, for I am sure that his real job is to watch the bathers in summer and save the drowners—when the nation is in the water. For they would never trust a Jew.

Dear Mo and I lie in bed, or on the beds and read Virgil aloud—also Le Nôtre and the journals. She has her meals sent up—so far—but I descend into the amphibious theater and prowl amid the animals. The young I like. They submit to caresses and their parents are pleased. The young have aplomb as well as the old in Judea.

Food, cigars, clothing, bien-être—this people understands enjoyment. They are uncritical: life is a simple matter to them:—a bank account and the larder. No, they will never rule the world. They are too easily deflected—absorbed and satisfied. It is foolish to rule the world, and the Jew knows it. They are crumbling material for the hands of their leaders and ropes of sand. They have too much sense—and will go for the glittering garments and not murder Progress. They strike me as an inferior race in spite of their great advantages. Did it ever occur to you how much Napoleon must have despised the French? He had not a drop of French blood in his veins, and was born just before or just after Corsica was ceded to France. What sort of nation must that be that can be ruled by such a shyster? At the time of his Brumaire coup d'etat, three or four men could have done for him. But Frenchmen cannot act together. He ruled them by terror and espionage, by flummery and *gloire*, by their vanity and their baseness. He made monkeys of them, and today they are proud of him! But I ought not to foment your critical dislike of the French—and their ways and vanities. You are young and easily influenced, and something I said might stick in your mind and cause a gangrene. But to return to the Jews, my long acquaintance with Klein and his club makes me at home with them—but I'm glad I haven't *more* Jewish blood in me than I have. I don't want any more. They are losing their quality by the loss of their education. These people don't know anything. They have no religion, no customs except eating and drinking.

Imagine the job of an American Jewish rabbi. They have good hearts and charities I know, but no thrills, and O my, they *look* so grotesque that I could never preach to them.

M. A. D. Howe, ed., *John Jay Chapman and His Letters* (Boston, 1937), p. 170.

Anti-Semitic sentiments, often of an extremely brazen type, also found widespread expression in literary form during the 1920s. Distressing in themselves, they are even more so in terms of the support they give to that gradual progression to a state of affair in which Jew-hatred actually becomes "fashionable," or at least acceptable. Particularly damaging, one supposes, are anti-Semitic elements in children's books. The following two extracts, from *Mother Goose* and *Grimm's Fairy Tales* respectively, were deleted from American editions shortly before the Second World War. But to what extent can we attribute American indifference to the fate of European Jewry during the 1930s and 1940s to the diet of hate which the adults of that time had been fed as children?[8]

"A Rogue of A Jew."

> Jack sold his egg
> To a rogue of a Jew,
> Who cheated him out
> Of half of his due.
>
> The Jew got his goose,
> Which he vowed he would kill,
> Resolving at once,
> His pockets to fill.

Quoted Sigmund Livingston, *Must Men Hate?* (New York, 1944), p. 18.

"The Jew Among the Thorns."

There was once a rich Man, and he had a Servant who served him well and faithfully. He was first up in the morning, and last to go to bed at night. If there was any hard work to be done which no one else would do, he was always ready to undertake it. He never made any complaint, but was always merry and content.

When his year of service was over, his Master did not give him any wages, thinking: "This is my wisest plan. I save by it, and he is not likely to run away."

The Servant said nothing, and served the second year like the first. And when at the end of the second he again received no wages, he still appeared contented, and stayed on. When the third year had passed, the Master bethought himself, and put his hand into his pocket, but he brought it out empty.

At last the Servant said: "Master, I have served you well and truly for three years; please pay me my wages. I want to go away and look about the world a bit."

The Miser answered: "Yes, my good fellow, you have served me honestly, and you shall be liberally rewarded."

Again he put his hand into his pocket, and counted three farthings, one by one, into the Servant's hand and said: "There, you have a farthing for every year; that is better wages than you would get from most masters."

The good Servant, who knew little about money, put away his fortune, and thought: "Now my pocket is well filled, I need no longer trouble myself about work." Then he left and went singing down the hill, and dancing, in the lightness of his heart.

Now it so happened that as he was passing a thicket, that a little Mannikin came out and cried: "Whither away, my merry fellow? I see your troubles are not too heavy to be borne."

"Why should I be sad?" answered the Servant. "I have three years' wages in my pocket."

"And how much is your treasure?" asked the Mannikin.

"How much? Why, three good farthings."

"Listen!" said the Mannikin. "I am a poor needy fellow; give me your three farthings. I can't work any more; but you are young and can easily earn your bread."

Now the Servant had a good heart, and he was sorry for the poor little man, so he gave him his three farthings, and said: "Take them, in the name of heaven! I shall not miss them."

"Then," said the Mannikin, "I see what a good heart you have. I will give you three wishes, one for each farthing; and every wish shall be fulfilled."

"Aha!" said the Servant, "you are a wonder-worker I see. Very well, then. First, I wish for a gun which will hit everything I aim at; secondly, for a fiddle which will make everyone dance when I play; and thirdly, if I ask anything of anyone, that he shall not be able to refuse my request."

"You shall have them all," said the Mannikin, diving into the bushes, where, wonderful to relate, lay the gun and the fiddle ready, just as if they had been ordered beforehand. He gave them to the Servant, and said, "No one will be able to refuse you anything you ask."

"Heart alive! What more can one desire," said the Servant to himself as he went merrily on.

Soon after, he met a Jew with a long goat's beard, who was standing still listening to the song of a bird sitting on the top of a tree. "Good heavens!" he was saying, "what a tremendous noise such a tiny creature makes. If only it were mine! If one could but put some salt upon its tail!"

"If that is all," said the Servant, "the bird shall soon come down."

He took aim, and down fell the bird into a quickset hedge.

"Go, you rogue," he said to the Jew, "and pick up the bird."

"Leave out the 'rogue,' young man. I will get the bird sure enough, as you have killed it for me," said the Jew.

He lay down on the ground and began to creep into the hedge. When he had got well among the thorns, a spirit of mischief seized the Servant, and he began to play his fiddle with all his might. The Jew was forced to spring up and begin to dance, and the more the Servant played, the faster he had to dance. The thorns tore his shabby coat, combed his goat's beard, and scratched him all over.

"Merciful Heavens!" cried the Jew. "Leave off that fiddling! I don't want to dance, my good fellow."

But the Servant paid no attention to him, but thought: "You have fleeced plenty of people in your time, my man, and the thorns shan't spare you now!" And he played on and on, so that the Jew had to jump higher and higher, till his coat hung in ribbons about him.

"I cry 'enough'!" screamed the Jew. "I will give you anything you like if you will only stop. Take the purse, it is full of gold."

"Oh, well, if you are so open-handed," said the Servant, "I am quite ready to stop my music, but I must say in praise of your dancing that it has quite a style of its own." Then he took the purse and went on his way.

The Jew stood still looking after him till he was a good way off, then he screamed with all his might: "You miserable fiddler! Just you wait till I find you alone! I will chase you till the soles of your shoes drop off—you rascal!" And he went on pouring out a stream of abuse. Having relieved himself by doing so, he hurried off to the Judge in the nearest town.

"Just look here, Your Worship," he said, "look how I have been attacked and ill-treated and robbed on the highroad by a wretch. My condition might melt the heart of a stone; my clothes and my body torn and scratched, and my purse with all my poor little savings taken away from me. All my beautiful ducats, each one prettier than the other. Oh dear! Oh dear! For heaven's sake, put the wretch in prison."

The Judge said: "Was it a soldier who punished you so with a sword?"

"Heaven preserve us!" cried the Jew, "he had no sword, but he had a gun on his shoulder and a fiddle round his neck. The villain is easily to be recognized."

So the Judge sent out men in pursuit of the honest Servant, who had walked on slowly. They soon overtook him, and the purse of gold was found on him. When he was brought before the Judge, he said: "I never touched the Jew, nor did I take his money away; he offered it to me of his own free will if I would only stop playing, because he could not bear my music."

"Heaven defend us!" screamed the Jew, "his lies are as thick as flies on the wall."

But the Judge did not believe him either, and said: "That is a very lame excuse; no Jew ever did such a thing." And he sentenced the honest Servant to the gallows for having committed a robbery upon the king's highway.

When he was being led away, the Jew screamed after him: "You vagabond, you dog of a fiddler, now you will get your deserts!"

The Servant mounted the ladder to the gallows quite quietly, with the halter round his neck; but at the last rung he turned round and said to the Judge: "Grant me one favor before I die."

"Certainly," said the Judge, "as long as you don't ask for your life."

"Not my life," answered the Servant. "I only ask to play my fiddle once more."

The Jew raised a tremendous cry. "Don't allow it, Your Worship, for heaven's sake, don't allow it!"

But the Judge said: "Why should I deny him that short pleasure? His wish is granted, and there's an end of the matter!"

He could not have refused even if he had wished, because of the Mannikin's gift to the Servant.

The Jew screamed, "Oh dear! Oh dear! Tie me tight, tie me tight!"

The good Servant took his fiddle from his neck, and put it into position, and at the first chord everybody began to wag their heads, the Judge, his Clerk, and all the Officers of Justice, and the rope fell out of the hand of the man about to bind the Jew.

At the second scrape, they all lifted their legs, and the Hangman let go his hold of the honest Servant, to make ready to dance.

At the third scrape they one and all leapt into the air, and began to caper about, the Judge and the Jew at the head, and they all leapt their best.

Soon, everyone who had come to the marketplace out of curiosity, old and young, fat and lean, were dancing as hard as they could; even the dogs got upon their hind legs and pranced about with the rest. The longer he played, the higher they jumped, till they knocked their heads together, and made each other cry out.

At last the Judge, quite out of breath, cried: "I give you your life, if only you will stop playing."

The honest Servant allowed himself to be prevailed upon, laid his fiddle aside, and dismounted the ladder. Then he went up to the Jew, who lay gasping upon the ground, and said to him: "You rascal, confess where you got the money, or I will begin to play again."

"I stole it! I stole it!" he screamed; "but you have honestly earned it."

The Judge then ordered the Jew to the gallows to be hanged as a thief.

> *Grimm's Fairy Tales,* any edition prior
> to 1935.

A Jew Lawyer from Memphis (1930).

At the other end of the table sat a man picking his teeth. His skull was capped closely by tightly curled black hair thinning upon a bald spot. He had a long, pale nose. He wore a tan palm beach suit; upon the table near him a smart leather briefcase and a straw hat with a rand-and-tan band, and he gazed lazily out of a window above the ranked heads, picking his teeth. Horace stopped just within the door. "It's a lawyer," he said, "a Jew lawyer from Memphis."

> From William Faulkner's *Sanctuary,*
> quoted by Alfred J. Durzch, "Faulkner
> and the Jews," *YIVO Annual of Jewish
> Social Science,* XIII (1965).

"The Most Unpleasant Race Ever Heard Of" (1922).

The Jews could be put down very plausibly as the most un-
pleasant race ever heard of. As commonly encountered they
lack many of the qualities that mark the civilized man: courage, dignity, incorruptibility, ease, confidence. They have
vanity without pride, voluptuousness without taste, and
learning without wisdom. Their fortitude, such as it is, is
wasted upon puerile objects, and their charity is mainly a
form of display.

> H. L. Mencken, "Treatise on the Gods,"
> quoted in Heywood Broun and George
> Britt, *Christians Only* (New York, 1931),
> p. 276.

"Mr. Wolfsheim" (1925).

Suddenly he looked at his watch, jumped up, and hurried
from the room, leaving me with Mr. Wolfsheim at the table.

"He has to telephone," said Mr. Wolfsheim, following him
with his eyes. "Fine fellow, isn't he? Handsome to look at and
a perfect gentlemen."

"Yes."

"He's an Oggsford man."

"Oh!"

"He went to Oggsford College in England. You know
Oggsford College?"

"I've heard of it."

"It's one of the most famous colleges in the world."

"Have you known Gatsby for a long time?" I inquired.

"Several years," he answered in a gratified way. "I made
the pleasure of his acquaintance just after the war. But I
knew I had discovered a man of fine breeding after I talked
with him an hour: 'There's the kind of man you'd like to take
home and introduce to your mother and sister.' " He paused.
"I see you're looking at my cuff buttons."

I hadn't been looking at them, but I did now. They were composed of oddly familiar pieces of ivory.

"Finest specimens of human molars," he informed me.

"Well!" I inspected them. "That's a very interesting idea."

"Yeah." He flipped his sleeves up under his coat. "Yeah, Gatsby's very careful about women. He would never so much as look at a friend's wife."

When the subject of this instinctive trust returned to the table and sat down Mr. Wolfsheim drank his coffee with a jerk and got to his feet.

"I have enjoyed my lunch," he said, "and I'm going to run off from you two young men before I outstay my welcome."

"Don't hurry, Meyer," said Gatsby, without enthusiasm. Mr. Wolfsheim raised his hand in a sort of benediction.

"You're very polite, but I belong to another generation," he announced solemnly. "You sit here and discuss your sports and your young ladies and your——" He supplied an imaginary noun with another wave of his hand. "As for me, I am fifty years old, and I won't impose myself on you any longer."

As he shook hands and turned away his tragic nose was trembling. I wondered whether I had said anything to offend him.

"He becomes very sentimental sometimes," explained Gatsby. "This is one of his sentimental days. He's quite a character around New York—a denizen of Broadway."

"Who is he, anyhow, an actor?"

"No."

"A dentist?"

"Meyer Wolfsheim? No, he's a gambler." Gatsby hesitated, then added coolly: "He's the man who fixed the World's Series back in 1919."

"Fixed the World's Series?" I repeated.

The idea staggered me. I remembered, of course, that the World's Series had been fixed in 1919, but if I had thought of it at all I would have thought of it as a thing that merely *happened*, the end of some inevitable chain. It never occurred to me that one man could start to play with the faith of fifty million people—with the single-mindedness of a burglar blowing a safe.

"How did he happen to do that?" I asked after a minute.

"He just saw the opportunity."

"Why isn't he in jail?"

"They can't get him, old sport. He's a smart man."

F. Scott Fitzgerald, *The Great Gatsby*
(New York, 1925), pp. 69–74.

5. American Anti-Semitism and European Fascism

Although the selections offered, without further comment, in this chapter may seem to belong to the ravings of the lunatic fringe, it would be a serious mistake to underestimate their importance. Lunatic these readings most certainly are; but the extent to which they reflect a mere "fringe" of American sentiment during the 1930s and the postwar period is open to question. As mentioned in the introductory essay, the 1930s and 1940s witnessed an extraordinary resurgence of anti-Semitic feeling in this country; the New Deal was a Jewish conspiracy, so was the entry of the United States into the Second World War; so was international communism. These beliefs, com-

bined with a racist disliking of Jews and widespread indifference to their plight in Europe, pervaded large sections of the
Gentile American community.[1]

"The World Hoax" (1938).

Try an experiment! Walk up to the average American today
and ask him to tell you what Communism is.

"Everybody knows what Communism is!" he responds,
surprised and not a little nettled at having a question so
childish put to him.

"Well, what is it?"

"It's a worldwide political party, originating in Russia,
that's fighting by revolutionary methods to destroy preda-
tory Capitalism. It invites the workers of the world to enjoy
the same rights that have always been enjoyed by the aristocratic classes with influence and money!"

"No more?"

"Whatta you mean, more?"

"But where do the Jews come in?"

"What Jews?"

"All Jews! All over the world. You know that Communism
with its ghastly bloodglut, wherever you find it, is confessedly
Jewish, don't you?"

"That's Jew-baiting Nazism—and I don't believe in Nazism. I believe every race has the right to worship God as it
pleases."

"What's worshiping God got to do with it?"

"Well, Jews are persecuted because of the way they worship God, aren't they? And that's against the Constitution.
It's un-American. Besides, it's race prejudice."

"But from what you've seen of Communism here in the
United States, you'll agree it's mostly Jew-financed and Jew-
led, won't you?"

"Well, the Jews have always been downtrodden and persecuted for their religion—just like the downtrodden in mass
production. It's not to be wondered at, that as a race they
make common cause with all enemies of Gentile capitalism."

"Then you believe in sticking up for Jews, regardless of

whether or not they are making 'common cause' with a 'political party' that is seeking to overthrow all governments by violence?"

Your average American suddenly becomes disgruntled then and warily angry. "Well, they're God's Chosen People, aren't they? The Bible says so."

"The Bible's been rewritten about seven times since the Ascension of Christ. How much investigating have you done, to find out whether the Jews are God's Chosen People or not —or whether that's something they've put forward themselves to gain a religious edge over Christians?"

"I see. You *are* one of them Nazis!"

"What's being a Nazi got to do with the facts behind this business of bogus claims by Jews, so they have an excuse to overthrow all governments by violence?"

"I dunno. And I don't care. But I'm an American and against race prejudice. You asked me what Communism is, and I answered you."

"No, you didn't answer me. You said Communism was merely a political party."

"Well. What else is it?"

"Karl Mordecai didn't say so. And he should have known."

"Who's Karl Mordecai?"

"The person you know as Karl Marx. Marx wasn't his real name, you understand. It was only an alias he used to cover up the fact that he was a Jew—the same as this 'Russian' Finkelstein gets himself accepted under the bogus name of Litvinoff."

"I never knew Marx's real name was Mordecai. What of it?"

"Mordecai—or Marx—never claimed that Communism was political. He had other ideas and said so frankly."

"What did he say?"

"He said that his Theory of 'Scientific' Socialism—that later became Communism in practice—was simply a means of smashing all Gentile governments so that the Jews might become 'emancipated'—and supreme over Gentiles."

"Marx said that!"

"It was the premise of his whole career. It resulted in Communism as you know it."

"The newspapers never put it so. I don't find it anywhere in the Communist literature."

"So you're familiar with Communist literature?"

"I try to keep up with what's going on."

"Then why haven't you kept up with what's going on in Germany? If you keep up with what's going on, and read Communist literature, why don't you read a bit of 'Nazi' literature to balance up and give you both sides?"

"I told you before, I'm against race prejudice."

"You believe in class prejudice?"

"Who said I did?"

"Well, you don't express the same angry opinion about the Communists' setting class against class. You don't say *that* is un-American."

"I didn't aim to start no argument. You asked me to tell you what I understood by Communism. I let you have it, and now you try to sell me on becoming a Nazi. Well, I couldn't be one if I thought you were right. I do businsss with Jews, and I owe 'em a lot o' money. The Jews get sore if you don't fall in with this panning of Hitler. And besides, I've got two boys and a brother on PWA. If the Administration heard I was anti-Jewish, it might make my relatives a lotta grief."

And determined to put a halt to your "Nazi Jew-baiting," Mr. Average Citizen stalks off and will have no more to do with you. His colossal ignorance about what is going on is not only tragic. It is heartbreakingly pathetic.

All that he has expressed in this conversation is a parroting of what he has had dinned into his ears so long and so insistently by America's kept press, tinctured with its "progressive" doctrines of "liberalism," that he actually believes he has been expressing his honest convictions—that on the whole you were disposed to see him on substituting some Fascist form of government for Constitutionalism.

Henceforth he recalls you as an exceedingly dangerous person to have running around loose in the Body Politic. Jews, in the aforesaid kept press, have contrived to create that conviction in him also.

To agitate for the overthrow of Constitutionalism by violence—or even through New-Deal legislation in the name of "liberalism"—makes no one particularly dangerous. But to imply that international Judah may have picked up and promoted the anti-Gentile system of Karl Mordecai, alias Marx, in order to pull down Christian culture and substitute the Jewish, exempting itself from any possible retributions by charging up the whole bloody business to the proletariat-of-the-world fighting for its "rights," converts you into a Public Enemy Number One. And the LaFollette Committee in the Senate, or the Dies Committee in the House of Representatives, should "investigate" you pronto.

You are engaged in preaching Fascism in this nation, and Fascism—holy horrors!—might succeed Constitutionalism!

Now America is filled with millions of the foregoing average citizens—whose attitudes on Communism, Fascism, and Nazism, are dictated by the fact that they do business with Jews daily, or owe them money, or concede that this current Administration is Yiddish, else a possible losing of their jobs on PWA would not be the implied penalty for talking against Jews openly. The nation is likewise filled with other millions of more erudite Gentiles, not beholden to PWA for any jobs, who are commencing to note the Jewishness of Communism, the Jewishness of our Federal government and its crackpot schemes for rescuing the country, and the well-nigh disgusting Jewishness of the representative daily press. These two classes are clashing hourly, with growing bellicosity, in every section of the public domain. Sooner or later this sort of thing is heard—

"You say Communism is Jewish?" challenges the Liberal-Minded Gullible.

"I certainly do!" the wiser man affirms.

"Well, *how can you prove it*, aside from the fact that great numbers of persecuted Jews flock into it to get them their rights the same as the workingman?"

In nine cases out of ten, the more educated Gentile is immediately nettled and at a slight loss. He knows that there are a hundred instances where Jews themselves have boasted of the Jewish character of Communism and its sponsorship, but where and how to put his hands on such statements, or fetch forth documentary proof to support his contentions, is at the instant beyond him.

Truth to tell, he actually must search the press of the nation—and perhaps the politico-economic literature of the last generation—for the devastating weapons to show his scouring correctness of position.

Well, the time has come when such plight may be remedied.

"Why has no one written a book to date," exclaims the sincere critic of Communistic Jewry, "presenting the admitted hook-ups between Judah and Bolshevism?"

The demand is a fair one.

In response to its persistence, *this volume in your hand has found literal expression!*

Communism, as you will now be shown, was hatched by a Jew—and a particularly disgusting one at that—kept alive by Jews, financed by them at the close of the world war, is staffed by them, installed by them in every country wherein it has taken its blood-toll, and at the present moment is being promoted to a lecherous "victory" in our Christian land by certain especially rapacious Sons of Judah, whilst thousands of other Jews brag openly of its "success" and readily concede its Jewish character and purpose from hide to marrow.

The only way to convince the Gentile gullible that such statements are by no means Fascist propaganda, birthed in race prejudice or serving the execrations of religious persecution, is to give him the simple but devasting life-stories of the Jewish gentlemen who have been Communism's patrons from the first.

Who was Karl Mordecai Marx and how did he come to project Communism at the start? Who were Lenin, Trotsky, Bela Kun, the whole devil's spawn of apostate Jews—276 of them from New York's East Side—who swarmed into Russia at the birth of the Bolsheviki and clapped machine guns to the head of White Russian Christians? What hook-ups has

Stalin, the present Red Dictator, with officious world Jewry as we behold it today?

This volume puts the whole documented narrative into your hands *at last,* for instant reference henceforth when the enlightened non-Jew is challenged by his critics.

Endorse it or don't endorse it, as you prefer, but the Jew or non-Jew is not alive today who can refute the ensuing *facts!*

> Ernest F. Elmhurst, *The World Hoax* (Asheville, North Carolina, 1938), pp. 8–13.

"The Invisible Government of the Jews" (1935).

In spite of the fact that some of the leaders of Jewry openly confess their lack of loyalty to the countries in which they live, their unpatriotic spirit is not what is meant by the political element of the Jewish Question. That element is more carefully organized and more active among Christian nations. The political element of which I wish to speak belongs to the fact that the Jews form a *Nation in the midst of nations,* with a super-government which is allied to no government, yet has its hand in them all; that this secret government is playing a vast and closely organized game with the world for its table and universal control of the money of the world and the vital resources for its stakes. This government of the Jews is said to have been the source of Bolshevism in Russia, to have been the cause of the collapse of the German Empire, and to have been the real ruler of both England and America during the World War, and is the cause of the unrest and depression which has followed the signing of the armistice; therefore the *Invisible Government of the Jews* is the cause of the rising feeling of anti-Semitism, and the cause of world unrest, past and present, although for nearly one hundred and fifty years it has remained discreetly in the background.

Evidence tends to show that writers, statesmen, and military leaders have for a long time known that there was an Invisible Government directing the affairs of nations.

(1) **Lafayette** July 24, 1789, Lafayette wrote, "An Invisible Hand rules the mob."

(2) **Acton** In his *Essay on the French Revolution,* Lord Acton says, "The appalling thing is not the tumult, but the design. Through all the fire and smoke, we perceive the evidence of calculating organization. The managers remained concealed or masked, but there is no doubt about their presence from the first."

(3) **Dumesnil** In his *Preface aux Memoirs de Senat,* Alexis Dumesnil says, "The party that pushed the Revolution to violence was directed by a Hidden Hand which until today could not be surmised."

(4) **Disraeli** The Jew Disraeli, in 1844, in his book, *Croningsby,* said, "The world is governed by very different personages from what is imagined by those who are not behind the scenes."

(5) **Mazzini** Giuseppe Mazzini, an Italian patriot, who died in 1872, said, "We wish to break every kind of yoke, yet there is one that is not seen that weighs on us. Whence comes it? Where is it? No one knows, or, at least, no one tells. The association is secret, even for us, the veterans of secret societies."

(6) **Merriam** Professor Charles E. Merriam, of the University of Chicago, in the *Chicago Tribune,* January 24, 1924, asked this pertinent question, "What advantage will we reap if science conquers all the world, except the World Government?"

(7) **Bryan** William Jennings Bryan said, "New York is the city of privilege. Here is the seat of that Invisible Power represented by the allied forces of finance and industry. This Invisible Government is reactionary, sinister, unscrupulous, mercenary, and sordid. It is wanting in national ideals and devoid of conscience. . . . This kind of government must be scourged and destroyed."

(8) **Francis** Phillip Francis, ex-editor of *The New York American* and author of *The Poison in America's Cup,* said,

"Nominally, we govern ourselves: actually, we are governed by an oligarchy of the American branch of the International Bankers."

Evidence tends to show that this "Invisible Government" is the government of the Jewish "nation."

(a) **Gooch** G. P. Gooch says, "The French Revolution brought the Jewish World Empire on the stage, and, molding the actions of men ever since, it has taken a permanent place among the formative influences of civilization. Each Revolution surrenders a country to its yoke."

(b) **Disraeli** In his book, entitled *Life of Lord George Betinck,* Disraeli says in regard to the revolutionary outbreaks of 1848: "The influence of the Jews may be traced in the last outbreak of the destructive principle in Europe. An insurrection takes place against tradition and aristocracy, against religion and property. Destruction of the Semitic principle, extirpation of the Jewish religion, whether in the Mosaic or in the Christian form, the natural equality of men and the abrogation of property, are proclaimed by the *secret societies who form provincial governments,* and men of *Jewish race* are found at the *head* of every one of them. The people of God cooperate with atheists; the most skillful accumulators of property ally themselves with Communists; the peculiar chosen Race touch the hand of all the scum and low castes of Europe! And all this because *they wish to destroy* that ungrateful *Christendom* which owes to them even its name, and whose tyranny they can no longer endure."

(c) **Hobart** Mary E. Hobart, in her book, *The Secret of the Rothschilds,* says, "The House of Rothschild with a few co-religionists conspire to own the world."

(d) **Hearst** In Hearst's *Chicago Evening American,* of December 3, 1923, was printed the following statement: "The Rothschilds can start or prevent wars. Their word could make or break Empires."

(e) **Rathenau** The Jew Walter Rathenau, in *Wienar Press,* December 24, 1912, said, "Only 300 men, each of whom knows all the others, govern the fate of Europe. They select their successors from their entourage. These German Jews have the means in their hands of putting an end to the form of any State which they find 'unreasonable.' "

Evidence tends to show that the Bolshevik movement in Russia is under Jewish leadership and may be regarded as primarily a Jewish movement.

(1) For proof of this statement we examine the testimonies of 1919, contained in the printed Senate Report (a public document) entitled *Bolshevik Propaganda*—"Hearings before a Senate committee of the Committee on the Judiciary, United States Senate, Sixty-fifth Congress, pursuant to S. Res. 439 and 469."

(a) Dr. George A. Simons, a Methodist clergyman, who had been for many years in charge of a church in Petrograd, said, in part, "that hundreds of Jews from the lower East Side of New York were among the agitators, and that in 1918, in the northern community of Petrograd, the Soviet regime was made up of 16 real Russians and 371 Jews, and 265 of that number came from the lower East Side of New York."

(b) Mr. William Chapin Huntington, Commercial Attaché of the United States Embassy at Petrograd from June 1916 until September 1918, stated before the Overman Committee that two-thirds of the Bolsheviks are Russian Jews.

(c) Theodore Kryshtofovich, who was at one time employed by the Russian Department of Agriculture, testified that the people governing Russia are now Jews, that although Lenine is a Russian all the constellations turning around this sun are Jews.

(2) In the *London Times* of March 29, 1919, this statement appeared: "One of the most curious features of the Bolshevist movement is that 75 per cent are Jews."

Other Evidence.

(a) George Pitter-Wilson, of the London *Globe*, wrote in April 1919, "Bolshevism is the dispossession of the Christian nations of the world to such an extent that no capital will remain in the hands of the Christians, that all Jews may jointly hold the world in their hands and reign wherever they choose."

(b) Mrs. Clare Sheridan, a friend of Trotsky, in the *New*

York World, December 15, 1923, said, "The communists are Jews, and Russia is being entirely administered by them. They are in every office, bureau, and newspaper. They are driving out the Russians and are responsible for the anti-Semitic feeling which is increasing."

(7) **Marx**   As far back as 1879, Wilhelm Marx wrote the following warning: "At the present hour, Russia alone of all the states of Europe is the last rampart against which the Jews have dug their last sap. The capitulation of Russia is only a question of time. When Russia has been laid low, it will fear the attacks of no one; then the Jews will officially set about the destruction of the society in Western Europe."

(b) **Dostoyefsky**   In 1880, F. M. Dostoyefsky, a Russian philosopher, wrote the following, "Yes, she is on the eve of her fall, your Europe, of a fall universal, general, terrible. Judaism and the *banks* reign now over everything, as much over Europe as over education, over the whole of civilization and socialism, particularly over socialism, because with its aid Judaism will tear out Christianity by the roots and destroy Christian culture. And if nothing comes of all this but anarchy, then at the head of all will be found the Jew, and when all the *wealth* of Europe has been pillaged, the *Jew bank* alone will remain. The Jew will lead Russia to her ruin."

Russia, the granary of Europe, has fallen and today is controlled by Jews who, with the support of their banks, now seek, according to Dostoyefsky, to pillage "all the wealth of Europe."

Anon., *The Cause of Anti-Jewism in the United States* (Boston, 1935), pp. 11–18.

The Jew Roosevelt (1943?).

On March 7, 1934, there was released to the Associated Press a genealogical chart prepared in the Carnegie Institute of Washington, D.C., under direction of Dr. H. H. Laughlin, showing that the first Roosevelts to come to the United States were Claes Martenszen Van Rosenvelt (not Roosevelt) and

his wife, whose maiden name had been Jannetje *Samuels.*
Take note that the spelling of the name at that time was
Rosen-velt, not Roose-velt.

Claes' wife must have been a Jewess, for Samuels is by no
means a Dutch name.

Claes and Jannetje thereupon had a son, Nicholas Rosenvelt, who subsequently married Heyltje *Kunst*—obviously
another Jewess. Thereupon there were five generations of
Rosen-velts before Franklin Delano came upon the scene.

Early in 1934 Chase S. Osborn, ex-Governor of Michigan
gave, in an interview at St. Petersburg, Fla., the results of his
researches into the Roosevelt—or Rosenvelt—genealogy.
Printed in the St. Petersburg *Times,* the Osborn interview
made reference to the Jewish ancestry of the President, the
Governor declaring that Franklin D. Roosevelt is the living
descendant of the Rossocampo family, expelled from Spain in
1620. Seeking safety in Germany, Holland, and other countries, members of the family, he said, changed their names
to Rosenberg, Rosenbaum, Rosenblum, Rosenvelt, and Ro-
senthal. Quoting ex-Governor Osborn directly—"The Rosen-
velts in North Holland finally became Roosevelt, some
becoming apostates with the first generation, and others following suit until, in the fourth generation, a little storekeeper
by the name of Jacobus Rosenvelt was the only one who
remained true to his Jewish faith."

Besides these contentions of the Carnegie Institute and
ex-Governor Osborn, the following is from the book, *The
House of Roosevelt,* by Paul Haber, said to be a Jewish author,
1936 edition: "Claes Rosenvelt entered the cloth business in
New York and married in 1682. He accumulated a fortune.
He then changed his name to Nicholas Rosenvelt. Of his four
sons, Isaac died young, Nicholas married a Sarah Solomons,
Jacobus married Catherine Hardenburg. . . . Isaac became a
capitalist. He founded the Bank of New York in 1790." *In the
Roosevelt family tree there are 351 persons bearing Biblical
names of the Tribe of Israel!*

If Roosevelt of today claims Dutch ancestry, how happens
it that there cannot be located any true Dutch families in

Holland by that name, and why, on all the old records, is the family name consistently spelled Rosenvelt?

It is interesting to note that no matter what the origin of the family name, it means in all languages, "Field of Roses." Even Rossocampo, the Spanish translation, means Field of Roses. Changed to German it becomes Rosenfeld. Evidently, the spelling of the name with two "o's" and no "n" *was an alteration made long after the family had become domiciled here in America.* One wonders why.

> Anon., *New Dealers in Office, with Their Red Front Personnel. The Amazing Roster of Persons with Strange Names Ascending into Vital Federal Positions Since 1933* (New York?, 1943?), pp. 8–9.

The "Jew Deal" (1940).

The New Deal, through its leader, President Roosevelt and the chorus of his satellites, warns us that we must prepare to "defend" ourselves against a foreign aggressor. A tremendous drive is under way to arm this nation on a scale as never before in our history, with a Stalin-like regimentation of men, women, children, and all industry.

Leave out of the discussion for the moment whether this danger is real or just another grossly exaggerated New Deal "emergency" and whether these billions are for defense or for Roosevelt aggression on foreign soil for World Jewry and the British Jewish Empire. Let us concern ourselves with the question: "What have Roosevelt and the New Dealers done, in terms of domestic policy, to prepare us for this hysterical effort?"

Franklin Delano Roosevelt went into office in March 1933, with a tremendous majority in both houses of Congress, the enthusiastic support of the entire country, the hopes of the people, and a platform which, he told the nominating convention, "I endorse 100 per cent."

Six months later that platform looked like Belgium when

Hitler got through with it. Its authors would not have recognized its mangled remains. With that event the tried, experienced, and trusted Democratic Party—the Party the people thought they voted into office in November 1932—died. Its historic functions were taken over by a crowd of invaders who no more resemble true Democrats than Felix Frankfurter resembles Thomas Jefferson. Bull-Moosers and professional social workers, reformers, revolutionaries, visionaries, radicals, communists, the "president-can-do-no-wrongers," political bankrupts and political prostitutes, a generous sprinkling of bemused Southern hereditary Democrats, the Hague machine, the Kelly-Nash machine, the Pendergast machine, some loose cogs from Tammany Hall, the Huey Long gang, the promoters of the millennium, the opportunists, the McCoy machine of Rhode Island, the Creel-McAdoo-Olsen machine of California, the pinks and Reds, the Youth Congress and the Communist Party, the professional nostrum dispensers, and a potent fringe of "Big Business" who are selling all sorts of machines to the New Deal bureaus, *buying insurance from* Jimmy Roosevelt and licking their chops in anticipation of war profits on munitions, etc.

Add to this galaxy the habitual malingerers who always infest every nation, the Fifth Column of professional "foreigners," a swarm of termite Jews, the professional reliefers and indigents, the subsidized propagandists for the higher life, and a lunatic fringe of chronic malcontents.

We have already mentioned some of the more prominent Jews who led this army of invaders of the Government. Among the better known or more influential of those not yet mentioned, were: Justice Sam Rosenmen of New York, credited by Raymond Moley in *After Seven Years* as one of Roosevelt's real intimates; Gerard Swope, rich industrialist, said by many to have been the father of the unconstitutional NRA if not of much of the New Deal itself; his brother, Herbert Bayard Swope, racetrack owner and publicity man; Gov. Herbert Lehman of New York, long ago described by Roosevelt as "My good right arm"; Prof. Harold Laski of Oxford,

British-Jew radical and powerful in the New Deal background; David Lilienthal, head of TVA, one of the New Deal's socialistic experiments; J. David Stern, radical publisher, now on the Federal Reserve Board; Nathan Straus, advisor on housing; Jesse Strauss, first New Deal Ambassador to France; E. A. Goldenweiser, Russian-Jew director of the Federal Reserve Board; David Dubinsky, Polish-Jewish advisor on labor problems and C. I. O. leader; Lee Pressman, pro-Communist labor leader and now counsel for C. I. O; Abe Fortas, counsel to several New Deal bureaus; Charles Michaelson, former Republican publicity man, then smearer of Hoover administration, now in charge of publicity for Democratic National Committee; Lawrence Steinhardt, now Ambassador to Soviet Russia; Harry F. Guggenheim, heir to copper millions, advisor on aviation; Arthur Garfield Hays, advisor on civil liberties, active in defense of Scottsboro rapists and Communist defender; Mordecai Ezekial, most influential in agricultural matters under New Deal, now an official of Department of Agriculture; David Lasser, head of radical Worker's Alliance, who has strongly influenced New Deal in keeping relief rolls at highest possible peak; Emanuel Celler, head of House Judiciary Committee; Sol Bloom, head of House Foreign Affairs Committee and traducer of George Washington; Henry Morgenthau, gentleman-farmer and Secretary of the Treasury; Herbert Feis, State Department counsel, whose voice, according to Moley, Alsop, and Kintner, and other writers, has colored New Deal foreign policy; Prof. Albert Einstein, German-Jew and refugee "scientist," member of several pro-Communist organizations and often a White House guest; Rabbi Stephen S. Wise, radical propagandist who has coerced New Deal immigration policies and who once said that he was a "Jew first—an American after that"; Rose Schneidermann, called, in New York, "Red Rose," dominant in labor politics; Max Zaritsky, left-wing labor advisor; James P. Warburg, heir to Warburg millions, who, after giving early aid to New Deal, fled to shelter of Republican Party and is today back in New Deal favor; Adolph Sabath, Chairman of all-powerful House Rules Committee; Isador Lubin, statistician of Department of Labor; Nathan Margold, counsel to several New Deal bureaus and accused by Indians of trying to "communize" them while he was counsel to Indian Bureau; the late William I. Sirovich, one-time head of House Patents Committee; the late Samuel Untermyer, credited by Moley and others with sponsoring much of early New Deal and its radical legislation; Leo Wolman, labor advisor and active in labor legislation; Sidney Hillman, C. I. O. leader, *very recently anti-Communist,* now one of Roosevelt's seven leaders of "preparedness" drive; Bennie Cohen, driving force of New Deal "must" legislation and lobbyist for Roosevelt; Louis Kirstein, associate of late A. L. Filene, Jew Boston millionaire for whose company young John Roosevelt is now an executive; Samuel Dickstein, Chairman of the House Immigration Committee, whose efforts have hamstrung every patriotic attempt to restrict immigration in both quantity and quality; Charles Wyzanski, Jr., former Counsel to Madame Perkins' Department of Labor; Chas. Taussig, molasses millionaire, advisor to the New Deal in its early days and now the employer of Dr. Rex Tugwell, the young Brain Truster whose stay in Washington was devoted to "making America over." Among the hundreds of other Jews now in the Government or who flit in and out at intervals, and who have been employed at one time or another, are: Jacob Straus; Lucian Koch, thrown out of his job as head of the notorious Commonwealth College of Mena, Arkansas, of which the wife and sister of Mr. Justice Brandeis were financial supporters, and given a job in the New Deal; Jerome Frank, present head of the S.E.C.; Louis H. Bean of the Department of Agriculture; Abraham M. Fox, former research director of the Tariff Commission; Benedict Wolf of the National Labor Relations Board; William Leiserson of the National Labor Relations Board; David J. Saposs of the National Labor Relations Board; L. H. Seltzer, head economist of the Treasury; Edward Berman, Department of Labor; Jacob Perlman of the Department of Labor; Morris L. Jacobson, chief statistician of the Government Research Project; A. H. Meyers, New England division of the National Labor Relations Board; Jack Levin, assistant general manager of the Rural Electrification Authority; Harold Loeb, economic consultant for the N.R.P; William Seagle, attorney for the Petroleum Labor Policy Board; Herman A. Gray, member policy committee of the National Housing Conference; Alexander Sachs of Lehman Bros., early consultant of the New Deal, as was Paul Mazur, also of Lehman Bros.

The list is as long, if not longer, today than it was in 1933. To name them all would claim a substantial part of the New York and Washington City directories and most of the B'nai B'rith. Like Hitler on the Western Front, swarms of Jews have consolidated their positions in the New Deal and are taking over Americans to die for World Jewry.

Under the influence of these Jews and some "liberal" Gentile Fronts, the New Deal proceeded to make America over. One of their first acts was to debase our currency by reducing the value of the dollar to 59¢; then to repudiate our obligations, domestic and international, by going off the gold standard. In an alleged attempt to raise agricultural prices, great fields of grain were plowed under, and millions of pigs and cattle were destroyed. The relief rolls were padded by the addition of thousands of persons whose jobs or relief checks depended upon their voting for the New Deal.

By crying "Emergency" the President took away from Congress its Constitutional duty to write all legislation and shoved down the throats of the crying representatives of the people scores of bills written by the sly and facile pens of the "Happy Hot-Dogs" of Felix Frankfurter.

Hundreds of illegally appointed publicity men were encouraged to belabor the brains and ability of true Americans and assault the ideas and ideals of the sober, hard-working middle classes, while the President himself took the lead in mocking the "economic royalists" and "princes of privilege."

Billions of dollars, today needed for a defense program, were squandered on boondoggling. Just a few samples follow:

Thousands of dollars were spent for a community service campaign in Tempe, Arizona; to drain a piggery in Massachusetts, and to measure the area and cubic contents of buildings in Allegheny County, Pennsylvania.

Uncle Sam hired a fan-dancer to entertain the C.C.C. in Minnesota, and $19,000 was spent in Memphis to buy a dog-pound.

A Guide Book to the United States—in one of which George Washington Parke Custis was vilely slandered by a Jew author on "information" furnished by a negro research "expert"—cost you and me $2,689,000, or one dollar per word.

Johnston City, Illinois, asked for money to erect a flood control project but was refused and thousands of dollars were given to teach its unemployed how to play checkers, and to teach dancing, bridge, and pinochle.

More thousands was the cost to the W.P.A. to relocate a brook at Winchester, Massachusetts.

It cost us several thousand more to take a census of the trees in Harrisburg, Pennsylvania.

We spent still more thousands to build a waterhole on a fox-farm in Everett, Massachusetts, and to blow away an overhanging rock at Buncombe, Wisconsin.

And while this was going on, our President says he knew that we were facing the greatest crisis of our existence in which we would, as we are now told, need uncounted billions for defense!

The worst of the New Deal's many offenses against the people took place under the W.P.A. The most lurid of these were the so-called Arts Projects, under which writers, painters, musicians, actors, and playwrights were paid to libel America and its citizens and to conduct open Communistic propaganda. Its director was Hallie Flanagan, frequent guest of Stalin in the Soviet and member of the board of editors of the Communistic magazine, *New Theatre*. She was given an initial fund of $27,000,000. Among those pro-Communist and radical theater workers to whom Mrs. Flangan gave immediate employment were Virgil Geddes, Alfred Kreymbourgh (Jewish author of a foul revolutionary poem "America"), Meyer Levin, one of whose plays was so obscene that even the "liberal" city administration of Chicago banned it; Langston Hughes, negro fellow-traveler; Michael Gold, recently convicted of labor blackmail in New York, and a Communist-Jew on the staff of the *Daily Worker*; Upton Sinclair; Ben Blake, Elmer Rice (Reizenstein), Jewish playwright; Jacob Baker, Jewish assistant to Harry Hopkins when he was head of the W.P.A., and Clifford Odets, Communistic-Jew playwright; Philip Barber, John Bonn, John Howard Lawson, Albert Maltz, Augustus Smith, M. Blankfort, H. W. L. Dana (radical Boston professor hauled up several years ago on a perversion charge), George Sklar, P. & C. Sifton—all members of the American branch of the International Union of the Revolutionary Theater—went to work under Mrs. Flanagan. The "P. Sifton" mentioned was later appointed as Assistant Administrator of the Wages and Hour Act.

Under the "Arts Project" division of the W.P.A., Jacob Baker appointed, as head of the Music Division, Nikolai Sokoloff, Russian-American director, and as head of the Creative Arts section, Holger Cahill, "fellow-traveler" and former member of the I.W.W.

The Writer's Project was headed by Henry Alsberg, the Jew traducer of George Washington Parke Custis, father of Mrs. Robert E. Lee. Alsberg's right bower was Orrick Johns of the Communist magazine *New Masses*; Reed Harris, too red even for Columbia University and expelled for that reason; Leonard D. Abbott, Alsberg's field supervisor, an outstanding Anarchist; George Cronyn, "fellow traveler," and Floyd Dell of the American Society for Cultural Relations with Soviet Russia. One anti-Communist, Samuel Duff McCoy, accidentally got a job with the Writers' Project, but was kicked out by Alsberg and Johns, as was Major William L. Ball, treasurer of the Theater Project, who made the mistake of protesting against the Communistic nature of Mrs. Flanagan's plays.

Among the flagrantly Communistic plays produced under Mrs. Flanagan, who, incidentally, is an intimate friend of Mrs. Eleanor Roosevelt, were:

"Triple A, Plowed Under," in which Earl Browder, head of the Communist Party of America is depicted as reversing a Supreme Court decision;

"Battle Hymn," by Mike Gold and Michael Blankfort, a play whose set-model was displayed in New York's Communist Worker's Bookshop;

"Turpentine," a story about negro revolt in the South, in which religion is mocked and the negroes depicted as shooting the white "bosses";

"We Live and Laugh," produced by the Yiddish Theater Unit and praised by the *Daily Worker*;

"Prisoner 1936," a review produced by the Yiddish Unit whose keynote is put in the words of one of its characters: "We love America as one of the most beautiful flowers in the bouquet of the world Soviets of tomorrow."

"America, America," an obscene argument for revolution;

"The Dance of Death," which not even the *Daily Worker* could pretend to explain;

"Class of '29," also praised by the *Daily Worker*.

It is a matter of record that the W.P.A. Theater Project did not produce in all of its all-too-long existence—a single anti-Communist play or production.

The Jewish-controlled Press and Radio concealed or played down these facts from Gentile America.

The Theater Project was particularly active in making propaganda movies for use in C.C.C. camps. Aroused by a flood of protests, Congress recently refused further funds for these "creative" arms of the Communist movement.

Roosevelt's R.E.R.A. appointed Hilda Smith, described by Drew Pearson and Robert Allen, Washington columnists, as Harry Hopkins' "Professor of Communism," as director of worker's education. Her job was to teach the teachers of some 50,000 American workers enrolled in work-projects schools. She was a member of the board of the notorious Commonwealth College of Mena, Arkansas, and though she denied teaching Communism, she ordered the use of Earl Browder's books as textbooks, as well as the *Moscow Primer*. Mrs. Smith was defended by Mrs. Roosevelt when she was criticized for her acts.

The Rev. Joseph Thorning, S. J., writing in *America* (Oct. 5, 1935), stated that under Mrs. Smith, students in the worker's schools were forbidden to sing the "Star Spangled Banner" and encouraged to sing the "Internationale."

The *New Republic* for June 10, 1936, states that both President and Mrs. Roosevelt opposed "social discrimination" against the negro, and Mrs. Roosevelt, on numerous occasions encouraged Government agencies to banish all "discrimination" against the colored race. The *Times* of Avon Park, Florida, says of this state of affairs: "The South has much reason to love the Democratic Party. It will not vote for alien ideas of the 'Dictatorship of Bums' . . . and the 'negro supremacy' regardless of . . . attempts to purchase millions of votes with . . . government funds or of the sacred name of Democracy which has been stolen by the New Dealists. The New Deal is not only Communism but it is black Communism."

Incidentally, Mr. Roosevelt appointed Lucien Koch (head of Commonwealth College) to the consumer's division of the short-lived N.R.A. after the Arkansas Legislature had closed the school because of its almost indescribable immorality.

The story of the New Deal support to the radical Youth Congress is recent news. It is enough to point out that, despite the fact that Mrs. Roosevelt got young William Hinckley, head of the Youth Congress, a job on the Federal payroll as assistant to the head of the Department of Education, the Congress, in its recent Washington meeting, was so embarrassingly blatant in its sympathies for Soviet Russia that the President was forced to administer a mild spanking on the White House lawn and Mrs. Roosevelt to withdraw her more overt support of the body. During their stay in the Capitol, she entertained several of the officers of the Congress in the White House and even provided overnight hospitality to some of them.

In 1936, Roosevelt, after receiving high praise from the left-wing Co-operative League of the U. S. A., sent a three-man delegation to Europe to study the cooperative movement. The men he selected were all known left-wingers:

1. Charles E. Stuart, vice-president of the Export-Import Bank, set up to facilitate loans to Soviet Russia, director of the

Russian-American Chamber of Commerce, the lecturer at the New School for Social Research of which Mrs. Roosevelt is a director;

2. The ineffable Mr. Jacob Baker, vice-president of the Communist-aiding Garland Fund, a radical backlog for several communist organizations; and

3. Leland Olds, former industrial editor of the Communist Federated Press, the Soviet-Russian news-agency in the United States, of which William Z. Foster, Chairman of the Communist Party in this country, was the head. In mid-June of 1940 Roosevelt gave Olds—one-time Industrial Editor of the pro-Communist Federated Press, the delicate task of "protecting" our entire electric power system from sabotage by the "Fifth Column."

Probably the most serious of all these attacks upon the American form of Government and our way of life have been the President's unconcealed attempts to stimulate class warfare, by methods both direct—such as attacks upon individuals who opposed his policies—and indirect, by coddling of aliens, agitators, and radicals to conduct their own foul brand of warfare. He allowed his alien-minded Secretary of Labor to grant unlimited visas to hordes of Jews, European scum, and criminals, and encouraged her to defy those who fought such action.

While professing to be "profoundly disturbed" by the aggression of anti-Semitic Germany, he continued his special friendship for Soviet Russia after its attacks upon Outer Mongolia, Poland, and Finland. Professing an adoration for "democracy" he refused to invoke the Neutrality Act against Japan in its war on China and against Russia when, with Germany, she invaded Poland and attacked Finland. He extended a warm welcome to the Communist Ambassador Oumansky when he presented his credentials and, on the same day, displayed marked coldness toward the newly appointed Ambassador from Christian Spain.

Within the last few days Joe Davies (who says he is not a Jew), guardian of Post Toasties millions, former Ambassador to Russia and Belgium, now special assistant to the Secretary of State, honored at a royal entertainment Oumansky, Ambassador from Soviet Russia, and Joe Stalin.

Roosevelt's official subordinates have persecuted honest opponents of the New Deal through abuse of the Income Tax Statutes, and dropped charges against the Huey Long machine, based on those statutes, when Long died, and his political heirs rushed to Washington to make peace.

He winked at the W.P.A. when it openly and brazenly coerced votes of the poor and needy on behalf of New Deal candidates for the Senate and House of Representatives.

He allowed the Democratic National Committee to borrow an immense sum from the radical and Communist-penetrated C.I.O.—and used that money for campaign purposes. He paid off this debt in part by blandly looking the other way when the C.I.O. began its war on industry by means of sit-down strikes. He rewarded the outstanding apologist of the sit-down, Governor Frank Murphy, by making him first Attorney General and then a Justice of the Supreme Court.

He protected and defended his National Labor Relations Board when its illegal assumptions of authority and abuse of the statutes became a public scandal.

He refused to entertain patriotic protest when Madame Perkins admitted such notorious revolutionaries as John Strachey and Tom Mann, English-Communists; Henri Barbusse, French-Communist; "Red" Emma Goldman, anarchist; Sandor Garbai, Hungarian-Jewish Communist and associate of the murderer Bela Kun; and Hans Eisler, writer of Communist songs, a German-Jew refugee, who, incidentally, is now a lecturer at the radical New School for Social Research, of which Mrs. Roosevelt is a director.

He ardently supported the Socialist Party's recommendation for the cancellation of the war debts by taking no steps to collect them. He gagged the Naval Intelligence Department when it disclosed the extent of the Communist movement.

No greater offense to this nation could have been committed than Roosevelt's recognition of Soviet Russia from the bloody hands of Comrade Litvinoff (Finklestein). As he later told the radical American Youth Congress, he took the stand that the Russian Revolution—he did not the mention the over 5,000,000,000 persons shot and starved to death by its leaders—was a force "for great good."

He denounced the Supreme Court and mocked one of its decisions as of "the horse and buggy days" and, failing in his effort to destroy it by a change in the Constitution, managed eventually to pack it with a Ku Kluxer, an Austrian-born Jew, a principal apologist of the sit-down strike, a professor who never tried a case, and a political appointee: all this in order to get a Court that would determine what the Constitution is and interpret the law of the land à la Brandeis, Frankfurter, and Roosevelt.

He made a violent and overt attack upon certain members of Congress—distinguished figures of his own party—in order to punish them for their opposition to his extra-legal activities and political conduct. This was, in effect, an assault upon the voter and an attempt to hamper his right to vote as he chose.

The net result of these acts, plus their inevitable failure to restore industrial production, put the workless to work, and protect the rightful interests of the farmer, was to create class warfare of the bitterest sort, pile up the greatest debt in all history, undermine internal stability, and water the blood of independence of the individual citizen. Added up, they have brought us to the verge of another and even greater "emergency" than any we have ever known—the threat of a great war: a nation torn by internal dissension and debt, dominated by radical bureaus and anti-American bureaucrats; a nation little prepared to defend itself against a formidable enemy.

Even this new threat, the President and the New Deal have turned to political and selfish purposes. Crying for "unity" and the support of all the people, it is now proposed that we get ready for Armageddon under the direction of Franklin D. Roosevelt, Harry Hopkins, Henry Morgenthau, and the team of Cohen & Corcoran.

The New Deal and the New Dealers have systematically conducted a wordy warfare with nations with whom we are at peace. The President, the Secretary of State, and the bureaucrats have preached a neutrality which they do not even pretend to practice.

Through his aides and claque the President has let it be known that he "foresaw" this great war, which is not at all remarkable since his every act indicates that he encouraged it by interfering with the foreign policies of the belligerents —supporting one and flouting the other—while at the same time weakening this nation's capacity to defend itself.

The President has made several offers of "mediation for peace." None of the belligerents, and particularly Germany and Italy, paid the slightest attention to these proffers; for the very good reason that the President by his many angry expressions of prejudice had disqualified himself of all capacity to honestly mediate the differences between the quarreling nations.

When the President "foresaw" our need for guns, tanks, airplanes, and bombers, and the probable necessity of calling on America's sons to fight and die in Europe, he asked Congress for a blank check and, getting it, allowed it to be spent on monkey-houses, fan-dancing, leaf raking, garden cities for job holders, free golf links, radical theaters, and other vote baits for loafers and ne'er-do-wells.

These are the facts as we consider Roosevelt's foreign policy and its danger to the American people.

"Cincinnatus," *War! War! War!* (1940?), pp. 134–144.

A Bumper Sticker (c.1944).

First man killed—Mike Murphy
First man to sink a Jap warship—Collin Kelly
First man to down five Jap planes—Eddie O'Hara
First man to get four new tires—Abie Cohen.

Quoted in Sigmund Livingston, *Must Men Hate?* (New York, 1944), p. 213.

The *"Jewish" Atom (1946).*

The first choice of pro-Russian liberal, Henry A. Wallace, for head of our Civilian Atomic Energy Control Commission was the Jew, David Lilienthal, and he so recommended to Mr. Truman; who very obligingly appointed Mr. Lilienthal together with two other Jews, and two non-Jews. Now isn't that just dandy? Especially since it was Jews, both in the U.S. and otherwise, who financed the Bolshevik Revolution in Russia, and whose first love is Russia. Former head of this Commission was the Jew, Bernard M. Baruch (close friend of the veto-man, Andrei Gromyko) whom Henry J. Klein, American-Jewish writer, says is the head of the Jewish Sanhedrin in America.

Here is the present line-up of this life-and-death commission, which is "vested" with extraordinary powers covering the entire range of atomic research, production application, and information:

David E. Lilienthal, (Jew) Chairman, who has been running Tennessee Valley Authority with a high hand: Lewis A. Strauss, (Jew), New York banker, member Army-Navy Munitions Board, who financed Lise Meitner, one of Jewish inventors of atom bomb; and partner in Kuhn Loeb & Co., Jewish International Bankers who helped finance Russian Revolution and who control (according to Mr. Chas. B. Hudson) about half of the U. S. A. railroads, our telegraph system, etc.: Robt. Fox Bacher (Jew) physicist and consultant of Bernard M. Baruch; New Deal non-Jews W. W. Wymack, editor of Des Moines, Ia. *Register;* and Sumner T. Pike, former member of Securities and Exchange Commission—which latter two form a minority.

A fine bunch, if you ask me: why not put all-Americans on guard, and particularly one or more able officers of our Navy and Armed Forces: they who by their brilliant strategy, courage, and patriotism fought for America and won? Answer: The Judeo-Reds objected to representatives of our Armed Forces on this life-and-death Commission. They prefer their own people, and innocents who know nothing about the subject.

Russia's German stooge-scientists in Germany are now turning out about 300 rocket planes per month (as fast or faster than anything we have): there is a city of 400,000 in Russia (well blocked off and top-drawer secret), probably somewhere in the vast stretches of Siberia-Asia, called Atomgrad, where atom bombs are being manufactured. In the meantime, Russia's Bolshevik leaders stall around in the U.N. until they have had time to manufacture a sufficient stockpile of these bombs to blot out American cities. Were you one of those simple folks who believed Stalin's utterance (just smoke in your eyes) on the subject of the bombs and peace, recently? When the Russians begin dropping atom bombs on your heads, just remember who is largely responsible: also remember that you were told about them in advance, and what did you do about it??? Beware of anyone who tells you there is no danger from Russia: they are betraying you.

The able columnist, Paul Mallon, has the Bolsheviks down pat: he knows their tricky double-dealing, and the virtue they make of perverting all facts and figures to suit their own purpose. (For them, figures do lie.) His column of 10-31-46 is headed: "U.S. Would Be Very Foolish to Match Russ Fund Cuts" for defense and armament. As he explains, their monetary system is different from ours: besides, they have two budgets (just as they have two political policies): one for home consumption and the other for the poor dumb foreigners. Actually, no expert could possibly figure out their system of bookkeeping: and the main purpose of their budget is to fool others, if not themselves. "A Russian budget is no more like a budget than Russian democracy is like American democracy." They also have three different values for their rubles (money): so there is no possible basis of comparison between what we mean by a budget and what they mean by one. Therefore, they can issue meaningless statements in their Government-controlled press, stating that they are cutting down their budgets for military expenditures (when they are actually doing no such thing), with the hope of getting us to follow suit, and we, no doubt, will fall for it.

Jews continually scream that they are being persecuted and abused: yet here on what is said to be the most important commission in the world, the Jews are three to two, in what is supposed to be a Christian non-Jew nation. This same sort of thing prevails throughout our government. The same thing is also true in Britain today. International Jews (plus the help of Kuhn-Loeb and other U. S. Jews) overthrew the Russian government, and control that country today, as well as many of the smaller nations of Europe. It was these same people who endeavored to take control of Germany and her economy: it is the Ashkenaz Russian-Jew who is endeavoring to take over Palestine. It is a Jew-Bolshevik, Dmitri Z. Manuilsky, who is head of United Nations Atomic Energy Commission, who is close friend of U. S. delegate Bernard M. Baruch. Louis F. Budenz says Manuilsky is real head of Communist International today.

When a certain racial minority holds this record for continual agitation; seizing of control of governments and a nation's economy; for violence and smear campaigns against native citizens: for warfare against Christians: for introducing such pro-Jewish legislation as HR Bill 6897; for tampering with U. S. mail, ad infinitum; it is not to be expected that they can forever escape retribution for their deeds. Especially when they freely admit in their literature that their first allegiance is always to the Jews as a nation, and not to the country of which they are residents; and their favored avocation is collecting huge sums of money for their own purposes, usually to be sent abroad. Has anyone ever heard of the Jews collecting millions of dollars for non-Jew, or strictly American projects?

In his unimportant little smear sheet, *Propaganda Battlefront,* L. M. Birkhead (whose organization and sheet is part of the Un-American Gestapo) says that I "fanatically berate the Jews." This is a lie: I do no such thing. I merely state facts and truth, which anyone can verify for themselves, from the record, who is not a Jew-Communist advocate like Birkhead; or who is not so emotionally and mentally biased and prejudiced as not to be able to see the truth. I favor no group of people in the United States who, as a whole, care so little for our ideals, institutions, and blessings, and who work so feverishly and continually for outside interests. I am heartily in favor of them having their own country (outside of the continental limits of the U.S.A.) and let them fight among themselves, as Dr. Paul Hutchinson (quoted herein) suggests they will do.

One grants that there are some noble, fearless, unselfish Jews (such as Henry H. Klein, author of *The Sanhedrin Produced World Destruction*) truly devoted to American interests, who warn their people against the danger to themselves in working against America's best interests: but too many of the Jews work hand-in-glove with Communism: inciting the Negroes against the Whites: fomenting trouble and strikes among the labor unions. They work for the Sanhedrin; for the Kehillah: for a foreign state: for their own selfish interests: for aid in smuggling 60,000 illegal refugees, mostly Russian-Communist-Jews, into this country every month: this in addition to the number already coming in under quota. This situation is appallingly serious, and threatens the jobs, security, rights, liberty, homes, and lives of every genuine American. Already we have reaped a vicious crop of paralyzing strikes, due largely to this foreign element in labor unions. Fortunately, some of the unions are beginning to wake up, and rid themselves of this menace.

Over a year after war's end, our whole life is shot through with Sovietized regimentation: our money buys less and less of what there is to buy: it is a struggle for the average person to exist. Who shall say that the International Moneychanger is not responsible? And at the same time there are more able-bodied folks doing nothing and living like parasites on doles—which means off the rest of us. A foreign ideology has sapped our enterprise, our free spirit, our self-respect and self-reliance. As Mr. Henry J. Taylor so aptly says: We have become a nation of "pants-pressers."

Instead of coming here where they are not wanted, or going to Palestine where they also are not wanted, why do not all the European Jews go to Russia, which country they love so well? Which country they control and for which they are always working in this country? There is infinitely more room in huge Russia: there are incalculably rich natural resources (which might require hard work to develop): besides that, there already is a well-established homeland for Jews, called Birobidjan, in Russia, for which Jews in America collect money.

There is much talk of the *Protocols of the Elders of Zion* being a forgery. Is this why the powerful Jewish B'nai B'rith, Anti-Defamation League, Civil Liberties League, and innumerable other hundreds of organizations and publications spend millions to try to prove it is a forgery? The only adequate answer is that the Jews' actions are themselves the best possible proof of the authenticity of the *Protocols:* they live up (or down) to them in every particular. Anyone who is an open-minded observer and student—not merely swayed by his emotions and all the sentimental gush gotten out by the Jews themselves re the "poor persecuted Jew" can readily ascertain the truth. But we Americans love to be deceived by our emotions. Is it because of their tolerance and firm belief in their own innocence that Jew-Communists rob the mails of my booklets, particularly the two titles: *The Jewish Protocols and Their Application to Present Times,* and *My Country, Right or Wrong, My Country;* the latter containing discussion of Pro-Jew Bill 6897?

The people's safety and security is fast disappearing in the United States! If we keep on importing more revolutionists from Europe and Asia, and placing our welfare and security at home in the hands of these people, the honest, decent, native Christian American will have no rights in his own country. If you think this is just propaganda, you had better wake up and get hep to what is going on in America, not abroad. Write your Congressmen and Senators against importing any more foreigners until we have made this country

safe for Americans: also write them objecting to the personnel of the Atomic Energy Commission.

M. R. Allen, *Judaic-Communism Versus
Christian Americanism: A Pro-Ameri-
can Publication* (Salt Lake City, 1946),
pp. 42–45.

The Indictment (1935).

We the American people, sworn to uphold the Constitution of the United States and all that it stands for, as the sons
of the patiots of 1776, desiring to preserve the nation founded
by George Washington and Thomas Jefferson and per-
petuated by their successors, hereby present the indictment
against the members of a race known as the Jews who have
consistently and persistently opposed the doctrines of which
American life subsists.

That they have failed to discard their alliances with members of their race in foreign lands.

That they are considered by Americans, and other peoples
likewise, to be a distinct people and not a religious sect.

That they are an international people having never
pledged their allegiance to any one nation, which is based on
their history that reveals their nomadic tendencies.

That their internationalism is extirpating the roots of
Americanism, which will result in the destruction of those
abstract and undefinable principles which are so vital to the
existence of Democracy.

That their international interests have undeniably caused
much of the unrest and ill-feeling that prevails throughout
the world.

That a number of their race in America, in conspiracy with
others of the same race in foreign lands, precipitated the
World War and therefore, resulting in an excessive financial
burden for the United States, causing untold hardships and
sufferings for the American people.

That their control of international finance is leading the
peoples of the world to certain suicide.

That their race is planning the next holocaust for the purpose of subjecting the Gentile governments of the world to their dominance.

That their international financiers have literally mortgaged the United States to their foreign co-conspirators.

That they were instrumental in bringing excessive taxation upon the American people, to pay for the killing of Gentile soldiers, which is estimated to be about $25,000 per head in the last war, to make the world safe for the Jewish bankers.

That their national bankers have cornered the money market, while our real wealth is over-abundant, causing unnecessary privation and suffering.

That their international bankers are backing the tyrannical rule of a Communist-Jewish minority in Russia.

That their financial princes supplied the money for the Communist usurpation of authority and law in Germany and Hungary, and are behind the Socialist Goverment of Mexico.

That they are preparing to foment another war with Germany to execute the salvation of the Jewish money-changers and political racketeers who have been driven out of Germany by Adolf Hitler.

That their finance mongers have provoked the reign of terror and anarchy in China by their exploitation of the Chinese, with the hope of subjecting the yellow peoples to their financial rule.

That they have given the world the most dreaded of social diseases—Communism, and are the foremost carriers of its germs.

That they have installed themselves as the rulers of the Gentile majority in Russia, and are determined to undermine and destroy every other government opposed to Bolshevism.

That the Jews resident in America have disregarded the international courtesies of nations, by interfering with the domestic affairs of other nations.

That the Jews in America have refused to be assimilated with other peoples in our country.

That the Jews in America have overstepped their proportionate representation in the Government of the United States.

That they have used their offices of public trust to further the interests of their own race.

That by refusing to be assimilated, they have created a State of their own within the United States.

That they have lent assistance and given shelter to most subversive movements in the country.

That they have opposed the Christian basis upon which our executive, legislative, and judicial departments are founded.

That they violate and disdain the Sunday tradition of the American people, by engaging in their business pursuits on the Lord's day.

That they have introduced doctrines into our institutions of learning which are inimical to Americanism and Christianity.

That members of their race, like Bernard M. Baruch, have intentionally mislead the chief executive of the United States Government in the performance of his duties for the purpose of advancing their own interests, to the detriment of the people.

That they have given carriage to atheism which is affiliated with Communism.

That they have been an important factor in the development of the white slave traffic in the United States.

That they have employed their influence in their monopoly of the moving picture industry, to tear down the moral casting of the American people.

That their representation in the professions in certain sections of the country have brought about a laxity in the voluntary enforcement of ethical laws, and have lowered the public's esteem and confidence in them.

That they have given to America and the world a new "liberalism," which is destroying the peaceful homes of America by encouraging an irreligious and unsocial attitude.

That they have tried to "liberalize" the immigration laws to permit more of their race to enter the United States and to deprive the already prostrate Gentile workingman of his meagre earnings.

That their un-Christian methods of business has destroyed the background of the small industries in the country.

That they have disfranchised the Gentiles in many instances in certain sections of the country, by gaining a monopoly on the political offices and hence denying the Gentile people of representation.

That they have aided radical agitators in aggravating the sore spots of labor disputes and are well represented in the strike-breaking field which adds to the general unrest of the country.

That they are a non-laboring class and prefer to live on the profits which they extract from the exploited farmer and laborer.

That they are the spearhead of attack of the Bolshevists upon the government and its institutions.

That the wealth of the nation is concentrated in the hands of the Jews.

That they object to any moral restrictions being incorporated within the law.

That the oath of the land, a Christian institution, is not tenable in the eyes of the Jewish people.

That they are opposed to military training as a measure of self-defense, and wage a constant battle against the increasing of the personnel of the military forces to meet the dangers of the present time.

That they do not distinguish themselves in the military affairs of the nation, and as a whole do not voluntarily subscribe themselves to the military forces in times of national emergency.

That the Jews adore the golden calf which satisfies the wants of their bodies.

Judaism is the antithesis of Americanism, both cannot survive in the same nation, if Americanism is to remain with us, the Jewish Problem must be solved.

Franklin Thompson, *America's Ju-Deal* (New York, 1935), pp. 195–200.

6. Selections from Contemporary Respondents' Replies

From the early 1940s on, a number of important studies of American anti-Semitism, utilizing survey research techniques, have been conducted; the most notable of these is the volume by Adorno and associates, entitled *The Authoritarian Personality*. The selections from respondents' replies, taken more or less at random from some of these studies, vividly portray the dimensions of anti-Semitism during the past three decades. They suggest that virtually the entire range of anti-Semitic attitudes, which we have documented in the preceeding chapters of this book, continue to be held by Americans today.

From The Authoritarian Personality *(1950)*.

"I think there is something that makes them all stick together and try to hold on to everything. I have Jewish friends and I have tried not to treat them antagonistically, but sooner or later they have also turned out to be aggressive and obnoxious. . . . I think the percentage of very bad Jews is very much greater than the percentage of bad Gentiles. . . . My husband feels exactly the same way on this whole problem. As a matter of fact, I don't go as far as he does. He didn't like many things about Hitler, but he did feel that Hitler did a good job on the Jews. He feels that we will come in this country to a place where we have to do something about it." (p. 614)

"I know very little, but I would be afraid to go into a synagogue. . . . I am not particularly sorry because of what the Germans did to the Jews. I feel Jews would do the same type of thing to me." (p. 615)

"I don't like Jews. The Jew is always crying. They are taking our country over from us. They are aggressive. They suffer from every lust. Last summer I met the famous musician *X*, and before I really knew him he wanted me to sign an affidavit to help bring his family into this country. Finally I had to flatly refuse and told him I want no more Jews here. Roosevelt started bringing the Jews into the government, and that is the chief cause of our difficulties today. The Jews arranged it so that they were discriminated for in the draft, I favor a legislative discrimination against the Jews along American, not Hitler lines. Everybody knows that the Jews are back of the Communists." (p. 615)

"Now this is where I really do have strong feeling. I am not very proud of it. I don't think it is good to be so prejudiced but I can't help it. [What do you dislike about Jews?] Everything. I can't say one good thing for them. [Are there any exceptions?] No, I have never met one single one that was an exception. I used to hope I would. It isn't pleasant to feel the way I do. I would be just as nice and civil as I could, but it would end the same way. They cheat, take advantage. [Is it possible that you know some Jewish people and like them without knowing they are Jews?] Oh no. I don't think any Jew can hide it. I always know them. [How do they look?] Attractive. Very well dressed. And as though they knew exactly what they wanted. [How well have you known Jews?] Well, I never knew any in childhood. In fact, I never knew one until we moved to San Francisco, ten years ago. He was our landlord. It was terrible. I had a lovely home in Denver and I hated to leave. And here I was stuck in an ugly apartment and he did everything to make it worse. If the rent was due on Sunday, he was there bright and early. After that I knew lots of them. I had Jewish bosses. There are Jews in the bank. They are everywhere—always in the money. My next-door neighbor is a Jew. I decided to be civil. After all, I can't move now and I might as well be neighborly. They borrow our lawn mower. They *say* it is because you can't buy one during the war. But of course lawn mowers cost money. . . ." (p. 621)

"I have an age-old feeling against Jews, some against Negroes. Jews stick together, are out for money: they gyp you. Jews are in big businesses. It seems they will be running the country before long. I know some people of Jewish descent who are very nice, but they're not full-blooded Jews. Jews have large noses, are slight in stature, little sly Jews. The women have dark hair, dark eyes, are sort of loud." (p. 265)

"I would like Jews as long as they don't reflect typical Jewish qualities. Typical Jewish nose, mouth, voice. The presence of a Jew creates feelings of tension. Squeaky voice, long, pointed nose." (pp. 625–626)

"I don't think there should be a Jewish problem. People should not be discriminated against, but judged on their individual merits. I don't like it to be called a problem. Certainly, I'm against prejudice. Jews are aggressive, bad-mannered, clannish, intellectual, clean, overcrowd neighborhoods, noisy, and oversexed. I will admit that my opinion is not based on much contact however. I hear these things all the time. There are a very few Jewish students in my school, and

I have already referred to my good contact with the one girl." (p. 629)

"I never understood why Hitler was so brutal toward them. There must have been some reason for it, something to provoke it. Some say he had to show his authority. But I doubt it. I suspect the Jews contributed a great deal to it." (p. 630)

"I don't blame the Nazis at all for what they did to the Jews. That sounds terrible, I know, but if the Jews acted the way they do here, I don't blame them. I've never had any bad personal experiences with Jews, it's just the way they act. Don't help your fellow man; that's their creed." (p. 632)

"They should be treated, I suppose, like individuals; but after all, they are all alike. . . . I think what Hitler did to the Jews was all right. When I was having trouble with a competing contractor, I often thought, I wish Hitler would come here. No, I don't favor discrimination by legislation. I think the time will come when we will have to kill the bastards." (p. 637)

"They get a soft life and they take over. You can't deal with one, and a lot of them are awful dirty, though they have money." (p. 460)

"I do not like their coercive aggression in business. They are not only aggressive, but they should also be segregated. They are always pushing people aside. I noticed nearly every time when there was pushing in the innumerable lines we had to wait in during the war, it was a Jew who started pushing. I feel a real revulsion towards Jews." (p. 641)

"The Jewish kids I knew in high school were the sons and daughters of the prominent Jewish businessmen, and they were very clannish. It's hard to say what ought to be done about it. It doesn't seem to bother them what people think. That is a natural characteristic. . . . Some are very crafty about sticking together and getting ahead in business, getting capital. . . . Some [Jewish women] are very attractive, and some are very clannish. They are dominated by the men; it's all in their creed." (p. 643)

"The worst experience with them I had was when I was overseas operator in Hawaii a couple of years ago. I had to monitor all the calls that went to New York so I listened to just thousands of conversations. And ninety per cent of them were rich Jews calling up their families. That is the only really good thing I can say for them—their devotion to their families. But all purely selfish. The money they spent—and the time—on just purely selfish calls. [Business calls?] Well I worked mostly at night. But the other girls said it was the same people making business calls during the day. [How did you know they were Jews?] Their voices and the things they said. Selfish. [Could there have been Jews you didn't recognize?] I don't think so. You get so you always know a Jewish voice." (p. 643)

T. W. Adorno *et al.*, *The Authoritarian Personality* (New York, 1950).

From **Dynamics of Prejudice** *(1950).*

". . . the Hebes [get all the breaks]. I think Hitler did a good thing. They're born that way, they can make a dollar where a white person starves. Where they come in, the niggers follow and knock the property down. They're awfully clannish for another thing. Take the Irish, they don't trust each other. The Jews patronize each other." (p. 121)

"They usually go into business for themselves. They have money and stick together. I've known only two that ever worked in a factory. The Gentiles will stick to a job, while if a Jew gets $500 he'll quit and open a store. . . . The Jews in the army did right well for themselves. They were treated all right. Our first sergeant was Jewish. He didn't qualify for it, he got it through drag. . . . Personally, I would send them all back to Jerusalem. They're not a creative race, they're always counting their money. It was the Germans, Irish, and the

Italians and the Russians that built up this country. These races aren't too proud to work. The Jews control the money and stick together." (p. 124)

"We didn't see many of them in the front lines. Those that were there had all the privileges anyone else did. I don't believe they were mistreated. Most of them were in the Medical Corps and base sections . . . a Jew tries to use his brain to get him out of things and is sly. . . . They got hold of all the financial ends in this country. I don't dislike them, but I don't like them, because a Jew has no scruples when he's out to get ahead. It's at his best friend's expense that he'll get ahead. I don't care to deal with Jews, but nowadays you can't help it because they're in every business field." (p. 126)

"If there was a Jewish officer in the outfit he'd have a Jewish fellow with him; if there was any easy work to be done, he'd get a Jewish fellow to do it. I don't know what there is in it, but they always think they're superior. There was one Jewish fellow in our outfit whom I liked especially. He wasn't like the ordinary run of Jews, that's why I remember him." (p. 137)

"They shirk their duty, they're not combat men. Some will fight, I'll give them that credit, but most of them are out for themselves. If he has a chance to save himself, he'll save himself. A Jew will never give you nothing for nothing either." (p. 139)

"The Jewish [*sic*] are cliquish. I heard that they have a lodge that will appropriate money for one of its members to start a business and then he repays it. If we're all created equal, it looks like the Jewish are in the driver's seat. . . ." (p. 140)

"They're pretty shrewd operators, I guess. Maybe I'm prejudiced against them. The one that screwed me up was a guy from California who said he had more reason than anybody to go back because he had a business to take care of. No family or anything else. He was a smart fellow, had a college education. He had a lot of money and would loan it to the guys and charge them interest. Any other guy would just hand it out and if he forgot to pay it back, O.K., you never asked him for it. Money is their God. This one got more passes than anyone else. Of course he was in the orderly room so he just wrote one for himself whenever he wanted one. He had a brand-new Buick up at camp and drove it all around. He managed to get out before it was over. He went to the hospital every day; said it was his nerves. Probably was worrying about his business." (p. 141)

"Everybody blames the Jews. In a way that's right because they have everything. They control everything. They're in the right places—in the offices, in politics. They're the ones running things. They always manage to get in at the top of everything. Like the Jews in the army. There was just three Jewish boys in our company anyway. Then at the point of embarkation, just when we were ready to ship out, what did they do but yank them two off the ship. So those two Jews got left behind—no reasons given, they weren't sick or anything. That's the way it is with them all the time." (p. 142)

"They control all the liquor—that's one I know about. Just take a look around at the liquor stores, see one on this corner run by a Dago and he ain't got nothing, neither has the Irish or whatever else he may be—but look at the one that's got plenty and you'll see it's a Jewish place. They control it all. If you name is Goldberg, you get all you want—otherwise you don't get nothing . . . 95 per cent of the liquor companies they still keep the same names, but the Jews got them now. It's the same in all business; but the liquor business is the one I know about." (p. 142)

"They have power all over the world—in all the industries. Everything is Jewish. Marshall Field and all the big stores in Chicago are Jewish." (p. 142)

"I have a lot of trouble with Jews, too. They're hard to deal with. They're too tight. Every time you go up to deliver something to them you have to have a fight with them first before you can collect your money." (p. 143)

"The Jews always seem to have a name for going some-where, they're go-getters. I don't know how, but they get there. In a lot of cases, the Jews use a lot of underhanded methods. They're always blamed for it, then I feel sorry for that. The Jews don't get along with anybody but themselves. Well, the way they have of getting places irks me most. I wouldn't care to have them use underhanded ways to push me out. As individuals they have a right to take a job." (p. 230)

"There should be no discrimination just because a man is a Jew. He's a member of the white race. He's of the Semitic branch and we're the Caucasians. But I don't want any busi-ness dealings with a Jew. He has an inherent something in him that will always cause him to win, but I have no preju-dice because of that. Much of the problem is due to the individual Jew. The cultured, refined Jew doesn't see what the kike is doing for his race. The kikes do a great deal of harm. They're overdressed, noisy, and loud." (p. 231)

"As for the Jews, run them out of business because they already control most of the business in the United States. Or make them work as anybody else. In the army there were no Jews in our outfit, but when we were inducted, I know the Jews angled around and got out of it. When they were in, they always got the best jobs. Send the Jews back where they came from because they don't get along over here. All the people are against them because of how they do business and control most business." (p. 236)

"They don't work or fight. I'd always give preference to a non-Jew. In the army the Jews weren't treated very nice. There was always a grudge, the Jews against the Gentiles. There was a grudge against the Jew because of his being intelligent and getting ahead faster. The Jews always held down good jobs and good ratings, and the boys disliked them for that. They made good clerks. As field soldiers, no. They don't fall into the routine, they were bad combat soldiers because they'd never stick. To their face we seemed to get along with them, but behind their backs we raised cain.

There are too many of the Jews around here now. They should never have allowed so many in here. Their population is too great. You can't chase them out—then we'd be another Hitler. We should close immigration to them. They're producing so fast that we'll have trouble with them here, a great deal. There's no place to send them. They're not even wanted in Palestine." (p. 238)

"I'd object against a Jew moving next door. They raise too much stink and too much commotion. The low Jews are filthy, and the higher class always think you're doing wrong. Those who own stores on Milwaukee Avenue are filthy, and you should see the alleys behind the stores—they're terrible. I wouldn't want to work with a Jew because he wouldn't want to do the manual labor. He wouldn't share in the work. I just can't get along with them. I can't get accustomed to the way they do things—they always want to take advantage." (p. 238)

"They should run all the Jews out of this country. On jobs, Gentiles should always get preference. Well, most of the Jewish people have all the factories, so the white people are working for them. You don't see Jews working. Another thing, how about this Jewish boat that came across—what was it?—with fifty thousand of them. Why are they bringing them in here? They just persecute us Gentiles." (p. 243)

"[Jews in the army] were treated like kings. They got away with more stuff than we did. They were poor soldiers. They haven't got the fighting ability. The best thing would be to get rid of them, export them. Well, if they'd move all the Jews out, I've reasoned it out—if they moved them all out, there'd be no more wars." (p. 243)

"I'm not against talking to niggers and Jews—I have several times—I talk to them at work and joke with them, but as for living next door to them or going around with them, I can't see that." (p. 299)

"The Jews always seem to get to the top; and that's because they stick together and help one another." (p. 299)

"The way to solve the Jewish problem is to get a Hitler over here, and then forget about the whole business once and for all." (p. 299)

Bruno Bettelheim and Morris Janowitz, *Dynamics of Prejudice* (New York, 1950).

From a Study in Employment Discrimination (1968).

QUESTION: Could you tell me any ways you feel Jewish people differ from non-Jewish people?

A: Generally they are more pushy.

Q: How do you mean "pushy"?

A: They will get right in front of you if you are standing in line in a cafeteria for instance. They are born with a desire to "get theirs"—this is real true of the New York Jews. The smart, clever Jew has more respect for his fellowman than other people. Braggadocio. The fast-buck guy, a little slippery—watch them. The smart Jew develops this complete faith and trust.

A: They are more aggressive.

Q: How do you mean "aggressive"?

A: They are harder to insult. They tend to go for the bundle —all or nothing at all. Are pushers. They are very intelligent. Much more willing to take a risk. They like to connive more than Gentiles.

Q: How do you mean?

A: A Gentile will tend to be a little more honest. A Jew, to make a sale, may tend to leave out a few statements or make statements that are not true.

A: Prouder.

Q: What do you mean by "prouder"?

A: Don't care for criticism. Resist criticism about their own work. Tend to want to work on their own. Tend to resist change. Rather high in creativity and overall intelligence. Cooperation is not as good as it should be—as good as with others.

A: I don't know very many Jewish people, but one who worked for me was a demanding person—not a polite type of person.

Q: Do you think this is true of them in general?

A: From what I hear, yes. When we took trips out of town he always seemed to spend more money than most people on expense reports. He wanted to put on an air of a big-shot—spend more money on customers than he had to. Another talked down to people when he realized they couldn't follow him, and he made sure they didn't follow him.

Q: You are talking about only two men. Do you think these would apply to Jewish people in general?

A: Probably generally true from what I have heard.

"To get their objectives some other people may suffer and this doesn't seem a big concern with them."

"More forward to the point of being overbearing."

"Due to the fact that they are Jewish they have a self-centered personality. They feel they are on display and have to make a showing. They have to do better than average to stand out."

"Generally they are more aggressive. They force themselves into situations that non-Jewish people would be reluctant to do."

"They have a high regard for external appearances. They show a greater tendency than other groups to maintain certain devices or ways of showing themselves off."

"I have high respect and regard for Jewish people as a race. I believe that some of their objectionable traits are less palatable in society than they are in business."

"Ethically they do not worry too much when it tends to make a buck. In a business-type position this could be a short-time advantage."

Q: Could you tell me any ways you feel Jewish people differ from non-Jewish people?
A: Obnoxious attitude of the large group.
Q: What do you mean?
A: Boisterous, egotistical comes to my mind's eye when I see Miami-Brooklyn Jew. General appearance, physical.
Q: What do you mean?
A: Skin color, nose and dress.
Q: What do you mean by "dress"?
A: Flashy-gaudy. . . . I have two feelings. What I call the Miami or Brooklyn group bother me. They are very disturbing to me. Another group you'd never recognize any difference in them in any way.

R. P. Quinn *et al.*, *The Chosen Few: A Study of Discrimination in Executive Selection* (Ann Arbor, Michigan, 1968), pp. 19–36.

From Christian Beliefs and Anti-Semitism (1966).

"This questionnaire is apparently for the use of finding out if I am prejudiced against Negroes or Jews *which I can say I am not.* I feel that they should have a place in the community if they earn the right. So far the Negroes are uneducated and unclean and haven't earned their place in the average community. The Jews are neither and they fit in most places, *but they are underhanded and sneaky.*" (p. 105)

"Some of my replies in connection with races and faiths, other than my own, might seem prejudiced to some. But during my forty years of business life I have had a very good opportunity to observe the characteristics of the Negro and the Jew. Granted that some are much better men and women than I am. However, in my opinion, by far more than the majority of them retain the distinctive traits attributed to their race and/or faith. . . . Jews as a rule try almost every devious trick in the book to alleviate themselves from the fulfillment of their just obligations." (p. 106)

C. Y. Glock and R. Stark, *Christian Beliefs and Anti-Semitism* (New York, 1966).

7. Anti-Semitism Today

In the second half of the 1960s anti-Semitism once again became a prominent issue in the public life of America. That this should have happened is in many ways baffling. Jews were by now enjoying unprecedented acceptance in American society. Ethnic differences, which had before been feared, now became fashionable; the Jewish identity, in particular, had come to exercise widespread appeal among non-Jews. In literature, in the theater and cinema, and in academic life, Jews, as Jews, were encountering receptive audiences where before there had been at best indifference.

In business and commerce Jews were making impressive gains, despite lingering instances of discrimination. Jews were also to be found in large numbers in prominent political positions. All in all, then, Jews were partaking of the wealth and bounty of American life as fancied in the American dream. So much progress in overcoming hostility had, indeed, been made that assimilation and intermarriage, rather than anti-Semitism, appeared to be the greatest dangers confronting American Jewry. Unquestionably, it was good to be a Jew in America.

Within a very short period of time, from about 1967 on, this halcyon state of affairs seemed to have vanished. Jewish life was suddenly considered to be beset by grave danger; everywhere, the most ominous signs were becoming evident. Alarming as it was, this situation was also baffling. The anti-Semitic menace to which attention was being called was not erupting from the right, or from the churches, or from other traditional breeding grounds of Jew hatred. Rather, it was coming from the groups which had previously been seen as the natural allies of the Jews—namely the radical left and the blacks: groups working for social justice, for brotherhood, equality, and peace. That *they* should have turned their fury on to the Jews seemed to make no sense whatsoever. It also seemed like a cruel irony.

But no matter how absurd or ironic, the public was being told, facts are facts and cannot be denied. The anti-Semitic nuances of the catalog of the Metropolitan Museum's "Harlem on My Mind" exhibition; the reaction to the New York City teachers' strike; the famous poem read on Julius Lester's program on WBAI; the incessant denunciations of Israeli "aggression" in the Middle East by the Black Panthers, SNCC, and the New Left groups, and their openly declared sympathy for the Arab guerrilla movement; the assault on "Jewish control" of public hospitals, and on Jewish landlords and shopkeepers in the large metropolises—are not these all facts which point to the existence of sustained and purposeful anti-Semitism in the militant communities of America today?

I think not; and it is for this reason that I have chosen to discuss the *contexts* of anti-Semitism in America today at the conclusion of this book, rather than presenting the kind of documentation contained in the preceding chapters. If one can lie with statistics one can also lie with quotations—or at least greatly distort the reality which they represent. And it is precisely this that I believe has happened in the past few years.

This is not to suggest that there is no anti-Semitism among blacks (whether militantly radical or not) or among the members of the radical left. The notorious poem read on the Julius Lester show, "dedicated" to Albert Shanker, which declared in part,

> Hey, Jew Boy, with that yarmulka on your head
> You pale-faced Jew Boy—I wish you were dead

is, by any standards, anti-Semitic.

However, to point to such manifestations of anti-Semitism is one thing. To suggest that they are in any way typical of the groups to whom they are attributed is quite another matter. A black anti-Semite does not make all blacks anti-Semitic. Indeed, the few studies which have been made of black attitudes have indicated that blacks are *less* anti-Semitic than white Gentiles *and* that blacks tend to entertain significantly more favorable attitudes toward Jews than they do toward white Gentiles.[1] Surely, such data should make one wonder at the motives of those so-called "defense" agencies which, in the name of American Jewry, seek vociferously to call attention to black anti-Semitism. Presumably the fact that these agencies—notably the American Jewish Committee and the Anti-Defamation League—are bastions of white, middle-class American values, rather than of Jewish values, provides at least some of the explanation of this fact. . . .

Incidentally, it is not entirely inappropriate to note at this point that these so-called defense agencies do not conduct studies of *Jewish* attitudes toward, for example, the blacks. But a reference to one study that I have come across indicates that in quantitative terms Jews tend to be as anti-black as blacks tend to be anti-Jewish.[2] This does not justify either bigotry, of course; but it is clearly a situation in which, if the metaphor be pardoned, the pot is calling the kettle black.

However misguided it may be (for too often opponents of others' power are merely seeking power for themselves), much radical support for the Palestinian guerrillas against the Israeli government is nothing more than the product of identification with a revolutionary life-style and, particularly in the case of the blacks, of identification with nonwhite victims of Western-sponsored aggression. But the connection goes deeper than that, too. Radicals noting Israel's endorsement of the American position in Vietnam cannot help but feel a strong antipathy toward that country. Only a demagogue could accuse them of being anti-Semitic as a result. In fact they are no more anti-Semitic than others who support both American aggression against Vietnam *and* the Israeli position in the Middle East—I am thinking of such fervent anti-Communists as Senator Goldwater of Arizona and Senator Jackson of Washington—are philo-Semitic.

Criticism of the Israeli position in the Middle East is of course not always warranted: Israel's critics, no less than Israel's supporters, are frequently the victims of their own rhetoric. But such criticism must be *shown* to be anti-Semitic rather than merely glibly accepted as such. Of course, it is convenient for Zionists to cloud the issue by accusing their detractors of anti-Semitism—Israel is the Jewish state, so the argument goes: and anyone who is against the Jewish state is against the Jews. But others' convenience should not be allowed to define our truths.

All this, I emphasize, is not to deny the existence of anti-Semitism in the radical movement. I only question whether anti-Semitism is anywhere as pervasive and intense as is frequently suggested. Indeed, it is difficult to escape the conclusion that certain Jewish interests are themselves the purveyors of militant anti-Semitism. During the Ocean Hill-Brownsville dispute in New York a few copies of an anti-Semitic flier were distributed in the mailboxes of union teachers. The United Federation of Teachers then printed "hundreds of thousands of copies"[3] of this document and circulated them far and wide. Commenting on this and similar practices, the New York Civil Liberties Union observed that "The UFT leadership, and in particular Albert Shanker, systematically accused the Ocean Hill-Brownsville Board and Rhody McCoy of anti-Semitism and extremism, and then 'proved' those accusations only with half truths, innuendos, and outright lies."[4]

Again, the *facts* should be seen clearly. People *who happen to be Jews* are attacked by parties against whom they have offended. The former then find it convenient to defend themselves by accusing their opponents of anti-Semitism. But life is really much less simple than this; and the strategy is too transparent to require further comment. Nor should we overlook another consideration. The multimillion-dollar business of "defending" Jews against anti-Semitism requires that there be anti-Semitism against which to defend them. Harmonious times do not make for good Anti-Defamation League fund-raising drives (not to mention recruitment to the ranks of the Jewish Defense League). And so, from time to time, anti-Semitism is invented by these organizations to justify their continued existence, as, for example, with the ADL's outcry of anti-Semitism against groups seeking community control of ghetto hospitals, which Nat Hentoff so effectively exposed in a series in *The Village Voice*. In thus fabricating threats the Jewish "defense" organizations are no different from other "defense" organizations of whose antics we hear from time to time: the Pentagon, for example, or the FBI.

Anti-Semitism has frequently nourished itself on a paranoic delusion that the world was controlled by, and that its numerous upheavals were caused by, a secret and massively powerful Jewish conspiracy. This fact should not lead us to assume that attacks on Jewish institutions in our own day are necessarily fostered by the same paranoia and prompted by the same anti-Semitic antipathy. Where Jews lack power but are condemned for possessing and misusing it, we may reasonably talk of anti-Semitism. Where the Jews possess power, on the other hand, the accusation that they are misusing it may be perfectly warranted—indeed, in view of the nature of power as such *is likely to be warranted*—and the charge of anti-Semitism must be demonstrated rather than merely asserted.

The possession by Jews of power in these senses is a modern phenomenon which goes back at the most half a century, and the growth of which has received its most striking impetus in the past quarter of a century or so. Zionism and the *embourgeoisification* of what had hitherto been a poor and powerless people are, after all, the distinctive marks of contemporary Jewish history. Jewish power, then, is not an illusion fostered by paranoics but a fact.

Power—which has been regarded with great suspicion in many streams of normative Jewish thought across the ages[5] —is that which makes it possible for its possessor to secure outcomes which he desires in face of opposition to them. It is, in other words, in the very nature of power that it engenders opposition and, under most circumstances, it is morally desirable that it should do so.

Where Jews possess power, then, it is inevitable and morally desirable that such possession should not exempt them from critical judgment. And each of us, likewise, must make the crucial distinction between such moral judgment—a judgment to be made equally upon all human beings—and the authentic anti-Semitism documented in this book.

Notes

Introduction

1. See Chapter 2.
2. See Chapter 3.
3. See Chapter 4.
4. See Chapter 5.
5. Charles Stember *et al.*, *Jews in the Mind of America* (New York, 1966), pp. 208ff.
6. Heywood Broun and George Britt, *Christians Only: A Study in Prejudice* (New York, 1931); Carey McWilliams, *A Mask for Privilege: Anti-Semitism in America* (Boston, 1948), *passim.*
7. American Jewish Committee, *Jews in College and University Administration* (New York, 1966).

8. E. Digby Baltzell, *The Protestant Establishment: Aristocracy and Caste in America* (New York, 1964), p. 211.
9. See Chapter 1.
10. Charles Glock and Rodney Stark, *Christian Beliefs and Anti-Semitism* (New York, 1966), p. 110.
11. *Ibid.*
12. *Ibid.*
13. Glock and Stark, *Christian Beliefs*, p. 128.
14. Stember, *Jews in the Mind of America*, p. 128.
15. Ann Wolfe, *Why the Swastika? A Study of Young American Vandals* (New York, 1962); David Capolwitz and Candace Rogers, *Swastika 1960: The Epidemic of Anti-Semitic Vandalism in America* (New York, 1960); Joseph Kampf, *The Bigots Behind the Swastika Spree* (New York, 1960).
16. This is quite literally the case, as Gentiles who grew up in small Midwestern towns without ever having seen a Jew have told me.
17. Ernst Simmel, ed., *Anti-Semitism: A Social Disease* (New York, 1946).
18. Cf., Maimonides' *Iggeret Teman, passim*, for an authoritative Jewish view of anti-Semitism.
19. I have discussed anti-Semitism, and the Jewish response to it, more fully in the introduction to *Zionism Reconsidered* (New York, 1970) and *The Wineskin and the Wizard: The Problem of Jewish Power in the Context of East European Jewish History* (New York, 1970), *passim.*

Chapter 1

1. Samuel Oppenheim, "The Early History of the Jews in New York, 1654–1664," *Publications of the American Jewish Historical Society*, XVIII (1909).
2. Cf. Charles C. Jones, Jr., *History of Savannah, Ga.* (Syracuse, 1890), pp. 50ff.
3. John Higham, "American Anti-Semitism Historically Reconsidered," in Charles Stember *et al., Jews in the Mind of America* (New York, 1966), p. 244.
4. L. J. Levinger, *A History of the Jews in the United States* (New York, 1954), pp. 72ff; Morris Jastrow, "References to the Jews in

the Diary of Ezra Stiles," *Publications of the American Jewish Historical Society,* X (1902).

Chapter 2

1. The best account of Jewish immigration to the United States is Moses Rischin, *The Promised City: New York's Jews, 1870–1914* (Cambridge, Massachusetts, 1962). Cf. also Mark Wischnitzer, *To Dwell in Safety: The Story of the Jewish Migration Since 1800* (Philadelphia, 1948).
2. Morris U. Schappes, *A Documentary History of the Jews in the United States* (New York, 1950), p. 511, gives an extensive list of references relating to this episode; cf. also Rudolf Glanz, "German Jews in New York City in the Nineteenth Century," *YIVO Annual of Jewish Social Science,* XI (1956), p. 32.
3. Cf. B. W. Korn, *American Jewry and the Civil War* (New York, 1964), pp. 121–188.
4. Abraham Steinberg, "Jewish Characters in Fugitive American Novels of the Nineteenth Century," *YIVO Annual of Jewish Social Science,* XI (1956).

Chapter 3

1. See the discussion of this period in E. Digby Baltzell, *The Protestant Establishment: Aristocracy and Caste in America* (New York, 1964); Oscar Handlin, "American Views of the Jews at the Opening of the Twentieth Century," *Publications of the American Jewish Historical Society,* XL (1951); John Higham, "Anti-Semitism in the Gilded Age: A Reinterpretation," *Mississippi Valley Historical Review,* XLIII (1957).
2. Bingham's retraction is in *North American Review,* CLXXXVIII, October 1908. Cf. Arthur Gorenstein, "The Commissioner and the Community," *YIVO Annual of Jewish Social Science,* XIII (1965).
3. Cf. Baltzell, *The Protestant Establishment,* pp. 90ff.
4. *The Jewish Times* (New York), October 25, 1872.
5. "Club Candidates," *Evening Post* (New York), April 17, 1893.
6. Baltzell, *The Protestant Establishment,* p. 105.

7. E. A. Ross, *The Old World in the New* (New York, 1914).
8. *Ibid.*, p. 288.
9. *Ibid.*, p. 293.
10. *Ibid.*, p. 304.
11. *Ibid.*, p. 290.
12. On Grant, cf. Baltzell, *The Protestant Establishment, passim.*
13. Richard B. Hovey, *John Jay Chapman, An American Mind* (New York, 1959), p. 285.

Chapter 4

1. A classic study of this period is John Higham, *Strangers in the Land: Patterns of American Nativism, 1860–1925* (New Brunswick, New Jersey, 1955).
2. Cf. Richard B. Hovey, *John Jay Chapman, An American Mind* (New York, 1959).
3. The authoritative work on the *Protocols* is Norman Cohn, *Warrant for Genocide: The Myth of the World Jewish Conspiracy and the Protocols of the Elders of Zion* (New York, 1967). Cf. p. 158.
4. Cohn, *Warrant for Genocide*, p. 159.
5. *Ibid.*, pp. 159–160.
6. *Ibid.*, pp. 158–164.
7. Cf. Norman Hapgood, "The Inside Story of Henry Ford's Jew-Mania," six articles in *Hearst's International*, June to November 1922.
8. Cf. Bruno Lasker, *Race Attitudes in Children* (New York, 1929). Gordon Allport, *The Nature of Prejudice* (Anchor Books ed., Garden City, New York, 1958), p. 310, reports the following bizarre and sinister episode:

   Recently, in a waiting room, I watched three youngsters who sat at a table looking at a magazine. Suddenly the smaller boy said, "Here's a soldier and an airplane. He's a Jap." The girl said, "No, he's an American." The little fellow said, "Get him, soldier, get the Jap." The older boy added, "And Hitler too." "And Mussolini," said the girl. "And the Jews," said the big boy. Then the little fellow started a chant, the others joining in: "The Japs, Mussolini, and the Jews! The Japs, Hitler, Mussolini, and the Jews!"

Chapter 5

1. Donald Strong, *Organized Anti-Semitism in America: The Rise of Group Prejudice During the Decade 1930–1940* (Washington, D.C., 1941). Cf. also Charles Stember *et al.*, *Jews in the Mind of America* (New York, 1966), pp. 110ff.

Chapter 7

1. Gary T. Marx, *Protest and Prejudice, A Study of Belief in the Black Community* (New York, 1967), pp. 137ff.
2. Roland Gittelsohn in Shlomo Katz, ed., *Negro and Jew, An Encounter in America* (New York, 1967), p. 42.
3. Robert G. Weisbord and Arthur Stein, *Bittersweet Encounter: The Afro-American and the American Jew* (Westport, Connecticut, 1970), p. 170.
4. Quoted *ibid.*, p. 172n.
5. Michael Selzer, "Politics and Human Perfectibility: A Jewish Perspective," *Cross-Currents*, Spring, 1971.

Bibliography

It would be impossible to offer a comprehensive bibliography of anti-Semitism in the space available here. The following titles will, however, provide an adequate introduction to the literature.

Jewish History

The major general histories of the Jews, each of which contains extensive discussions of anti-Semitism through the ages, are:

Baron, Salo, *A Social and Religious History of the Jews*, 14 vols. (New York, 1937–).

Dubnow, Simon, *History of the Jews*, trans. Moshe Spiegel, 3 vols. (New York, 1967–).

Graetz, Heinrich, *History of the Jews*, trans. Bella Lowy *et al.*, 6 vols. (Philadelphia, 1891).

A useful, if rather flawed, one-volume study is:

Sachar, Howard, *The Course of Modern Jewish History* (Cleveland, 1958).

A number of excellent essays are contained in:

Finkelstein, Louis, ed., *The Jews: Their History and Culture*, 2 vols. (New York, 1960).

American Jewry: History and Institutions

Useful introductions include:

Glazer, Nathan, *American Judaism* (Chicago, 1957).

Janowsky, Oscar, ed., *The American Jew: A Reappraisal* (Philadelphia, 1965).

Learsi, Rufus, *Jews in America* (Cleveland, 1954).

Levinger, Lee, *History of the Jews in the United States* (New York, 1954).

Sklare, Marshall, ed., *The Jews: Social Patterns of an American Group* (Glencoe, Illinois, 1958).

The Jewish People: Past and Present, 4 vols. (New York, 1946–.)

Anti-Semitism: General

Of the vast literature on the subject the following are, perhaps, the most useful introductions:

Arendt, Hannah, *The Origins of Totalitarianism* (Cleveland, 1951).

Hay, Malcolm, *Europe and the Jews* (Boston, 1960); this work was originally published as *The Foot of Pride* (Boston, 1950).

Parkes, James, *Antisemitism* (Chicago, 1963).

Roth, Cecil, *The Ritual Murder Libel and the Jew* (London, 1935).

Sartre, Jean-Paul, *Anti-Semite and Jew*, trans. George Becker (New York, 1948).

Simmel, Ernst, ed., *Anti-Semitism: A Social Disease* (New York, 1946).

Trachtenberg, Joshua, *The Devil and the Jews* (New Haven, 1943).

Anti-Semitism: The United States

Although dated, the following are wide-ranging and compassionate studies of anti-Semitism, and chiefly of anti-Semitic discrimination, in the United States:

Broun, Heywood, and Britt, George, *Christians Only: A Study in Prejudice* (New York, 1931).

McWilliams, Carey, *A Mask for Privilege: Anti-Semitism in America* (Boston, 1948).

Major historical treatments of American anti-Semitism are:

Baltzell, E. Digby, *The Protestant Establishment: Aristocracy and Caste in America* (New York, 1964).

Handlin, Oscar, "American Views of the Jew at the Opening of the Twentieth Century," *Publications of the American Jewish Historical Society*, XL (1951).

Handlin, Oscar, and Handlin, Mary, *Danger in Discord: Origins of Anti-Semitism in the United States*, 3rd. ed. (New York, 1964).

Higham, John, "Anti-Semitism in the Gilded Age: A Reinterpretation," *Mississippi Valley Historical Review*, XLIII (1957).

———, "Social Discrimination Against Jews in America, 1830–1930," *Publications of the American Jewish Historical Society*, XLVII (1957).

Strong, Donald, *Organized Anti-Semitism in America: The Rise of Group Prejudice During the Decade 1930–1940* (Washington, D.C., 1941).

The specific contexts of Christian anti-Semitism are explored in:

Brown, James, "Christian Teaching and Anti-Semitism," *Commentary*, December 1957.

Glock, Charles, and Stark, Rodney, *Christian Beliefs and Anti-Semitism* (New York, 1966).

Olson, Bernhard E., *Faith and Prejudice* (New Haven, 1962).

Roy, Ralph, *Apostles of Discord: A Study of Organized Bigotry and Disruption on the Fringes of Protestantism* (Boston, 1953).

Much of the large number of survey and other research into anti-Semitism is listed in:

Tumin, Melvin, *An Inventory and Appraisal of Research on American Anti-Semitism* (New York, 1961).

Among the major inquiries into the nature of American anti-Semitism are:

Adorno, T. W. *et al.*, *The Authoritarian Personality* (New York, 1950).

Bettelheim, Bruno, and Janowitz, Morris, *Dynamics of Prejudice* (New York, 1950).

Galtung, Johan, *Anti-Semitism in the Making* (Oslo, 1960).

Lowenthal, Leo, and Guterman, Norbert, *Prophets of Deceit: A Study of the Techniques of the American Agitator* (New York, 1949).

Marx, Gary T., *Protest and Prejudice: A Study of Belief in the Black Community* (New York, 1967).

———, *The Social Basis of the Support for a Depression Era Extremist: Father Coughlin* (Berkeley, California, 1962).

Simpson, George, and Yinger, Milton, *Racial and Cultural Minorities: An Analysis of Prejudice and Discrimination*, 3rd. ed. (New York, 1965).

Stark, Rodney, and Steinberg, Stephen, *It Did Happen Here: An Investigation of Political Anti-Semitism, Wayne, N.J. 1967* (Berkeley, California, 1967).

Stember, Charles *et al.*, *Jews in the Mind of America* (New York, 1966).

Wolfe, Ann, *Why the Swastika? A Study of Young American Vandals* (New York, 1962).

Among the studies of discrimination against Jews in contemporary America are:

American Jewish Committee, *Patterns of Exclusion from the Executive Suite: Banking* (New York, 1966).

———, *Jews in College and University Administration* (New York, 1966).

Goldberg, Albert, "Jews in the Legal Profession: A Case of Adjustment to Discrimination," *Jewish Social Studies,* XXXII (1970).

Quinn, R. P. *et al., The Chosen Few: A Study of Discrimination in Executive Selection* (Ann Arbor, Michigan, 1968).

Waldman, Lois, "Employment Discrimination Against Jews in the United States—1955," *Jewish Social Studies,* XVIII (1956).

Novels

Finally, among a number of excellent novels depicting anti-Semitism in general, the following two are particularly to be recommended:

Malamud, Bernard, *The Fixer* (New York, 1966).

Schwartz-Bart, André, *The Last of the Just,* trans. Stephen Becker (New York, 1961).

PHOTO CREDITS

Page 1 (of insert): top, courtesy American Jewish Historical Society Archives; bottom, from *Puck*, January 19, 1881, courtesy American Jewish Historical Society Archives; page 2: from *Puck*, May 11, 1881, courtesy American Jewish Historical Society Archives; page 3: top, from *The Judge*, July 8, 1882, courtesy American Jewish Historical Society Archives; bottom, from *Puck*, April 17, 1889, courtesy American Jewish Historical Society Archives; pages 4–5: from *Dial*, June 26, 1894, courtesy American Jewish Historical Society Archives; page 5: from *Phil May's Illustrated Annual*, season 1900–1901, courtesy American Jewish Historical Society Archives; page 6: from *American Bulletin*, September 29, 1936, courtesy American Jewish Historical Society Archives; page 7: top, from *American Gentile*, November 1936, courtesy New York Public Library; bottom, from *Christian Bulletin*, January 1937, courtesy American Jewish Historical Society Archives; page 8: top, from *Christian Free Press*, November 1937, courtesy American Jewish Historical Society Archives; bottom, cover of a booklet distributed in the 1940s by Pelley Publishers, Asheville, N.C., courtesy American Jewish Historical Society Archives; page 9: from *National Renaissance Bulletin*, May–June 1963, courtesy New York Public Library; pages 10–11: from *Puck*, July 30, 1879, courtesy American Jewish Historical Society Archives; pages 12–13: from *The Judge*, July 22, 1882, courtesy American Jewish Historical Society Archives; pages 14–15: from *Puck*, November 30, 1881, courtesy American Jewish Historical Society Archives; page 16: from T. F. Timayenis, *The Original Mr. Jacobs*, courtesy New York Public Library.

The editor and publisher gratefully acknowledge permission to quote from the following works:

The Old World in the New by E. A. Ross, published by B. Appleton & Company. Reprinted courtesy of Appleton-Century-Crofts, successors to the Publisher.

John Jay Chapman and His Letters, M. A. D. Howe, ed., published by the Houghton Mifflin Company. Copyright © renewed 1965 by Quincy Howe, Helen Howe Allen, Mark De W. Howe.

The Great Gatsby by F. Scott Fitzgerald, published by Charles Scribner's Sons. Copyright 1925 by Charles Scribner's Sons; copyright renewed 1953 by Frances Scott Fitzgerald Lanahan.

The Authoritarian Personality by T. W. Adorno et al., published by Harper & Row. Copyright 1950 by The American Jewish Committee.

Dynamics of Prejudice by Bruno Bettelheim and Morris Janowitz, published by Harper & Row. Copyright 1950 by The American Jewish Committee.

The Chosen Few: A Study of Discrimination in Executive Selection by R. P. Quinn et al., published by The University of Michigan Institute for Social Research. Copyright © 1968 by The University of Michigan.